Design Attitude

To Alex, Mark and Gosia

Design Attitude

KAMIL MICHLEWSKI

GOWER

Published by
Gower Publishing Limited
Wey Court East
Union Road
Farnham
Surrey, GU9 7PT
England

Gower Publishing Company
110 Cherry Street
Suite 3-1
Burlington, VT 05401-3818
USA

www.gowerpublishing.com

British Library Cataloguing in Publication Data
A catalogue record for this book is available from the British Library

ISBN: 9781472421180 (hbk)
ISBN: 9781472421197 (ebk – ePDF)
ISBN: 9781472421203 (ebk – ePUB)

Library of Congress Cataloging-in-Publication Data
Michlewski, Kamil.
  Design attitude / by Kamil Michlewski.
    pages cm
  Includes bibliographical references and index.
  ISBN 978-1-4724-2118-0 (hardback) -- ISBN 978-1-4724-2120-3 (ebook) -- ISBN 978-1-4724-2119-7 (epub) 1. Creative ability. 2. Management. I. Title.
  BF408.M487 2015
  658.4--dc23

                                                                    2014037239

Printed in the United Kingdom by Henry Ling Limited, at the Dorset Press, Dorchester, DT1 1HD

Design Attitude

Design Attitude is a book for those who want to scratch beneath the surface and explore the impact design and designers have in organisations. It offers an alternative view on the sources of success and competitive advantage of companies such as Apple, where design plays a leading role. It sheds light on the cultural dynamics within organisations, where professional designers have a significant presence and influence.

At its heart, the book asks a question: what is the nature of designers' contribution that is truly unique to them as professionals?

To answer this deceptively simple question the author combines a multitude of hours of ethnographic study inside the design community, in-depth interviews with executives and designers from Apple, IDEO, Wolff Olins, Philips Design and Nissan Design and a follow-up quantitative study.

Since the author comes from a management and not a design background, the book offers a different perspective to most publications in the area of Design Thinking. It is a mirror held up to the community, rather than a voice from within.

Design Attitude makes the compelling argument that looking at the type of the culture designers produce, rather than the type of processes or products they create, is potentially a more fruitful way of profiling the impact of design in organisations.

With design being recognised as an important strategic framework by companies, not-for-profit organisations and governments alike, this book is a distinct and timely contribution to the debate.

Dr Kamil Michlewski was awarded a PhD by the School of Design at Northumbria University, having completed a programme supported by Oxford's Saïd Business School. In his academic capacity he has published on the role of design and designers in organisational settings, tacit knowledge and aesthetics in organisational learning. He has presented at international conferences including the European Academy of Management, European Group for Organisational Studies, Design Management Institute and European Academy of Design. Michlewski works at The Value Engineers – a strategic brand consultancy based in the UK. He advises a number of blue-chip clients on issue ranging from global consumer segmentation to brand strategy. Michlewski previously worked as a senior strategy lecturer at Newcastle Business School.

Contents

List of Figures

List of Tables

Acknowledgements

Writing a book like this one isn't a quick and simple process, and it certainly isn't one done in isolation. I was extremely fortunate to receive a great deal of help from a number of individuals and institutions in my quest to understand designers and publish this book. The School of Design at Northumbria University in Newcastle upon Tyne, UK, hosted my PhD research, which forms the backbone of this book, between 2001 and 2007. As a place that trained designers such as Sir Jonathan Ive of Apple, or Tim Brown of IDEO, it was an extremely conducive environment for my research.

I am indebted to the late Professor James More, Dean of the School at the time of my research, for his mentorship and the support of the entire doctorate. Professor Robert Young, who extended his counsel, was an important voice of design research and academia. I am very grateful to Dr Emma Jeffries, Dr Lauren Tan and Dr Joyce Yee who have encouraged me to pursue the subject matter and were a friendly sounding board for my ideas. Mark Illman, Jeremy Hildreth, Benedict Singleton and Nick Spencer – thank you for your support and help at various stages of the process.

On the business side, Professor Rafael Ramirez of the Saïd Business School, University of Oxford, provided an invaluable perspective as my second supervisor. His experience and wisdom were pivotal in key junctures of my investigation.

Most importantly, it was the assistance of the senior executives, consultants and designers from five design-intensive companies that proved vital to my studies. Apple, IDEO, Nissan Design, Philips Design and Wolff Olins all offered help and access to interviewees. I am very grateful to them for their generosity which made my study, and subsequently this book, possible. I especially would like to thank the late Wally Olins, OBE, for his time and patience over several interview sessions; Sir Jonathan Ive for entertaining my questions on a couple of occasions; Steven Kyffin, the head of Philips Design for arranging interviews with his staff and also for the time he spent answering my queries; and Colin Burns, director of IDEO London.

I would also like to extend my thanks to The Value Engineers, a brand strategy consultancy, based in the UK, which I was part of during the writing of this book. They kindly offered me a sabbatical, without which this project would not have seen the light of day.

Between November 2013 and February 2014, I partnered with a global research agency Toluna to conduct an extensive online survey. James Pickles and his company provided scripting and hosting services. I am very grateful for their help and support.

Over two hundred individuals have taken part in my survey. I would like to mention them all but that would be breaking my promise that they should remain anonymous. Thank you all, if you are reading this book.

Fred Collopy and Dick Boland of the Weatherhead School of Management, Case Western Reserve, Mariana Amatulo of Designmatters, Art Center College of Design and Christian Bason of MindLab all offered valuable words of wisdom and useful critique. I am much obliged to all of you.

I would also like to thank my editors, who have somehow managed to put up with me over the entire process. Naturally, they made this book what it is today. Christopher Murray, Cherry Mosteshar and Jonathan Norman, please accept my sincere thanks.

Finally, I would like to thank my wife, Dr Gosia Wamil, for giving me the space to write the book as well as for the great deal of constructive encouragement I've received from her over the years. You know this thing would not have happened if it wasn't for you. Thanks a million!

Foreword

This book is a welcome addition to the growing body of literature on design and innovation in organisations. It takes an unusual perspective, turning away from the many books and articles that attempt to describe a single method or process of designing. It focuses instead, on the culture of professional designers and the attitudes and values that stand behind their creative work. Studies of design method are common enough today, sometimes written by the leaders of design consultancies with a thinly disguised promotional purpose for the advance of their own commercial interests or by academics intent on impressing their ideas about design on the business community. The marketplace of ideas encourages such work, and the work does good in advancing the general cause of design as an important part of our technological culture. However, there are two areas for innovation that are important for revealing what design brings to organisations and leads to change and development. One area is the tough job of asking whether design is more than a set of steps or stages that anyone may follow on the road to innovation. It asks how principles and values are implicated in design as we seek to understand what design really contributes to our emerging world of technology and social development. The other area is the equally tough job of asking what values and attitudes are the foundation of imagination and creation in design. It asks what professional designers share, despite all of their individual differences of personality and approach, that makes them unconventional and valuable in the organisations that they serve. This is Kamil Michlewski's contribution in his book on design attitude and the professional culture of design.

Where other researchers have employed methods of cognitive psychology in an effort to explain what we mean by 'design thinking', Michlewski turns to a field study of design in practice, exploring what designers and managers actually say and do in their work. He employs ethnographic methods for a holistic understanding of the values and meanings of design thinking in organisations. Based on extensive interviews of designers and managers in different types of organisations, he identifies five shared values that, taken together, characterise what he calls the 'design attitude'. This book is organised around the five values, with descriptions and examples that help us to see what is different in the way designers approach the challenges of their work. For example, designers characteristically *embrace uncertainty and ambiguity* as part of their work. They are willing to take risks in exploring problems, leaving open the opportunity for discovering solutions that depart from the conventional and accepted solutions that surround them. They engage a *deep empathy* for understanding the interests, needs, and desires of customers and clients. They appreciate *the power of all five senses* when exploring design challenges, often leading to emotional as well as practical solutions that appeal to human beings. They delight in the *playful dimension of bringing ideas and strategies to concrete life* in products and services. Finally, they are willing to *engage and reconcile diverse perspectives* as they work toward solutions to complex problems, seeking new expressions of strongly held values and purposes among customers, clients and society. Designers have an intuitive understanding of these values in daily practice, but the importance of Michlewski's work lies in a thorough exploration of these values through research and in a careful articulation of the meaning of such values in action.

This book provides a powerful tool for managers who are charged with leading design and innovation in their organisations. It offers insight into a way of thinking and working that is often in sharp contrast to traditional management practices. Moreover, it provides the rationale for why this way of working belongs among the best practices of management in a highly competitive world. Indeed, it provides a useful framework for new approaches in the education of managers and designers. For several decades, the curricula of management education have focused primarily on analytical tools, neglecting the importance of synthesis and creative action in preparing new managers and leaders for a highly competitive world that stands in constant need of new ideas and innovation. Michlewski's work points toward a new perspective on the so-called 'learning outcomes' of management education. Closer attention to the concrete values of design culture will enhance all forms of education, whether in schools of management or schools of design or the many other disciplines of our colleges and universities.

Richard Buchanan, PhD
Professor and Chair, Department of Design and Innovation
Weatherhead School of Management
Case Western Reserve University

Preface

Let's make one thing clear straight away, to paraphrase Herbert Simon, we are ALL designers in a sense that we all apply our intellect and will to turning situations we find ourselves in into situations that we prefer to be in. From painting a living room, building a shed, designing our work presentation, organising a holiday to figuring out how we want to live our lives – we all design things.

In this book, however, I want to focus on a group of people who call themselves designers by profession. To be more precise, they are individuals who belong to a family of design professions ranging from graphic design, industrial design, multimedia and user interface design, right through to architecture.

The recognition of design-led methods, processes and ways of thinking has grown significantly in recent years. Chief Design Officers are being appointed in large organisations such as Barclays, Philips, 3M, PepsiCo and Kia. Leaders in the field of design, such as John Maeda, the graphic designer, computer scientist, academic and author, are being headhunted by venture capital firms to spot the next billion-dollar business opportunity. Designers are starting to be seen as crucial to the success of start-ups and new ventures. In companies such as Airbnb, Pinterest or Instagram designers played pivotal roles as founders and entrepreneurs. A whole industry of service design consultancies has sprung up – from live|work, Fjord to Engine and many others – with a style and substance that is distinct from other outlets. NGOs and public sector organisations are applying design thinking and methods to the challenges they face. From UNDP, Denmark's MindLab, California's Designmatters, through to the UK's Participle and the British government's GOV.UK and the Policy Lab – there is a broad spectrum of organisations that have been taking design methods very seriously indeed. Finally, in the domain of business schools, institutions such as the Weatherhead School of Management, Case Western Reserve University and the Rotman School of Management, University of Toronto, use design-inspired policies and curricula to position themselves in the marketplace.

The understanding of the discipline of design within the domain of the organisation has also deepened a great deal, not least thanks to the work of institutions such as the Design Council in the UK and the Design Management Institute in USA. There was also one, unequivocal event in 2012 that marked a very significant moment for design. It was when Apple overtook Exxon to become the most valuable company by market capitalisation in the world. After the partnership of Steve Jobs and Jonathan Ive created the largest company on the planet, it's no longer possible to dismiss design and designers as a superfluous accessory in a hard-core world of business. Those who have seen designing mainly as superficial attempts at prettifying objects have been forced to re-evaluate their thinking. Large organisations that had previously predominantly favoured engineering and marketing as the leading professions are taking a second look at the role design and designers play in their success.

Design Thinking could be described as a movement that promotes the philosophies, methods and tools that originate in the practice and culture of the design professions. It is often seen as a breath of fresh air in organisations that have for too long concentrated on technical or financial aspects to the detriment of a human-centred way of doing business.

The narrative of this book is, broadly speaking, part of this design thinking debate, where design methods, tools and ways of thinking are adopted by an ever-widening group of people – from managers to public health officials and politicians. There is, however, an important between how design thinking and how design attitude approaches the subject. Instead of focusing on what is being advocated in the name of design by numerous, disparate voices, I chose to use ethnographic-level research to specifically understand the unique aspects of the professional culture that designers themselves create. My primary objective was to uncover, understand and describe what was different and distinctive about this group, particularly from an organisational point of view.

As somebody who isn't a designer – I have both formal and informal management training, and over a decade as a consultant – I am effectively an outsider looking in. I would like to think that I have followed, to some small degree at least, in the footsteps of the father of ethnography, Bronisław Malinowski. Even though my subjects were not the inhabitants of the Trobriand Islands of Melanesia, but rather the tribe consisting of professional designers, I tried to be as true to their native ways of doing things as I could. As in Malinowski's case, my goal was to describe their culture from an embedded outsider's perspective in order to capture larger social themes, which may not appear immediately apparent to designers themselves.

My pursuit of the subject over a period of more than 10 years has led me to conclude that there are indeed distinctive aspects of the professional culture of designers that form what I call design attitude. With the help of Apple, IDEO, Nissan Design, Philips Design and Wolff Olins, I've identified five aspects of it. Each has a chapter devoted to it. They are, briefly:

- Embracing uncertainty and ambiguity – designers know that, when it comes to creating something completely new and original, there are no guarantees of success. They realise, and accept, that a really creative process is often discontinuous and messy. Pretending otherwise is counterproductive at best and very damaging at worst. Unlike many in the corporate world, they feel comfortable navigating the often multifaceted and complex reality without relying on seemingly bulletproof processes and management frameworks. This allows them to challenge the received wisdom with conviction and fearlessness. It is not difficult to see how this attitude may be a good basis for coming up with breakthrough ideas and innovation.

- Engaging deep empathy – using true empathy requires courage, honesty and abandoning one's mental models. It is not for those who, at the outset, consider themselves more knowledgeable or better informed as to the challenges faced by the customers/users they are meant to be serving. It certainly isn't for those who are not ready to exercise a great deal of personal and professional humility. Designers, in their professional nature, don't pretend they have all the answers. They are not limited by a rigid set of best-practice tools and instead rely on an instinct which pushes them to find out as much as they possibly can about their target consumers. Above all, they treat these consumers as real human beings and not simply as management abstractions.

- Embracing the power of the five senses – designers recognise that two senses, namely sight and hearing, are often not enough to create something that captivates people on a deep, visceral level. The best brands and experiences use many senses to create powerful neural pathways. When designers design, they consciously and unconsciously draw upon a plethora of senses to help them come up with better solutions. They acknowledge that we, as human beings, are complex creatures and we need to be treated as such. Their attitude towards using their sense of aesthetics (a deep and objective compass within each of us) is honest and open. Unlike many other professions in the corporate domain, designers are not afraid of this messy state. On the contrary, they are happy to use this apparent complexity to create surprise, delight and real emotions.

- Playfully bringing things to life – in order to create traction in an innovative process/dialogue designers believe in the power of playfulness, humour and a healthy dose of subversion. They often use the cloak of creativity and apparent silliness, projected onto them by other professions, to ask some profound questions and challenge entrenched ways of doing things. It helps them to tackle some of the politically sensitive issues without appearing threatening. Alongside deep empathy, this is one of the reasons that design-inspired methods and interventions have been gaining traction with NGOs and governments. Moreover, designers don't pay lip-service to the notion of early prototyping. They believe deeply that it is the only way to really make progress. Creatively manifesting potential products, services and future scenarios as quickly as possible is effectively their way of being.

- Creating new meaning from complexity – at the heart of designers' ways of doing things is the willingness to engage and to reconcile multiple, often contradictory, points of view and sources of information (not least the aforementioned five senses) in order to come up with an entirely new way of thinking about something. Strategy is one thing, but turning all of the disparate elements into a coherent and delightful whole – be it product, experience or a system – is something else entirely. Designers strive for progress in what things mean to people as much as they strive to create something valuable that works on many different levels.

Apart from exploring the aspects of design attitude mentioned already, the book attempts to untangle how design impacts organisations. Having studied the subject extensively, I believe there are essentially three ways in which design makes its mark on businesses and institutions. The first one is frameworks. Here design practitioners, theorists and scholars argue, persuade and reason with the public about the benefits and intricacies of the design-inspired frameworks. Design thinking and service design are only two such frameworks. Their adoption is based on how receptive the public is and how well the arguments and evidence are put forward. It usually takes time for the ideas to take root. The second way in which design impacts organisations is the effects of the designers' work, be they physical or digital objects, services, experiences or environments. The human impact is felt instantly – when we touch a phone, sit in an office or look at a building. Environmental impact is, naturally, something else entirely. We are physical beings and how we experience the world is very much led by what designers put in our hands or in front of our eyes. Thirdly, and from the point of view of design attitude, most importantly, the impact of design on organisations occurs directly through designers themselves and, in particular, through their professional culture. The way in which they are integrated into organisational structures is an important indicator of how effective their impact will be. They can be helped or hindered, their empathy bandwidth throttled or boosted. It all depends on their place in an organisation.

More than ever, the world of design is teeming with excitement and change. Its influence on the world of business is growing independently of marketing and other business functions. That is important as it allows designers a better, more direct, access to both customers/users and decision-makers.

I hope that through this book I managed to capture, to some degree at least, the nature of the culture that designers create. I also hope that it will help those who wish to understand designers better make up their mind about whether their ways are something useful and appealing to them.

I believe that adopting design attitude cannot be compared to, say, using a design thinking toolkit. For it to have a meaning, it needs to become a way of being. Yes, it's very prevalent among the design community, but it can also be embedded and adopted outside it. I am not suggesting that design attitude is something that everybody should embrace. It's not an innovation panacea – far from it. I believe that it has come about as a part of the professional culture of designers over a number of years and is intrinsically linked with who they are as professionals. It certainly isn't a quick-fix, off-the-shelf solution to increase competitiveness or creative proficiency of an organisation. Those who are interested in understanding and pursuing it should bear in mind that design attitude is a deeply held set of beliefs, attitudes and mental models; a cultural footprint left by the professional culture of designers; a way of doing things, and a way of making sense of the world around us.

Kamil Michlewski
Oxford, May 2014

PART I
Design in Context

Chapter 1
Design and the Design Profession

Professionally Speaking

Let's suppose that we asked people from three different professions, say tax lawyers, carers and psychiatrists, to each build an organisation of their own. We wouldn't expect that each would come up with the same formula for motivating people, approaching strategy or setting up an innovation framework. But often that's exactly what we do. We somehow skip past the fact that people spend their entire lives investing emotionally, mentally and socially into who they are as professionals, and focus instead on the organisations they currently are part of. We talk about building the right kind of cultures for our companies and institutions. Suffice it to say that with the cohort of Millennials, or Generation Y as they are known, this has never been more important.[1] Companies such as Zappos, the online shoe company, and Netflix, the online media streaming service, are very vocal about the importance of their cultures to their success, yet the issue of professions and their impact rarely enters the debate.

The central thrust of this book hinges on two observations. The first is that professional cultures are often the under-appreciated influencers inside organisations, despite the considerable impact they have on individuals' worldview and attitudes. The second is that professional designers play an increasingly important role in the success of businesses, non-profit and public sector ventures. These two observations form the framework for attempting to understand nature of the influence and impact of designers in today's, and very likely tomorrow's, organisations.

Professional cultures flow through companies and institutions like rivers carrying values, attitudes, mental models and the approaches of their members. Since there is no such thing as a job for life, and since most of us are more strongly linked with our profession than we are with the organisation – just ask which is easier to change – professional cultures have become powerful conduits of belief systems and the way they carry out their work. Consider Google, for example, with its strong engineering mind-set. Look closely and you'll notice that it's got a very strong bias towards the engineering profession. As Google grew, it considered dispensing with middle-level managers entirely, as the engineering culture was heavily focused on the actual work and concrete results. Based on a deeply analytical approach, which included sophisticated mathematical modelling, Google eventually relented and now there are about 5,000 managers, 1,000 directors, and 100 vice presidents in an organisation of 37,000.[2] This is a direct result of the impact the values of their founding engineers had on the company.

Naturally, there are organisations that are influenced by other professions, such as medics (National Health Service in the UK), marketers (P&G) and journalists (BBC). They all have their particular ways of solving problems, managing change and coming up with new products and services. Professional cultures significantly inform how these things are done. More to the point, there are companies and institutions where the family of design professions plays a large role. When looking at the role these professionals play, one needs to ask what happens to the organisations they inhabit. What are the beliefs and attitudes espoused by the design profession? Knowing that can help us to understand in what ways the design profession impacts the institutions it enters. This is precisely what this book is about.

Before we begin to examine what is so unique about the designers' contribution to organisations, and before we even look at the world of companies teeming with designers, we must look at the basics: what do we mean by *design?* What do we mean by their professional culture and whom are we actually talking about when we say designers? In Chapters 1, 2 and 3 we will dig deeper and tackle a few relatively heavy issues around definitions of design, culture and more specifically, professional cultures. Then in Chapter 4, we will start to examine the crux of the matter, namely the heart of *design attitude.*

CRACKING THE DESIGN NUT

Defining design is notoriously difficult, but let's do it anyway. The ambiguity of the term is almost legendary, not least because it's both a noun and a verb, and could refer to a process, an object or a function. Perhaps not surprisingly, given the rising profile of design, the number of definitions has exploded over time. In 1986, Peter Gorb counted 26 definitions of the term design. Twelve years later Olson et al.[3] found some 50 definitions.

Clearly, design can mean many things to many people. Herbert Simon[4] famously defined design as the process by which one devises 'courses of action aimed at changing existing situations into preferred ones'. This is the broadest, all-encompassing and, arguably, the most ubiquitous definition of design as a process. It is comprehensive in nature and most forms of design are included '… to the degree that creating something new (or reshaping something that exists) for a purpose, to meet a need to solve a problem are courses of action toward a preferred situation even though we may not yet be able to articulate the preferred situation'.[5]

This definition is still valid, but I can only use it as a starting point, in reference to the domain of the organisation and the commonly understood meaning of *design*. If we look at Simon's definition and ask, 'a situation preferred by whom?' we see the link between the generic understanding and more specific requirements on the level of an organisation in their particular culture.

According to Friedman[6] the verb *design*, describing a 'process of thought and planning', takes precedence over all other meanings of the term (ibid.: 200). He dates the usage of the verb from the early 1500s and it first appeared in written form in 1548. Merriam-Webster's[7] defines design as '… to conceive and plan out in the mind; to have a purpose; to devise for a specific function or end; to make a drawing, pattern or sketch; to draw the plans for; to create, fashion, execute or construct according to plan' (see also[8, 9]). In the early seventeenth century the word began to be used as a noun, describing 'a particular purpose held in view by an individual or group; deliberate, purposive planning; a mental project or scheme in which means to an end are laid down'.[7]

Despite the fact that the word *design* refers first and foremost to the process rather than an outcome, popular culture and the media have added to the complexity by using the adjective designer to denote an original form, such as found in furniture, lamps or fashion.[10] Even more confusingly, there are now new terms in popular use such as designer drugs or designer babies, leading to the proliferation of meanings and increase in ambiguity of the word. At the other end of the spectrum, we see the growth in importance of concepts such as Design Thinking or service design – now recognised by organisations and governments as very useful frameworks.

Cultured Design

It is unthinkable to separate design from culture in any imaginable form of inquiry. The two are interlinked and cannot exist as separate entities. This has far-reaching consequences for analysing any issues regarding design. As Buchanan puts it:

> *The principles of design are grounded in spiritual and cultural ideals, or in material conditions, or in the power of individuals to control nature and influence social life, or in the qualities of moral and intellectual character which stand behind the integrative discipline of design thinking and the productive arts. Such principles are presupposed and pre-existent in the concerns of each designer.*[11]

One of most influential design thinkers, Donald Schön, proposes to see design as a 'reflective action' in the context of a 'conversation with a problematic situation'.[12, 13] He recognises that one cannot extract the design process from a personal or professional context. By engaging the professional practice approach, he positions design squarely in the practical-cultural domain, and lays the foundations for understanding design in its situational dimension. Schön recognises the imperfect and 'swampy' grounds upon which all action is based. He compares decision-making and discovery in similar terms as the projection of metaphors with which we are familiar, onto new, unfamiliar situations. The act of designing involves the projection of a partial design onto a particular design situation.[14] Think about it this way, you create a sketch, or a graph or a business model and, in the process, these creations reveal new insights to which you instantly respond. This process is often unconscious but it can also be conscious and reflective.

As to the demands of professional knowledge, Schön claimed that Simon, in his *Sciences of the Artificial*,[4] saw designing as 'instrumental problem solving: a purest form of optimisation'. He explicitly challenged the positivist doctrine underpinning much of the design science movement and offered instead a constructivist/pragmatist interpretation. He believed that Simon's view focused too much on solving well-formed problems and not on the most important functions of designing in situations of uncertainty, uniqueness and conflict. [13] Schön proposed an 'epistemology of practice' originating in the artistic, intuitive processes practitioners bring with them. This argument has since been successfully pursued by other scholars.[11, 15–18] For example, Buchanan views design as '… partly rational and cognitive, and partly irrational, emotive, intuitive, and non-cognitive'.[11]

There exist two fairly distinct streams in thinking about design. One group of commentators favours the pursuit of a design science, where design is 'explicitly organised, rational and wholly systematic. It is not just the utilisation of scientific knowledge of artefacts, but design is, in some sense, a scientific activity itself.'[19] The other group subscribes to the view that designing is itself either non-scientific or a-scientific.[20] This is key to how both the designers view themselves and how the societies and organisations view them.

An argument could perhaps be made that the reasons behind the systemising and scientisising of design might be socio-political in nature. As Sargent and Road[21] poignantly suggest, 'chasing after an illusionary 'design science' is more a characteristic of engineering seeking enhanced status as physical scientists rather than emphasizing design creativity ...' (ibid.: 402). What appears to be happening is that design, being in the process of establishing itself as a highly regarded profession, strives to legitimise itself in the eyes of other professions, government bodies and the general public in order to achieve a certain social status. This process is called a professional project and I discuss it later in the chapter. In order to achieve this legitimisation within the science-based paradigm, design must portray itself as coherent, predictable and robustly grounded in a comprehensive body of knowledge. If, at any point, a consensus develops that there is no general, wholly rational, overarching set of finite methods which could be taught and examined and policed, it would more than likely have a negative effect on the project of design ever becoming a scientific and thus credible profession, in some people's eyes. Hence, some designers and design scholars seeking social status and recognition for their profession and themselves might, understandably, want to avoid presenting it as inherently ambiguous, subjective and unpredictable. We will examine this point in more detail later.

Schön's interpretation of design as a 'reflective dialogue with a situation' and, in a professional context, his analyses provide an important link between the enormity of the term design, with its overabundance of meanings and interpretations, and the focus of this book, which is predominantly concerned with the domain of an organisation. It offers a conceptual bridge between design, which is on a very basic level a process of mending our environment according to our will and is practised by virtually everyone, and the need to analyse it within a manageable context. The fact that Schön based his *Reflective Practitioner* on the premise of the importance of professions in societies and carried out empirical studies on a number of those, including management, gave me the confidence that following a similar approach can be a good starting point for analysing the design profession in organisations. Hence, it would seem vitally important to explain what is meant by the phrase the design profession, and to prepare the ground for understanding how it interfaces with an organisation.

Design as a Profession

I believe that the importance of professions in our societies cannot be overstated. Virtually everything we as humans do is inherently linked to professional life. As Schön remarks:

> We conduct society's principal business through professionals specially trained to carry out that business, whether it be making war or defending the nation, educating our children, diagnosing and curing disease … or helping those who for one reason or another are unable to fend for themselves. Our principal formal institutions – schools, hospitals, government agencies, courts of law, armies – are arenas for the exercise of professional activity.[12]

According to Simon[4] all professional practice is centrally concerned with design as a process of 'changing existing situations into preferred ones'. He believes that schools of engineering, as well as schools of architecture, business, education, law and medicine, are all, in effect, concerned with the process of design.

It's not, however, my intention to either analyse all those professions or to engage in a sociological debate around the formation of professions in society and the general mechanisms for their emergence. There are many excellent sources that deal with this topic.[22, 23, 24] My primary aim in this book is to examine the family of professions and not a single design profession. Since, from a general point of view at least, all the professions are inherently concerned with design, which of those should one choose for an investigation of the social impact of designers in an organisation? The answer to that question consists of a number of interrelated arguments.

Firstly, many scholars in design management, which is the field that bridges design and organisation, see that there are significant differences between managers and designers.[25–9] The way in which they use the word designer implies that he or she belongs to a family of design professions comprising, amongst others, architecture, product design, industrial design, graphic design and environmental design. These professions have their roots in crafts and guild-based disciplines[10, 30] and have undergone a very different evolutionary pattern to other professions – such as accounting, medicine or engineering.[24] In addition, a number of recent writings in the field of design management consistently refer to this latter group as *designers*.[10, 31–3]

Furthermore, Donald Schön, who like Herbert Simon, was a great enthusiast of the idea that design is something that all professionals do, decided to concentrate on architecture as the 'prototype of design'.[12] He noted that there is a tendency to think of policies, institutions and behaviours as objects of design. Schön stressed, however, that in doing so '… we risk ignoring or underestimating significant differences in media, contexts, goals, and bodies of knowledge specific to the professions' (ibid.). It is important to add that many scholars, Schön included, seem to believe that there is sufficient commonality amongst the design professions to address some of the issues relating to them as universal.[12]

Based on my understanding of both, the literature and the context I've embedded myself into (the school of design the design research unit), I have decided to focus on the family of design professions which includes, among others: industrial designers, multimedia designers, graphic designers, user interface designers and architects. Even though the list is not exhaustive, it provides an overview of the context for some of the research decisions. Consequently, when I refer to designers, I mean professionals trained and working in a family of design professions consisting particularly, but not exclusively, of those design activities. Due to variability within this group, I simplify things and choose not to focus on the many differences that exist between these design specialisms. However, there exists a good level of internal cohesion within this group, which can be tapped into and explored.

Before I explore the other reason why these professions can be grouped and looked at all at once, let's look at the reason that when academics and practitioners talk about designers, they rarely think of engineers, medics or accountants. The concept of a professional project, the process through which occupations become well-established professions, is at the heart of my distinction between professional designers the rest of us.

Brief History of Design Professions: The Professional Project's Point of View

This book will not engage in a comprehensive discussion of the evolution of the numerous design disciplines and the outcomes of historically bound design processes, which is an area that can be followed up elsewhere.[34, 35–52] However, it is important to outline a general tendency in the development of design professions as this will have a significant bearing on what follows and on the definition of the selection of the design professions.

Occupations, in an attempt to assert their place in a society, follow what Larson[53] calls 'a professional project'. During the project the occupations dynamically position themselves vis-à-vis Weberian Ideal Type definitions and negotiate their way from both economic and socio-cultural perspectives. Figure 1.1 presents an outline of the working theory of the professions.

I would like to briefly introduce three basic concepts – Ideal Type, professional project and social closure. They are the basic building blocks that help one understand the dynamics of occupations becoming professions. A more exhaustive discussion can be found elsewhere.[54, 53, 55, 56, 22, 23]

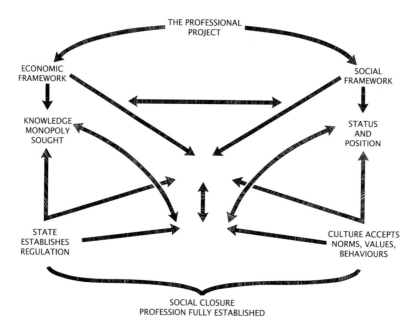

Figure 1.1   A working theory of the professions: Conceptual outline
Source: Adapted from K.M. MacDonald, *The Sociology of the Professions*, 1995.[23]

Firstly, Ideal Type is a concept that could be employed to interpret culture where the social actors project 'typical values and motivations to the supposed inner states of the actors under scrutiny'.[55] It enables the analysis of subjective meanings attached to objective social phenomena. Weber's[57] own definition of Ideal Type is that it 'is formed by the one-side accentuation of one or more points of view and by the synthesis of a great many diffuse, discrete, more or less present and occasionally absent concrete individual phenomena, which are arranged according to those one-sidedly emphasised viewpoints into a unified analytical construct' (ibid.: 90). It is a compilation of various observations to form an amalgamated understanding.

Ideal Type is:

- a heuristic device – which is a type of mental shortcut;

- a conceptual aid;

- not seeking to exhaust or understand its phenomenon;

- not a hypothesis;

- not lowest common denominator;

- not the 'core' – a selection of common elements;

- not an inductive generalisation;

- defined by what it is not.[56]

Secondly, professional project is the process by which occupations organise themselves to attain market power:[53]

> *Professionalization is … an attempt to translate one order of scarce resources – special knowledge and skills – into another – social and economic rewards. To maintain scarcity implies a tendency to monopoly: monopoly of expertise in the market, monopoly of status in a system of stratification. The focus on the constitution of professional markets leads to comparing different professions in terms of the 'marketability' of their specific cognitive resources. (ibid.: xvii)*

The process of professionalisation is generally described in terms of a sequence of often overlapping stages or events.[58] These events include:

- the formation of a professional association;

- attempts by members of the profession to gain control over their particular area of work;

- the development of minimum standard of professional training and the establishment of training facilities;

- the pursuit of a professional knowledge base;

- the development of a code of ethics;

- political agitation to gain public support for the claim to professional status and for affiliation with, and regulation by, the state.[59]

MacDonald[23] offers an updated model of the professional project whereby in addition to taking professions' 'official actions and pronouncements ... the ways in which professional behaviour is enacted and displayed to various appropriate publics by the professional body itself and by the constituent firms and individuals' are included (ibid.: 14).

According to MacDonald, the professional project approach offers good grounds for understanding how knowledge-based occupations that '... aspire to be accepted in society as professions set about achieving their goal' (ibid.: 34). This is why I believe using this concept to help us analyse designers in organisations can be helpful.

MacDonald's framework lists the following points with respect to a professional project:

1. Occupations must develop a special relationship with the state in order to achieve monopoly or at least licensure.

2. During and after securing a monopolistic position, a profession must strive in the arena or compete in the marketplace with others who can substitute its services. This means defending and probably enlarging the scope of its activities.

3.   The professions are not totally self-seeking and engage in 'reasonable altruism' to remain convincing to the general public.

4.   The overarching strategy of a professional group is best understood in terms of social closure (ibid.).

Thirdly, social closure is the means by which the professional project is pursued. 'The occupation and its organisation attempts to close access to the occupation, to its services and jobs; only "eligible" will be admitted ... Exclusion is aimed not only at the attainment and maintenance of monopoly, but also at the usurpation of the existing jurisdiction of others and at the upward social mobility of the whole group'.[23]

Show Me Your Values – Show Me Your Status

There are few occupations that fail to seek out professional status.[12] Virtually everyone wants to establish a profession based around their special skill. [60] This is not surprising, since the professional recognition means increased social status, and a monopoly for specialised knowledge. As Everett Hughes, cited by Schön,[12] states, we as a society, honour '... the profession's claim to extraordinary knowledge in matters of great social importance' (ibid.). Design is no exception in the quest for that elevated position in our society.

Design, as it currently appears, is a relatively young family of professions and dates back to the standardisation of production during the Industrial Revolution. Until that time, the processes of the conception of an object and its manufacture were embodied in the skill of the craftsman.[61] It can be said, perhaps, that if products and services did not have to be manufactured, prepared and eventually sold on the market for profit there would simply be no need for professional designers. As Forty[62] put it:

> In capitalist societies, the primary purpose of the manufacture of artefacts, a process of which design is a part, has to be to make a profit for the manufacturer. Whatever degree of artistic imagination is lavished upon the design of objects, it is done not to give expression to the designer's creativity and imagination, but to make products saleable and profitable. (ibid.: 7)

The same can, of course, be applied to services. Design and the family of design professions, emerged relatively late as a professional contender. This meant it had to recognise the fact that there were already established professions such as law, medicine and accounting. In the process of finding its own identity and recognition, design found itself wedged between what could be generally described as arts and science-based professional recognition. In the decades that followed, it silently split more or less into two sections – one aligning to the realm and values of fine arts, the other to the values and ways of natural sciences. This was accompanied by the development of two distinct educational pathways, different professional institutions and even different ways in which the two families have been incorporated into an organisation.[30] Nowadays, the difference between the cultures of engineering design – representing the science-based project – and design, as arguably still representing the *arts-based* project, is deeply entrenched. Ivor Owen, the former Design Council director said, 'I strongly believe that the schism between engineering design and industrial design has been one of the most damaging issues in manufacturing industry imaginable' (ibid.: 28).

The professional design project started in the craft-based roots of all design professions. It did, however, head in two different directions. One based on the social recognition of the high status of fine arts, the other based on the social recognition of the status of natural sciences. Those were the two Ideal Type paradigms recognised and highly regarded in the modern society. I emphasise here the Ideal Type[54] social recognition and associated identities and values rather than the philosophical debate about the nature of art and science as represented by Wittgenstein, Marleau-Ponty, Kuhn or Feyerabend. What is significant, from my perspective, is the social perception of its value. Is the value created through association with the technical revolution and its achievements, exemplified by people such as Darwin, Maxwell and Einstein? Or is it the through association with the achievements of a poetic and artistic human expression linked with the likes of Shakespeare, Mozart or Picasso? In both cases, those social role models represent and embody different aspirations, goals and values, and point to different models for the achievement of a higher societal status.

The professional design project needed to have a clear reference point that would leverage the quest for status and closure. Part of the profession followed the fine arts route, the other chose to align itself with natural sciences (see Table 1.1). Whether the choice was planned or simply emerged out of the dynamics in the field is less important. What is important, though, is how the design profession has constructed itself and how it now appears to society.

Table 1.1   Ideal Type models of distinct leverages in design's
                 professional project

Shared roots of the entire professional project of the design profession: Pottery, Embroidery, Jewellery, Calligraphy, Cart building, Thatching, Smithery, Weaving	
> *fine arts* as leverage to increased social status	> *natural science* as leverage to increased social status
Fine arts origins: Sculpture, Painting, Music, Photography, Dance, Literature, Poetry	*Natural sciences origins:* Mathematics, Physics, Chemistry, Biology
Design occupations: Installations design, fashion design, furniture, ceramics, industrial design automotive design, interior design, architecture, exhibition design, packaging design, layout, typography, service design	*Design occupations:* Systems design, electronics, structural engineering, electrical engineering, mechanical engineering, genetic engineering, chemical engineering, software engineering
Role models, social icons: Michelangelo, Mozart, Van Gogh, Picasso, Giugiaro, Starck	*Role models, social icons:* Newton, Darwin, Einstein, Hawking
Qualities highly regarded within the realm: Originality Nonconformism Improvisation User testing Variation and multiplicity Human-centrism Risk-taking Cross-breeding Projection Manifestation of values	*Qualities highly regarded within the realm:* Predictability Conformism Simulation Statistical modelling Statistical quality control Optimisation Techno-centrism Robust techniques and methods Formal structures and procedures Peer review Benchmarking Risk-aversion

Many commentators have argued that design emerged as an independent profession in the early part of the twentieth century.[63] In the UK, the Design and Industries Association was launched in 1915; while in the USA Susie Cooper, a ceramic designer, and Stanley Morison, a typographer, began their careers. A few years later, the world saw the rise of industrial design. In the context of the economic crisis of the 1930s in the United States, product design was starting to be recognised as uniquely important to commercial success. As a consequence, industrial designers – freelance consultants to industrial organisations – emerged. People such as Raymond Loewy and Walter Darwin Teague became the iconic personifications of the newly born profession.[46] At this time, particularly due to the demand for a more eye-catching packaging, the majority of the work done in design consultancies focused on styling and redesign without the more fundamental work on the product. This was already happening in an environment where engineering was staking a claim to making the product work, and design was doing what was left. This division was by no means accidental. According to the professional project, this was a consequence of the contrasting value bases corresponding with different social levers – natural sciences in the case of engineers and fine arts in the case of designers.

Further examples of this process can be found in the establishing of various professional bodies. In the UK during the WWII, the Ministry of Information set up the Design Research Unit, the UK's first design consultancy. It was set up to advise industry on matters regarding design. Despite the fact that there were some engineers involved, the work concentrated primarily on projects that involved interior design and graphic design,[63] thus reinforcing the argument among design professions about the bi-polarity regarding value models. In the USA, Aspen International Design Conference was established and in Japan the Japanese International Design Association – both having strong links with the arts side of the professional project.

During the 1950s, 60s and 70s the polarisation of the professional project increased.[10] This, I believe, was caused by the quest for social closure, i.e. societal acceptance and legitimisation, in two, entirely different ways.

Examples of the natural science led professional project included:

- The ULM school (Hochschule fur Gestaltung) in Germany, defending functional design, classic examples include Braun Design.

- The engineering design movement in the United States, creating convenient, vital products, particularly for the army, such as the Jeep in 1941 and Ranges in 1942.[10]

Examples of the fine-arts led projects included:

- The development of American Pop Art, and a mass culture that linked the new 'jean attitude'.

- The revival of crafts in London with the Biba store and the rebirth of an Art Deco style.

- The realisation of the Independent Group in London, which emphasised colours, decoration, surface, and pop fashion.

- In Italy, the Radical Design and Archizoom movements, inspired by Pop Art and Indian mystical culture.[10]

Also at that time, a number of design consultancies started to appear. Among those were Pentagram, Wolff Olins, Frog Design, Digital Design and others. Large corporations saw the need to incorporate design into their processes in order to support marketing function. These included organisations such as Herman Miller, Philips, Braun and BandO.

What Borja De Mozota[10] calls the return of ornamentalism to design between 1975 and 1990, I consider the triumph (if only temporary) of the fine arts-based design project. It succeeded at least in a sense of claiming the term design and disassociating itself from the natural science-based project. From this point it was clear that the term designers first and foremost described people and organisations such as Alessi, Issey Miyake, Giorgetto Giugiaro and Philippe Starck.

This is how Flusser explains the split in the profession:

> The words design, machine technology, ars and art are closely related to one another, one term being unthinkable without the others, and they all derive from the same existential view of the world. However, this internal connection has been denied for centuries (at least since the Renaissance). Modern bourgeois culture made a sharp division between the world of the arts and that of technology and machines; hence culture was split into two mutually exclusive branches: one scientific, quantifiable and 'hard', the other aesthetic, evaluative and 'soft'. This unfortunate split started to become irreversible towards the end of the nineteen century. In the gap, the word design formed a bridge between the two. It could do this since it is an expression of internal connection between art and technology. Hence in contemporary life, design more or less indicates the site where art and technology (along with their respective evaluative and scientific ways of thinking) come together as equals, making a new form of culture possible.[64]

Design Education: The Beating Heart of the Professional Project

From the design educator's point of view, one can see how the system has become the means by which the designers are imbued with their professional projects' values. In the UK, education initially followed a route of vocational skills training, developed in art schools and later in colleges of art and design. It later transformed to embrace more theoretically based courses with lesser emphasis on studio work. However, the core values as sketched out in Table 1.1 remained true to the fine art-based professional project. In 1996, the Design Council listed the following Art and Design courses:

- graphics – graphic design (general), book/magazine design, illustration, media/multimedia, packaging, photography, printing, typography;

- fashion/clothing – fashion/clothing design (general), theatre costume, footwear;

- textiles – textile design (general), carpet/rug embroidery, knitted textiles, printed textiles, surface pattern/decoration;

- 3D – products – product design (general), ceramics, furniture, glass industrial design, engineering design, jewellery/silver;

- spatial design – spatial design (general), architecture, building exhibition display, interior, landscape, theatre/stage;

- multidisciplinary;

- other.[63]

These days there is added emphasis on business studies and service design courses within the design curriculum, but these are a significant minority.

Looking at the list of US undergraduate majors offered by the 34 AICAD (Association of Independent Colleges of Art and Design) member colleges, it's clear which path the professional design project has taken (see Table 1.2). One could hardly imagine there would be a large number of students graduating from those courses who would choose their preferred values and methods from the right hand side of the Table 1.1, namely the natural sciences-based ones.

Table 1.2   US undergraduate majors offered at 34 AICAD (Association of
                 Independent Colleges of Art and Design) member colleges

Advertising	Animation	Architecture
Architectural Studies	Art Direction	Art Education
Art History	Art Therapy	Cartooning
Ceramics	Clay	Communication Design
Computer Animation	Computer Graphics	Design Marketing
Drawing	Enamelling	Environmental Design
Fashion Design	Fibres	Film
Filmmaking	Fine Arts	Furniture Design
Glass	Graphic Design	Illustration
Industrial Design	Interior Architecture	Interior Design
Jewellery	Landscape Architecture	Medical Illustration
Medical Photography	Metals	New Genres
Package Design	Painting	Papermaking
Performance	Photography	Printmaking
Sculpture	Textiles	Transportation Design
Video	Weaving	Wood

Source:[63]

It is apparent, even without taking a very detailed look at the individual courses that the educational arrangements must have added to the pre-eminence of the arts-based professional design project.

Design Research and the Professional Project

Reviewing the debate in design research from the professional project's point of view, one can observe a similar interplay of the two social projects.

Broadbent[65] presents a review of design methodologies suggesting there have been four different generations. Firstly, one based on craft method with some 250,000 years of history; the second being design-by-drawing, 550 years old; thirdly, one named 'hard systems' with 40 years of heritage; and finally 'soft systems' which is 20 years old. From the contemporary 'professional project's viewpoint, only the last two are significant. Those correspond respectively to the 'science' and 'art' based value sets of the proponents. This suggests that the design profession's struggle to establish itself is roughly as old as its methodological debate.

Cross[66] correctly predicted the 're-emergence' of the 'science-design' concerns in the 2000s (ibid.: 16) as a part of a cycle in the design field. The cycle began in the 1920s with the modernist movement, which tried to produce works of design based on the allegedly objective and rational science.[65] In the 1960s, a second wave of interest in design science arrived via the likes of Alexander, Simon and Rittel. The First Conference on Design Methods in 1962 recognised the need for a systematic approach to design practice which was sympathetic towards creative practices and was pursuing '… a unified system of design … that lies between the traditional methods, based on intuition and experience, on the one hand, and rigorous mathematical or logical treatment, on the other'.[67] It did, however, fail in this attempt (ibid.). Providing these goals might have been logically, philosophically and conceptually feasible, they might not have been socially feasible, precisely because holding contradictory sets of values while pursuing the professional project's agendas, may have been irreconcilable on an individual, human level.

There have been numerous attempts to bridge the gap between both projects in the sense of developing design's own knowledge base and methodologies. [5, 65, 66, 68–74] Despite the strong philosophical underpinnings of thinkers such as Dewey, Peirce, Habermas, Wittgenstein, and the post-modernist movement in the science debate, it still cannot find its voice on culturally-equal terms with that of natural science or fine arts. Judging by the current, very energetic, debate, the goal is as elusive as ever.

Broadbent[65] believes that the next step in the development of the design methodology, as an evolutionary system methodology, will position design as an evolutionary guidance system for socio-culture '… a much more socially central role in human affairs' (ibid.: 1). In this statement, we can clearly trace the signs of the professional projects manifesting itself in the pursuit of a higher social place based on perfecting the design method.

Similarly, Friedman[6, 75] has been advocating the dawn of the 'integrative discipline' of design. He has carried on the science baton after Fuller and Simon. Friedman presents a taxonomy of design knowledge domains as a framework within which a designer should act in order to give proper credit to the 'integrative' paradigm. Friedman asserts that the most common reasons for failure in design include 'lack of method and absence of systematic and comprehensive understanding' (ibid.: 5), thus echoing the values of the science-based professional project. In his view, design should integrate all the existing established disciplines and designers should be able to comprehend a large portion of the basic sciences. What he appears to be saying is that design, in order to be comprehensive, must to a large extent be predictable, and should first and foremost become a careful student and recipient of established professional knowledge.

This is but one out of the numerous attempts to tame design methods. However, instead of regarding it as concerned with better design scholarship, one could interpret it as yet unsuccessful attempts at making design matter in society in a politically driven bid to elevate design's role in society's eye.

Consequently, the common-ground agenda could have been championed by those circles associated with the 'design science' movement – who have failed to convince the rest of the community on two previous attempts (1920s and 1960s). To illustrate the point, one might use the following example.

Friedman,[6] in his attempt to justify the focus on the integrative interpretation of the new scientific approach to design, states, 'Past environments were simpler. They made simpler demands. Individual experience and personal development were sufficient for depth and substance in professional practice …' (ibid.: 212).

A very similar point was made by Alexander[73] precisely four decades ago when introducing pattern language as a now demonstrably failed aid to tackling the complexity in design. Back then he wrote:

> Today functional problems are becoming less simple all the time. But designers rarely confess their inability to solve them. Instead, when a designer does not understand a problem clearly enough to find the order it really calls for, he falls back on some arbitrarily chosen formal order. The problem, because of its complexity, remains unresolved. (ibid.: i)

This begs the question, are we seeing the new incarnation of the previously failed attempt at legitimising the scientific approach as the model for professional practice in design?

In order to convince sceptical designers and the rest of the professional community of the merits of design as science, this time scholars are invoking paradigms such as complexity theory, systems theory, artificial intelligence, evolutionary theory and neurobiology with the intention of structuring and strengthening the seemingly weak and fluctuating design methodology. Whether they fail or succeed remains to be seen. However, judging by the history of science and art in the design arena, there might be yet another cycle ahead – more as a result of political and social fashion then the merits of the argument.

It could be said that it would have to be real people who either accept the science of design message and its values or reject it. The theories and philosophical underpinnings might be ready, as some authors suggest, but the designers who are practising and researching in design may not be. As the state of the profession shows, they might want to embrace another set of values that do not carry with them a message of structure, cohesion, predictability and stability. Those individuals might want to live by other sets of rules and values. However, I believe that it will prove extremely difficult to find enough individuals willing and capable of carrying both sets of values simultaneously. And if we interpret this through the lens of the professional project, they might not have a socially based incentive to do so, since the adherence to the already established markers might give them better leverage in gaining social status.

It is difficult to speculate about whether there will come a time when design will no longer want, or need, to use either fine arts or natural sciences as a leverage to gaining social respect. Moreover, it is also not clear whether it will ever be recognised by society as something completely different – a third way of equal value. It appears, however, that since status and recognition depend to a large extent on external acknowledgement by other professions, it is unlikely that these will be willing to create a very attractive and practically-skilled competitor.

THE RISE OF DESIGN MANAGEMENT STUDIES, DESIGN THINKING AND SERVICE DESIGN

An even more recent phenomenon in the field of design is the emergence of the design management discipline to which this book is linked. The rise of design management dates back to 1980 in the UK, with the establishment of the Design Council. Although, as Press and Cooper[63] note, the term itself can be traced to the 1960s with the establishment of the RSA Design Management Award in 1965 and publication of Michael Farr's book *Design Management* in 1967, thus the real effort to put design on management's map began a little over two decades ago.

The professional project began with the formation of the Society of Industrial Artist and Designers (SIAD) Design Management Group in 1981. Peter Gorb, at the London Business School, pioneered the inclusion of the subject in the academic arena, which in turn resulted in the first MBA programmes. In the United States, a forum for discussing design in corporations has been established in the form of the Design Management Institute. In Europe the European Academy of Design was founded in 1995 (ibid.).

However, it is important to include a development that could prove to be very significant with respect to furthering the recognition of design in mainstream management studies. A realisation by a part of the organisational science community that design has something significant to offer, resulted in the first, and perhaps even seminal, compilation of articles by established scientists in the field. *Managing as Designing*, edited by Richard Boland Jr. and Fred Collopy,[32] is a significant development. In it, various authors show an unprecedented appreciation of the depth of the term design in connection with many key aspects of management studies. It would not be surprising if a critical and well-informed debate about the current, past and future place of design in organisations started in mainstream organisation studies from this publication.

The role of design and designers has since been recognised by the mainstream management domain, through the impact of people such as the Dean of Rotman School of Management, Roger Martin; IDEO's executives, including the Kelley brothers and Tim Brown; to the CEO of P&G. The increased profile of Apple and Sir Jonathan Ive has also helped elevate design's professional status significantly. There are numerous, high-profile start-ups established and run successfully by designers, including Nest, Airbnb, Flipboard, Pinterest and others.

The design professional project continues. Service design and the growing Design Thinking[76, 77] debate are just some examples of how design is attempting to broaden its domain. From the point of view of this book, however, it is more important to look at where the project has come from and not necessarily where it is going. The professional attitudes, values and mental models form over a long period of time. It is quite a challenge to the leaders in this field to create new reference points and new measures of success. The educational system is also a relatively big tanker that needs to be turned. This won't happen overnight. My intention is not to predict the future of the design project. My aim is to explain why, when I'm talking about designers, I've primarily got in mind the family of arts-based design professions.

Chapter 2
A Few Words about Cultures

Why Cultures Matter and How to Interpret Them

In the previous chapter I looked at design and the design profession. In order to understand the type of impact professional designers have on organisations we need to appreciate the arena in which it all happens, namely within the context of a *culture* – organisational culture. It is such a slippery subject, that I felt it warranted explaining what we actually mean by it.

Defining the term culture, as with design, is an exceptionally difficult task. Apart from being 'one of the two or three most complicated words in the English language'[1, in 2] the term *culture* has no broadly agreed meaning, even in anthropology, the field which most deals with its study.[3, 4] According to Mats Alvesson,[5] the variation in use of the word is particularly noticeable in the literature on organisational cultures. He argues that the heterogeneity of the studies stems not only from the different purposes and depths of books and articles, but also from the variation in scientific disciplines and philosophical orientations. The very broad use of the term often results in it covering everything and, consequently, nothing. Although there are many researchers who express an interest in culture, this does not translate into a uniform description.[6–8]

Understanding of the term culture was historically informed by anthropology, in which culture is a way of life.[9] The most widely accepted definitions of organisational culture are, 'the way we do things here';[10] and 'a set of shared basic assumptions, values and artefacts which developed whilst dealing with problems of external adaptation and internal integration'.[11] These definitions may sound puzzling, but in reality, everybody can begin to analyse the organisational cultures of the companies they interact with. By observing and noting cultural manifestations, they can begin to understand what their cultural make-up is. Take, for example, the look and feel of the offices. You can, sometimes, immediately sense the type of an organisation just by noticing things like office plan and desk arrangement. Is the MD sitting in a separate space or is he or she physically part of the team? Are the offices sparsely decorated or are they teaming with artefacts and colour? All these elements, if looked at systematically and alongside corporate tales, stories, myths, organisational hierarchies and others, can paint a picture of the organisational culture.

From the point of view of this book, it's important to establish the link between organisational and professional culture, in order to uncover what the culture of designers stands for. There is an agreement among scientists that professional, or occupational cultures have significant importance in relation to organisational cultures when compared to other types of subcultures.[12–16] As John Van Maanen and Stephen Barley[13] would have it, occupations are probably the most distinctive subcultures in organisational life. Once formed, professional groups develop not only different knowledge bases, but also different codes for constructing meaningful interpretations of persons, events, and objects commonly encountered in their professional world (ibid.). According to the authors, an occupational community is: '… a group of people who consider themselves to be engaged in the same sort of work; who identify (more or less positively) with their work; who share with one another a set of values, norms and perspectives that apply to, but extend beyond, work related matters and whose social relationships merge the realms of work and leisure'.[13]

Well-established occupations have cultures just as organisations do.[15] Specialisms can be said to consist of a variety of basic components, having the character of their work and forming their own culture.[17, 18] Hansen believes that, 'Like national cultures, occupational subcultures, too, develop distinct languages or jargon that can reveal much about how members prioritise and interpret work responsibilities, processes, and relationships.'[19]

For a quick and convenient example of an organisation shaped by one particular culture, let's look at Google. It has developed on the back of an engineering culture with heavy emphasis on quantification and statistical proof. In Google's case, the subculture of engineers actually became the dominant and overarching culture. An example of how this manifested itself was the case of Google's methods of choosing the right type of shade of blue for its advertising links. It is thought that Google has methodically tested 50 shades of the colour in order to check which one had the best saliency. This process has overridden any recommendations or concerns from the design team.

A plethora of subcultures could, for example, be found in the NHS. There are subcultures of the management staff, nurses and doctors. Within groups of doctors there are the even more specific cultures of the different specialties – interventionists are very different to general medicine doctors, for example. The former value clear, black-and-white decisions and work with sedated patients. The latter depend on a nuanced and fluid diagnosis, often over an extended period of time and deal with complex human emotions.

Given that there are as many different subcultures within organisations as there are professions, which are 'hosted' by the organisation, a question can be asked: what aspects of these overarching organisational cultures are truly unique and actually shared, as opposed to genetic and experienced elsewhere?

Joanne Martin[8] when analysing definitions of the term 'organizational culture' (see ibid.: 57–64), highlighted some common characteristics such as focus on sharedness, uniqueness and distinctiveness and also breadth – how many manifestations of culture (organisational artefacts, stories, routines, rituals) are being studied and the depth of their interpretation – the level of embeddedness of those manifestations. There were, however, a number of theoretical disagreements with respect to these characteristics being inherent in culture. Martin consequently questioned those allegedly common descriptors of an organisational culture such as sharedness or uniqueness. In her view, there was a great deal of confusion among cultural researchers over those issues.

Her assessment of the variety and widespread inconsistency in defining culture led her to put more emphasis on analysing what is actually being studied, how it is being operationalised and what sorts of cultural manifestations are being studied. As a result, Martin[7] devised a framework, now broadly recognised by organisational researchers, which includes three perspectives: integrative, differentiation and fragmentation perspective.

Integrative perspective – here those who study culture see it as primarily homogeneous. The 'sharedness' characteristic is underlined as a mark of the existence of culture. It focuses on those manifestations that have 'mutually consistent interpretations'. Above all the culture is clear and non-ambiguous. The culture is like a monolith seen identically by all.[8] There are numerous examples of this approach.[20, 10, 21, 22, 23, 11] The way in which these studies talk about organisational cultures is as though they were monolithic and totally coherent. They would, for example, say that Microsoft has a particular culture ignoring the fact that Microsoft consists of multiple divisions. Xbox division will be very different to Office division, and those two will be very different to the newly acquired Nokia. Integrative perspective is more interested in describing an entire organisation as a single cultural unit, disregarding internal differences even if those are quite significant.

Differentiation perspective – this concentrates on the subcultural level of inconsistencies within an organisation. From this perspective, consensus is present in organisations but only at lower levels of analysis. As Martin[8] says, 'within a subculture, all is clear; ambiguity is banished to the interstices between subcultures' (ibid.: 94). The ambiguity here resides outside subcultures. Few exemplars include.[12, 24–27] In this perspective, it is common to see differences between parts of an organisation acknowledged. Organisations aren't treated here as solid blocks of people thinking and behaving in exactly the same way. Commentators adhering to the spirit of this perspective discuss nuances and differences present between smaller units of analysis within organisations. Big multinationals, such as P&G, Samsung, Google, would be treated as collections of discrete social groupings, be they professional cultures (engineers, accountants, designers, blue-collar, etc.), national cultures or business unit cultures.

Fragmentation perspective – here the ambiguity of the culture is seen as its core. In this perspective 'consensus is transient and issue specific'.[8] There are patterns of different interpretations and every time they are examined, depending on the situation, these patterns are different. Individuals are each given a voice that could sometimes be supportive, condescending or indifferent to what is happening in their organisation. Sharedness, on any level, if present at all, is to be seen as situated and temporary. Again, there are many studies that espouse this approach.[28–32] It is not that difficult to imagine where this way of looking at cultures comes from. After all, all of us like to think about ourselves as unique individuals with our own backgrounds and life stories, value systems and quirks. The proponents of this perspective are of the view that any coherence and sharedness of values, attitudes and beliefs between individuals is at best temporary, but most likely it's only imagined by the researcher. Therefore, they are, in effect, of the view that there is no such construct as a culture.

Particularly significant from the point of view of this book is the differentiation perspective. Here, various authors emphasise that in many organisations their employees perceive their culture to be unique, whereas in fact there are very similar cultures present in other organisations. In many circumstances it is the professional or occupational cultures that exist independently of the organisation that give a strong identity and value base to the people involved.

Differentiation perspective, therefore, provides the best link between professional culture and the organisation. Looking at it from this angle, the unity and cohesion is delegated to the subcultural level. Occasionally, the ambiguities and inconsistencies are left outside of a subculture.

Uniqueness Paradox: No Organisation is an Island

What if what we think was unique was quite common elsewhere? Many organisations think of themselves and their cultures as unique. Can they, in fact, simply be the spaces where other cultures reside? Is it possible that organisations are the vessels where subcultures mix and collide?

Martin's 'uniqueness paradox', as she calls it, points us to exactly that viewpoint. She cites several studies which found that what researchers and members of the studied organisations perceived to be unique was in fact present in a number of cases. For example, Bockus[33] reviewed 13 different qualitative case studies of the cultures of large firms. All of them had a subset of the same content themes found in Martin et al.[34] content analysis of the annual reports of 100 large corporations. The consequence of this can be the absence of organisational culture, if, in fact, there are very few elements which are unique.

One study that influenced this area was conducted by Kathleen Gregory who looked at the occupational culture of programmers in Silicon Valley in California.[12] She noticed that programmers had a similar subculture in each of the organisations she studied. Her conclusion was that organisations do not have cultures. Rather an organisation is a meeting point of a number of occupational subcultures crossing organisational boundaries (ibid.: 374). There are a number of other writers who similarly conclude that occupational or professional cultures are often stronger (and more coherent) than other groupings, due to having extra-organisational associations.[13–15, 35] I intend to return to this point but firstly we need to examine the ramifications of the 'uniqueness paradox'.

Nexus Approach: Organisation as a Cultural Melting Pot

As Mills[36] points out, people do not leave their own cultural perspective at the gates of their place of work, but bring them to bear when they interact with their colleagues and build their organisations. In a response to the ambiguities and problems of uniqueness, or rather lack of it in organisational cultures, Martin proposes what she calls the 'nexus approach' to the study of culture.[7] A nexus occurs when a variety of internal and external influences come together and interact. She distinguishes between three types of cultural manifestations: manifestations that are truly unique; those that are acknowledged to be unique; and those that are mistakenly believed to be unique (see Figure 2.1). Every organisation has a combination of those and as she admits, 'strictly speaking we should say 'cultures in organisations' and not organizational culture'.[8] This implies that one could tap into the non-unique manifestations of culture that are more closely linked with the external environment, i.e. professional cultures, and analyse those through their manifestations in organisations. For example, we could look at the NHS (National Health Service in the UK) not as one culture but a series of professional cultures of nurses, doctors, managers, top executives and others. This approach does not assume that the different external influences are consistent, nor does it prevent us from exploring the unique parts of an individual organisational culture.

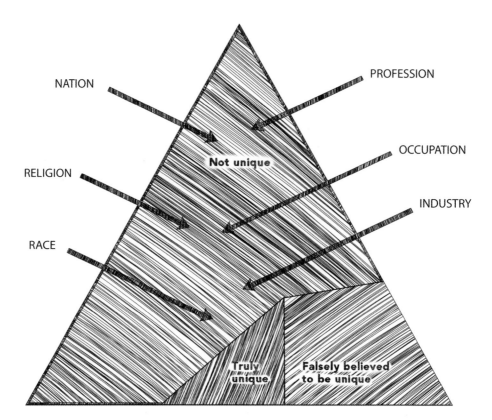

Figure 2.1   The Nexus approach to cultures in organisations

Source: Adapted from J. Martin, *Cultures in Organisations: Three perspectives.*[7]

Professional Culture: A River Flows Through

As noted already, it is difficult to overstate the importance of professional cultures in the light of their relatively low profile. If we reflect on the apparent marginal treatment they have received, the following observation by Geoffrey Bloor and Patrick Dawson appears rather significant, 'Professional subcultures are often stronger than other groupings within an organization in the sense of having extra-organizational associations and peers to aid them in shaping new cultures and codes of conduct, and resisting the imposition of other cultural values and practices.' In other words, professional cultures that reside outside organisations are central to sustaining professional subcultures within organisations.[14]

The prominent sociologist Emile Durkheim (1964) emphasised the importance of occupational life by suggesting that in societies, both nation states and work organisations are too far removed from individuals to offer them a sense of place, and that the institutions of traditional society, including family and religion, had become too weak to do so. Subsequently, he saw modern life concentrated more intensely around occupations.

Arguably, nowadays people are willing to define themselves more often through what they do as a part of an occupation or a profession rather than through the espoused values required of them in their organisational setting. If this were so, it would not be surprising that professions and occupations are forming stronger and more coherent bounds than those in organisations. One might reasonably expect to see people adhering more strongly to their professional cultures rather than their places of employment. Consider this – would a professional accountant, engineer or medic change their basic beliefs, values which they have grown-up with in their professional career in response to the requirement of the organisation, or is it more likely that they would bring those values with them to bear on their new organisation? Let's think for a moment about the ever-increasing workers' mobility, the fact that the job-for-life model is exceedingly difficult to come by, or the proliferation of flexible working arrangements (i.e. people working remotely, hot-desking, frequent rotations between teams). All these taken together contribute even more to the situation where employees would prefer to carry with them their sense of professional skill and pride and only after that consider adjusting to the values of their current employer. I would suggest, therefore, that what is unique in an organisational culture, especially in a company with one dominant profession, will be increasingly difficult to develop and maintain. Instead, professions or occupations will be seen as carriers of what is perceived as unique, but in fact, to a considerable extent is common. A group of accountants preferring structure, sporting great attention to detail or exercising a degree of risk-aversion (one would hope), having acquired these preferences professionally, would likely, overall, have more culturally in common with other groups of accountants from similar organisations than with, say, HR professionals from their own organisation.

The professional culture crosses organisational boundaries, leaving its signature values, attitudes and beliefs inside organisations. This suggests that looking at companies that all have a design culture can provide information regarding what is unique and what is non-unique when it comes to aspects and elements of this culture. This forms the framework for analysing the professional culture of designers. By looking at several organisations saturated with professional designers, I believe it is possible to identify and define the special characteristics of their culture.

Chapter 3
The Making of a Designer

Before we can really start to grasp the nature of design culture, we must first understand the main reference points relevant to the design profession. Before I move on to focus on the specific aspects of design attitude, I wanted to grapple with the issues of designerly ways of knowing – the skills that are unique to designers and the very nature of the activity of design.

Let us take a moment to really look at the characteristics, skills, and attitudes of designers. The best way to do this is to look at the field from three different perspectives – firstly, it is important to discuss the architectural/educational perspective; then I propose to review the psychological school, and finally I examine the design management approach.

What It Takes to Be a Designer

A designer makes things. Sometimes she makes the final product but, more often, she makes a representation – a plan, program or image – of an artefact to be constructed by others. She works in particular situations, uses particular materials, and employs a distinctive medium and language. Typically, this design process is complex. Because of this complexity, the designer's actions tend to produce unexpected consequences. When this happens, the designer may take account of the unintended changes she has made in the situation by forming new appreciations and understandings, thus producing something new she had not anticipated.[1] There have been volumes written on the traits, skills and thinking of designers.[1–24] I believe that, in essence, the literature could be divided into three different strands of analysing designers and their skills.

Firstly, there is the architectural studio tradition with a strong emphasis on design education. This approach looks predominantly at the design activity and design process through the lens of designer-learner, designer-educator or designer-practitioner perspective – that is to say the student, the teacher and the qualified designer.[1, 25, 26, 27, 28, 29, 24, 30, 5, 6, 8, 31, 32] Secondly, there is psychologically based research into designers' abilities and thinking. Here the accent is placed more on the cognitive styles and personality traits of designers.[2, 4, 13, 10, 33, 34, 35] Thirdly, there is a category that offers a more management-based viewpoint. This is a perspective that sees designers as contributors to the commercially based aims of an organisation. The research in this tradition is largely done by design managers, design consultants, organisational researchers or designers who are strongly connected with the area of management.[16, 36, 19, 37, 38,[6, 39, 18, 40, 41, 42, 43, 44, 45]

Architects of Their Own Success

According to Alexander,[46, 47] the design process has become too complex to be handled in its totality by any single designer-architect relying solely on the visual feedback he or she receives while designing. Therefore, a designer needs to be able to divide the project up into smaller parts – semi-independent subsystems, which could be dealt with separately. He proposes using 'a pattern language' in order to aid a designer in the demanding process of optimising his or her work. His view is that designers, and indeed all humans, are connected to one source that has a 'central value' which helps to make judgements and decisions about the 'fit' or, for that matter, 'miss-fit' of the solution presenting itself to this central value.

Schön also discusses design ability from the architectural perspective. In *The Reflective Practitioner* (1983) he gives a seminal account of the dynamics of working and learning within the professional design environment. Schön's description of the rather generic qualities of a designer includes first and foremost the ability to engage in a reflective conversation with a problematic situation. In his view, all practitioners must, to a certain degree, develop this capacity. When they do engage wholeheartedly with the reflective process they make use of their tacit knowledge and non-logical processes in order to swiftly operate in a tight feedback loop.

The designer listens to the situation's back-talk and reflects accordingly. Back-talk happens, for example, when, while sketching, we see unexpected patterns emerge and so we respond to them. It is an interplay between the designer, the materials at her disposal and the situational constraints. A designer will most likely use a central idea as a guiding principle in order to give the otherwise unstructured and fluid process a central spine. While making on-the-fly adaptations, the designer encounters both anticipated and unanticipated consequences. It's a situation we all recognise. When we develop presentations, plans or write proposals those things make us reflect on their various aspects and we often change course or make significant changes mid-flow. Designers, thanks to their obsession with prototyping early and often, engage very intensively and consciously in the reflective process where the developing solution becomes part of the purposeful conversation.

One of the most commonly referred to voices in the debate on the skills, abilities and thinking of designers has been that of Nigel Cross.[5–7, 32, 48] In Cross's view, all professionals are designers and indeed, all of us possess some form of design ability. This is consistent with what Schön[1] and Simon[49] advocate. Cross suggests that while this is true, some designers are better than others in the act of designing.[6] Although his later work appears to be sympathetic towards defining design ability within an organisational setting, the fact that his study, in general, is more concerned with an independent-of-the-economic-realm design ability – as a type and distinct form of intelligence – it is categorised along with the more generalist and educationally-based tradition.

Cross[6] has compiled a meta-analysis of the nature of design thinking and designerly ways of knowing, based on his own and other researchers' interviews with famous designers (architects, engineers and product designers), observations and case studies, protocol studies, reflections and theories, and simulation trials (ibid.: 22). Cross argues that design is rhetorical, which means it is persuasive. Design is also rhetorical 'in the sense that the designer, in constructing a design proposal, constructs a particular kind of argument, in which a final conclusion is developed and evaluated as it develops against known goals and previously unsuspected implications' (ibid.: 28). Cross summarises the rhetorical nature of design by quoting the architect Denys Lasdun, who says, 'Our job is to give the client … not what he wants, but what he never dreamed he wanted; and when he gets it, he recognizes it as something he wanted all the time' (ibid.)

Another characteristic of design is that it is not a simple exercise in optimisation. Design is exploratory and messy. The way in which a designer interprets a design brief is open and fluid. The true nature of the problem is often not entirely known until the actual solution is found and tested in real-life conditions. A classic example of this is the process of designing a new building. The initial constraints and expectations are only able to give an outline of the challenge. As the project progresses, the architect, contractors and the client encounter issues such as unexpected problems with the planning process, terrain, budget constraints, availability of materials and so forth. Only through these things revealing themselves at various stages, are they able to truly appreciate the problems and create solutions. This is a relatively simple design challenge. The truly perplexing and taxing design problems are ambiguous, open-ended and 'wicked'.[50] The good designer does not see an early brief as a given but rather tries to discover something new that is hidden in the assignment. Cross asserts that the vagueness of the relationship between problem and solution is reconciled by the emergent nature of the latter.

Design is emergent, the solution and the problem develop concurrently. Schön[1] further endorsed these ideas, stating that a designer in a problem-solution-space engages in a reflective conversation with the circumstances and often changes the early goals and constraints. The problem only becomes apparent when you are trying to solve it.

According to Cross, as a result of the fact that all the relevant information cannot be predicted in advance of the design activity, the decisions and directions taken during the design process occur partially by chance. This, he argues, means that design is opportunistic.

Cross also believes that intuition plays an important role in the process of design and that it is shorthand for what really happens – the reasoning in design is to him abductive. This is 'a type of reasoning different from the more familiar concepts of inductive and deductive reasoning, but which is the necessary logic of design – the necessary step from function to form'.[6]

In Cross's view, another characteristic of design thinking is its reflective nature. There is a conversation taking place where a designer is engaging both the 'external' and the 'internal' representations of a problem. She needs to have a medium – which, for example, could be a sketch – to 'converse' with. This argument therefore leads us to conclude that the design process is ambiguous. Ted Happold, a structural engineering designer puts it thus, 'I really have, perhaps, one real talent; which is that I don't mind at all living in the area of total uncertainty' (ibid.: 30).

Uncertainty within the design process, in the sense of leaving open alterative avenues of exploration until the last possible moment, is what Cross means by it being ambiguous. To him, 'designers will generate early tentative solutions … and are prepared to regard solution concepts as necessary, but imprecise and often inconclusive' (op. cit.). Lastly, design is risky. The process of design it is not easy and comfortable. Often design reputation is made by taking considerable risks.[6]

In addition to all of these statements about the nature of design intelligence, Cross stresses the importance of drawing and visualising during the process of design. He says that, to a certain extent, everyone possesses design 'intelligence' is possessed and that this 'highest form of human intelligence' – the best design intelligence – is possessed by the best professional designers.[6]

The themes that Cross presents suffer from at least one problem. His characteristics overlap heavily and are not of the same kind. For example, some of them refer to situations a designer finds herself in (for example: ambiguously set goals will lead to an ambiguous situation), others relate to the goals of design and others, such as emergent, opportunistic and reflective, concern the *modus operandi* of design.

One could ask the question, is it always like that? Does designing always have to be ambiguous, risky, abductive and so forth? Cross's description seems to be rather 'static' in the sense that he shows a snapshot of the various statements made by famous designers by extracting those out of the contexts in which they were (or are being) made, so that we do not know what the circumstances were in which these statements were made. What is also absent from the commentary is whether they referred to specific organisational settings. The way they are presented suggests he puts forward those characteristics as dispositional statements relating to a static, Ideal Type descriptions.

We can, for example, see how other designers might think that design is divergent and/or convergent, open, transparent, multifaceted, rapid, and so forth. In fact, there are a number of statements made by Smythe[51] that could make an equally compelling list that is representative of design thinking.

Table 3.1 shows what a number of authors think characteristics of designers are.

Table 3.1   Examples of analysis of designers' abilities and thinking

Alexander[46, 47, 52] designer is:	Schön[1] designer is:	Cross[5] Designer must be able to:	Chandran[27] designers competences:	Cross[6] designers thinking is:
Attentive to the 'central value'. Persuasive. Uses 'pattern language' to simplify the process. Tries to achieve the 'good fit' between problem and solution.	Listening to 'back-talk' in the problem-solution-space. Engaged in deep reflection. Thinking-by-drawing. Aesthetically judging the 'goodness of fit'. Working with the material.	Produce novel, unexpected solutions. Tolerate uncertainty, work with incomplete information. Apply imagination and constructive forethought to practical problems. Use drawings and other modelling media as means of problem-solving. Resolve ill-defined problems. Adopt solution-focusing strategies. Employ abuctive/ productive. appositional thinking. Use nonverbal, graphic/spacial modelling media. Work with several alternative design solutions in parallel in order to understand the problem-solution-space.	Core Knowledge Competence. Problem-solving. Critical Thinking. Creativity. Engineering Judgement.	Rhetorical. Exploratory. Emergent. Opportunistic. Abductive. Reflective. Ambiguous. Risky.

Psychological School Perspective

The second approach to analysing design ability stems mostly from the experiential method in psychology. There are a number of studies engaged in studying designers from a cognitive ability or cognitive and learning styles perspective (see Table 3.2). These studies are usually drawn from work in psychology on cognitive styles which use categories such as: convergent/ divergent; linear/lateral; serialist/holist; appositional/propositional; focused/ flexible.

One interesting example is provided by Lawson,[2] in where he examined the way students of engineering, architecture and science were dealing with an abstracted design problem. He was specifically interested in investigating different problem-solving strategies. Lawson found that scientists were more interested in discovering the underlying structure of the problem in order to generate a solution, while architects tested sequences of high-scoring solutions until one was accepted. In an additional experiment, he found that different strategies developed in the course of their education. The difference was clear among fifth-year and postgraduate students, but it was not observed among first-year students. Lawson concluded that the architects had therefore learned this strategy during their design-based education as a response to the nature of the problems they had to deal with.

In a different study, Cross and Nathenson[9] identified that it is important to study cognitive styles in order to inform design education and design methods. Newland, Powell and Creed[13] continued this work by studying learning styles among architects. The authors used Kolb's[53, 54] learning styles as the foundation of their study. Kolb's classification contrasts various aspects of learning. He juxtaposes 'abstract conceptualisation' and 'concrete experience'; 'active experimentation' and 'reflective observation'. Consequently, these extremes provide four types of learning styles. People who prefer to learn through active experimentation and concrete experience are labelled 'accommodators'; those who favour abstract conceptualisation and active experimentation are called 'convergers'; if they are more prone to using reflective observation and abstract conceptualisation they are 'assimilators'; and those people who prefer reflective observation and concrete experience are labelled 'divergers'. Based on those abstracted categories, Newland et al.[13] distinguish four types of designers by their preferred learning style:

- *Common-sense designer-learners* – are abstract thinkers; combine abstract thinking with experimentation or concrete experience – usually efficient architectural planners.

- *Dynamic designer-learners* – learn from dynamic incidents in life; are aware of opportunities, seek constant feedback.

- *Contemplative designer-learners* – combine reflective observation and abstract conceptualisation.

- *Zealous designer-learners* – actively experiment and observe reflectively; are practically driven.

In yet another investigation, Durling, Cross and Johnson[10, 33] conducted a study in which they explored cognitive styles among art-based design students. As with Newland et al.,[13] these authors decided to employ a well-known method as a backdrop to their investigation. Durling et al. used Myers-Briggs Type Indicator, a tool extensively tested in the field of the psychology of personality. They concluded that there is a match between students' preferred way of learning design and the preferred way of teaching design in the UK educational system. Another important outcome was that over three quarters of design students (including: graphic design, furniture design, interior design and design marketing) have a preference for Intuition and a majority also preferred Perception. A quarter of the design students included in the study were of just one (out of 16!) personality type – ENTP (Extroversion, Intuition, Thinking, Perception). This suggests they are more interested in intuition than thinking and will strive for maximum freedom and flexibility in the pursuit of intuitive goals.

Durling et al.[10] also concluded that designers prefer training which begins with abstractions and a general overview and then proceeds to explaining details; has a light structure that allows for exploration; focuses on possible future scenarios while giving alternative viewpoints and is based on exemplars of displayed things. A third of designers are additionally inclined towards a person-centred approach and value judgements. In contrast, non-designers favour teaching that begins with details and facts, and then engages in generalisations using a step-by-step process. The authors stress that no single kind of design learning is suitable for all designers.

Table 3.2   Psychological studies of designers

Carrol[55] in Arvola[56] investigates cognitive abilities of designers:	Durling et al.[10, 33] cognitive styles among art-based design students (Myers-Briggs Type Indicator), preferred teaching styles:	Newland et al.[13] learning styles among architects based on Kolb's[53, 54] learning styles; similar –[57]	Kirton[12, 58] cognitive styles in[59] Two overarching cognitive types. Designers belong to 'Innovators'
Communication ability. Inductive reasoning. Associative memory. Visual memory. Manipulating spatial relations. Perceiving gestalts or closures. Gestalt or closure flexibility. Visualisation. Perceptual speed. Associational fluency. Sensitivity to problems. Originality/creativity. Figural fluency. Figural flexibility.	Intuition over thinking. Feeling. Maximum freedom in the pursuit of intuitive goals. Perceptive attitude. Broad picture in the early stages then details. Focused on future possibilities. Lightweight structure allowing exploration. Logical and analytical based on exemplars showing things. Prefer teaching which begins with general picture and then it focuses on details and facts and more guided instruction. No single learning style is suitable for all designers. ENTP ¼ of all designers (Extroversion, Intuition, Thinking, Perception).	Common-sense designer-learners. Dynamic designer-learners. Contemplative designer-learners. Zealous designer-learners.	Adaptors. Innovators.

Design Management Perspective

The design management perspective presents the study of designers from a point of view where they are contributors to building commercial value within organisations. Since the emergence of design management in the 1980s, there have been several investigations into the place of design in business and the character of the designer's input.[16, 36, 38, 43, 60–67] Some of those studies have been associated with either the Design Council in Europe or the Design Management Institute in the US that have either commissioned the work or were affiliated with the authors. Almost without exception, these studies point to the positive financial consequences of engaging design and designers in organisations.

In the early days, Lorenz[16] identified a number of skills of designers in the organisational context. He argued that the designer's most fundamental skill is synthesis, or, as he calls it 'Cross pollination' from one field to another.

The second most important skill is that of visualisation – the ability to visualise shapes and the relationship between objects in three dimensions. He emphasises the use of imagination (after Theodore Levitt) as 'the construction of mental pictures of what is or is not actually present, what has never been actually experienced' (ibid.: 20). Furthermore, designers act as interpreters and stimulators in the product development process. Lorenz[16] underlined the importance of designers in an organisation and their role as that of 'facilitators' rather than 'stylists' (ibid.: 7). His list of skills was based on a number of case studies of design-minded organisations and interviews with well-regarded designers.

At the same time, Gorb,[38] who is responsible for setting up the first design management courses at the London Business School, defines designers as people who, work with artefacts, have special skills relating to manipulating artefacts and operate under a distinct methodology (ibid.: 107).

Walker[59] juxtaposes designers with managers by presenting a list of corresponding characteristics in a series of categories. He suggests that designers are concerned, among other things with short-term aims, reform, prestige and environments. Their education is in crafts, arts, visuals and geometric shapes. Walker also lists designers' thinking styles as holistic, lateral, synthetic and solution-led. As aspects relating to designers' culture and behaviour, he lists optimism, innovativeness, diversity and experimentation. It is, however, unclear how he has reached his conclusions. Apart from one source, a study of managers' styles of problem-solving by Kirton,[11] he provides no references regarding designers themselves. We can perhaps presume that those are based on his personal experiences in the field. To a certain extent, we can also see them as an expression of a stereotypical view of the differences expressed by someone coming from the management studies perspective.

Bruce and Harun[40] in a study commissioned by the Design Council, have highlighted the distinctive skills of professional designers. The report outlined designers' strategic and tacit skills grouped in four areas:

- applied skills such as creative techniques, commercial skills;

- knowledge including process, material and technical competences;

- processing in the form of visualising, researching, analysing and prioritising;

- values/perspectives that encompass risk taking, originality and anticipating future trends among other things.

The attempts of the authors, however, did not focus on distinct set of shared values, which designers possess and bring with them to organisations. Without any additional research one can state that non-designers are also thinking creatively, taking difficult decisions and managing considerable risks in their work.

Designers, according to Bruce and Bessant,[18] are good at drawing and model-making, have a visual imagination and sensitivity and are commercially-oriented. In addition the authors state that, 'A good designer has the ability to integrate, interpret and conceptualise solutions. Designers are under constant pressure to develop new skills and re-train in new technology, and they can harness technology and 'couple' this with user needs, to create novel products and/or services' (ibid.: 48).

Borja de Mozota[39] builds a set of in-house design competencies on Cooper and Press's[61] classification into design, relational qualities, business sense, project management, and the capacity to generate a perspective. The authors believe that designers' ability to generate concepts must be complemented by management abilities and relational abilities. According to Borja de Mozota there are certain competencies that should be required of an in-house designer. As with other scholars in the field, the list appears not to be supported by a methodologically-grounded empirical study but rather proposed by the author based on her experience and understanding. She lists commitment, enthusiasm, self-confidence, team orientation, objective creativity, strategic thinking and many similar competencies, as she calls them. These could quite easily be attributed to a number of other professions or persons.

Press and Cooper[43] divide the 'attributes' of a professional designer into two categories. Firstly, they list those skills that relate to the act of designing including manipulation of colour, texture, shape, space, odour, etc.; and visualisation of concepts using context-specific materials and media (ibid.: 179). Secondly, the authors feature skills/attributes which relate to the process of designing, the designer should be able to research, question, integrate, isolate and to be intuitive, sensitive, holistic, divergent and convergent; they should also be prepared to deconstruct, synthesise, reconstruct, innovate and create as well as to communicate verbally and non-verbally in words, images and forms (op. cit.). If designers were to acquire all of these skills, they would be one of the most multifaceted and talented professional groups in the world. However, the skills lists seem to have been derived from an act of thinking about, rather than researching among, designers.

Table 3.3 includes a summary of some of the features attributed to design and designers made by the commentators in the design management field.

Table 3.3 Examples of the descriptions of the skills and qualities of designers

Gorb[38] designers:	Bruce and Harun[40] distinctive skills of professional designers:	Lorenz[16] attributes and skills of a designer:	Press and Cooper[43] skills/ attitudes of a professional designer:	Bernstein[19] characteristics of a designer:	Borja de Mozota[39] designers' and qualities:
Work with artefacts. Have special skills relating to artefacts. Operate under a distinct methodology.	Creative thinking. Decision-making. Risk taking. User focus. Relating to processing: visualising. researching. analysing. scenario building. adapting and inventing. presenting and persuading. synthesising information. balancing stakeholder requirements. intuitive thinking.	Imagination. The ability to visualise shapes and the relationship between objects in three dimensions. Creativity. Natural unwillingness to accept obvious solutions. The ability to communicate through words and sketches. The ability and versatility to synthesise all sorts of multidisciplinary factors and influences into a coherent whole.	Relating to the *act* of designing: Manipulation of colour, texture, shape, sound, space, odour, etc. Visualisation of concepts using context-specific materials and media. Relating to the *process* of designing: Research, question, integrate, convergent. Be intuitive, sensitive, holistic, divergent, convergent. Deconstruct, synthesise, reconstruct, innovate, and create. Communicate verbally, non-verbally, in words, images and forms.	Designer as synthesiser. Sees new associations, Explainer – uses visual thinking to understand and communicate. Loves things, has product passion. Imagination. Creativity. Lateral thinking. Curiosity. Employs seemingly illogical means to reach the solution.	Not afraid to make mistakes. Simplify work presses. Work fast. Do not accept clients briefs as givens. Able to generate concepts. Management abilities: sense of dialogue. creative imagination. capacity to influence and listen.

Views of Designers' Skills and Roles

There are several issues that should be raised. There is much confusion with regard to the level of conceptual decomposition of these 'characteristics' among scholars. Often, a single contributor will discuss things which relate to the skills of designers, the nature of design activity, design intelligence and the nature of the process of design in the same paper without distinguishing between them appropriately, and when the author creates categories to accommodate any differences-in-kind among them, they end up classed in an even more misleading and confusing way. In order to clarify the matter, I attempted to organise most of the characteristics and skills present in the review into conceptually symmetrical groups (see Figure 3.1).

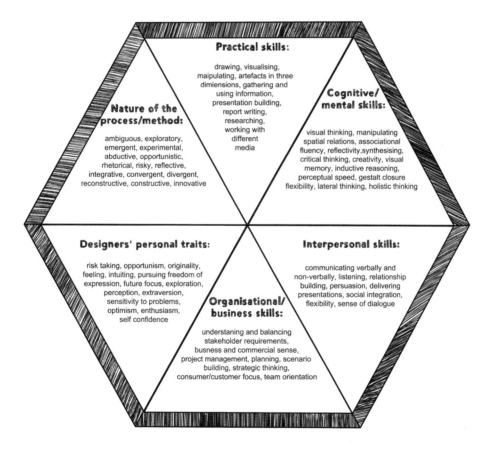

Figure 3.1   Designers' skills and characteristics

These groups are:

- practical skills: drawing, visualising, manipulating artefacts in three dimensions, gathering and using information, presentation building, report writing, researching, working with different media;

- cognitive/mental skills: visual thinking, manipulating spatial relations, associational fluency, reflectivity, synthesising, critical thinking, creativity, visual memory, inductive reasoning, perceptual speed, Gestalt closure flexibility, lateral thinking, holistic thinking;

- interpersonal skills: communicating verbally and non-verbally, listening, relationship building, persuasion, delivering presentations, social integration, flexibility, sense of dialogue;

- organisational/business skills: understanding and balancing stakeholder requirements, business and commercial sense, project management, planning, scenario building, strategic thinking, consumer/customer focus, team orientation;

- designers' personal preferences/traits both stemming from socialisation and inherited: risk taking, opportunism, originality, feeling, intuiting, pursuing freedom of expression, future focus, exploration, perception, extraversion, sensitivity to problems, optimism, enthusiasm, self-confidence;

- nature of the process/method: ambiguous, exploratory, emergent, experimental, abductive, opportunistic, rhetorical, risky, reflective, integrative, convergent, divergent reconstructive, constructive, innovative.

What is worth noting is that the authors rarely attach caveats to their lists, as though to suggest they are universally applicable. The situations and circumstances in which these skills are used seem to have no impact on them. It is impossible to say, for instance, which combinations of skills would be necessary, desirable or indeed redundant in relation to different circumstances. We can anticipate that not all of those skills and characteristics will be present at all times. There are virtually no references, except for a number of psychological studies, as to when, and if, some of these skills and characteristics would not be applicable.

What is missing in this debate is an ethnographically-based understanding of the influence and composition of the design profession. There has been a lot of focus in design management literature on selling design as a tool or a mode of thinking. It is only natural that organisations such as the Design Council or DMI, or design-led consultancies, including IDEO and Frog, would try to convince the public of the virtues of the design approach. There is nothing wrong with them pursuing their interest and lobbying on behalf of the design profession.

My aim is to examine design professionals more like an ethnographer rather than as an evangelist. The primary concern is to bring to the table what I know about other professions and to investigate designers as objectively as I possibly can (accepting that there is no such thing as objectivity in this type of research).

As outlined in the previously, designers are in a process of forming a profession (or a family of professions) and thus are engaged in a project that sees them adhere to certain values as a means of gaining social and economic recognition. In order to achieve closure and position themselves high in the professional pecking order, designers socialise themselves in accordance with certain values, attitudes, assumptions and ways of doing things. The design's educational systems and their professional institutions are being deployed to aid in this process.

Since a thorough understanding of the entirety of this dynamic phenomenon would be too ambitious for any one person, a situated and grounded study of these values might be feasible. This particularly relates to the organisational level where a better-targeted understanding of things such as the values, attitudes and behaviours of designers as a group might help dispel confusion and the common misapprehension of the place and role of designers in an organisational setting.

I intend, therefore, to investigate designers not only as individuals, but also as a professional group, with respect to the nature of their contribution to organisations. I hope that this group-level analysis has the potential to untangle some of the complex issues associated with the make-up of designers' professional culture. The overarching aim behind this book was to investigate the nature of the art-based professional design culture through its place in a design-intensive organisation.

PART II
Five Aspects of Design Attitude

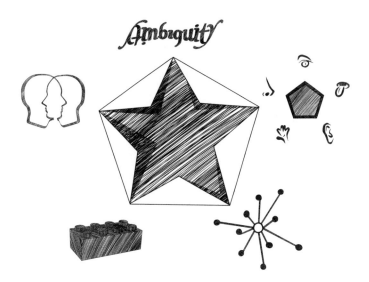

Having looked at the family of design professions and the arts-based professional project, we now turn to the heart of the matter, namely design attitude itself. When I first came across a professional design environment, I instantly felt that the culture created by the people working in it was very different to the professional culture I had come from. My business and management background moulded me in a way that put emphasis on structures, procedures and clear processes. The design environment struck me as unkempt, messy and highly irregular, if not irrational, at times. My initial sense of bewilderment gave way to a desire to find out more about designers as a professional group. I then started what was to become a four-year ethnographic project to uncover what distinctive and unique qualities inherent in the professional culture of the design profession. What I knew I didn't want to do was to collect a superficial list of attributes primarily based on my own assumptions of how things work. Having spent a couple of years embedded in a culture full of design professionals, I felt that the descriptions and analysis of designers in organisations didn't quite do justice to their apparently unique way of influencing the world. I would hear things like, creativity, synthesis, visualising, imagination, curiosity etc. All of them felt as though they could also be applied to other people and professions.

However, none of this quite put the finger on what was distinctive about them. Much of what I'd read and heard wasn't especially helpful either. It also occurred to me that a lot of the studies of the design profession were often very self-referential. Until I read Boland and Collopy's book *Managing as Designing*, I don't think I found a single in-depth book describing the impact of design and designers in organisations that didn't originate from within the design profession itself. This meant that a truly ethnographic perspective of an *in-situ* outsider wasn't available.

The following chapters are a culmination of a number of years studying professional designers by somebody who does not belong to their profession.

Over the course of the research which culminated in this book, I had countless formal and informal conversations with the staff and students of the School of Design at Northumbria University in the UK. Having been based in its Centre for Design Research, I had the opportunity to observe, interact and query designers daily. This formed the bedrock of my understanding and provided me with a rich environment to hone my thinking. The more formal and structured part of the research involved talking to roughly 20 top executives from design-intensive organisations between 2003 and 2007. Those businesses included Apple, IDEO, Nissan Design, Philips Design and Wolff Olins. When I interviewed individuals in these companies, I wasn't trying to describe the company cultures, but I was looking for what they had in common. I used them to unearth what was central to the culture of professional designers that flows through them. The other piece of formal research that fed into the findings of this book was an online survey tool, based on original insights. I'd developed it with the help and support of a global research agency, Toluna. It was rolled out internationally between November 2013 and February 2014. The total sample was N=235. Approximately half of the respondents were based in the United Kingdom and United States of America. The rest were from 30 other countries. The participants were not incentivised, but were told the study was about design. N=174 respondents classified themselves as designers, the rest identified themselves as non-designers. The bulk of the participants were recruited on a voluntary basis from LinkedIn design forums. The non-design sample consisted of a mixture of professionals, many of them having an interest in design.

The following chapters explore the design attitude and the culture of professional designers. Although my gaze is firmly fixed on this group, I'm also using examples from other areas to illustrate how design attitude is embraced and acted upon by others.

Chapter 4
Embracing Uncertainty and Ambiguity

'In our world, "prove it" is the absolute enemy of innovation. You can only prove things that have happened in the past. A business person who wants innovation has to be open to the logic of what might be, not just the logic of what is.' Roger Martin, Dean, Rotman School of Management.[1]

Tolerance of uncertainty is partly the effect of our genes[2] and partly our culture. In my experience, and based on all the research I have done, the profession of design both attracts and produces people who happily embrace uncertainty and fuzzy processes. For years, the management domain and business schools have based their philosophy on taming chaos, using prescribed and rigid frameworks and generally exuded an aura of the invincibility of the method they've been teaching. It's hardly surprising, then, that supporting or embracing ambiguity and uncertainty goes against their very foundations. Yet it is precisely what lies at the heart of design attitude. To put it simply, designers cannot afford to deceive themselves that there exist some universal and unshakeable set of tools and principles for creating entirely novel products and services. They know, in their heart of hearts, that there are no rules for creating something that has never been proposed before. Sure, they have lots of rules of thumb and useful frameworks, but they know that, all too often, those have to be ignored in order to achieve a creative leap.

In my survey, four out of six attitudinal statements relating to embracing ambiguity and uncertainty differed significantly between designers and non-designers. Designers agreed more strongly with, 'I am comfortable with an ambiguous and uncertain process' – 66 per cent designers agreed as opposed to 41 per cent others. 'Experimentation through trial-and-error is something

I value highly', was almost unanimously endorsed by designers (90 per cent agreed versus 72 per cent of non-designers). Non-designers, on the other hand, leaned more positively towards the statements, 'Not knowing precisely how a project is going to unfold makes me uncomfortable' (30 per cent vs 20 per cent) and 'I prefer a sequential, properly laid-out process to get things done efficiently' (64 per cent vs 43 per cent).

It is this acceptance of inherent uncertainty among designers that I found quite remarkable and different to other professions. It has to be noted, though, that this aspect of their culture still produces convulsions within their own profession. On the one hand, designers are attempting to formalise their discipline by creating, for example, countless toolkits and ideal process schematics. On the other hand, designers are happy to drop them instantly, if those formal models don't fit with their intuitive and immediate assessment of the situation. The latter actually reveals the true nature of the professional culture that designers create. They live and breathe uncertainty and ambiguity. With so many diverse inputs to their work, ranging from colours, shapes, textures, people's feelings, their desires and needs, to manufacturing constraints and brand strategy, designers are in an almost constant state of ambiguity and flux. This state is only temporarily resolved by a prototype or a final product or service. It is, undoubtedly, the language of the art-based professional project that has designers value originality over predictability and standardisation. This manifests itself in their relationship with uncertainty and an uneven, stop-start approach to problem-solving. Instead of fighting with uncertainty and discontinuity, they surf it.

To embrace discontinuity and risk is one of the most notable features of the culture of designers. The organisations with this attitude do not reject planning, however they are willing to go off-plan and venture to places where the outcomes are uncertain. For designers a plan is a preliminary guide and not a map cast in stone. They have the ability and willingness to stray from the predetermined path and into the unknown. Such an attitude entails risks, of course. As one senior manager from IDEO told me, 'It's about people who are willing to be risky and comfortable with not knowing exactly what the outcome of the project is going to be'. While the eventual path of a project may be unknown – that is, the exact nature or shape of the eventual outcome may be a mystery – those who espouse design attitude are comfortable with the feeling of ambiguity inherent in it. While many leaders strive to control all facets and factors of a process, believing that such control helps to ensure success, designers believe that the chances for success increase by actually letting go. They are more flexible and open than rigid. It is this very flexibility that is the strength of the design approach, since it allows practitioners to adjust to different developments and unexpected circumstances. The flip side of that is that we can no longer kid ourselves that having the perfect process will shield us from the messiness and complexities of those truly ambitious projects. The best entrepreneurs, scientists, artists and, it appears, many designers, learn to live with ambiguity and uncertainty. That is to say they always have one eye on the methods, hypotheses and structures and the other on the unknown, untested and original thoughts. They are always vigilant, always ready for serendipity or the wildcard idea to offer the unanticipated but brilliant solution. Then, when it comes, they don't dismiss it because it doesn't fit their predefined model. Quite the opposite, because their attitude is one that embraces useful accidents, they jump at the opportunity to try things out.

It's important to note that design attitude organisations, ones where the culture of designers is a significant force, embrace the open-endedness of the designer. They need to do it, however, without losing the commercial imperative of their business or despite funding constraints in case of public services organisations. They realise that if unchecked by a set process within an organisational culture (such as the one present at the companies I've looked at that included Apple, IDEO, Philips, Nissan or Wolff Olins), ambiguity and uncertainty could jeopardise commercial objectives. This might happen in part due to a prolonged search for the so-called perfect solution that results in overdesigning. As Weick[3] puts it, 'Designers fail because they don't know when to stop. The trick in designing is to stop while the design still has life'. It may also be caused by the blind faith in the inevitability of inspiration.

The IDEO process is a good example of how to introduce rigour into a design attitude infused culture while still encouraging exploration, creativity and acceptance of ambiguity. At IDEO, the attitude of keeping an open mind is balanced on a project level by the generic design process. This process consists of five distinctive parts:

1. observation – utilising cognitive psychologists, anthropologists, sociologists in conjunction with the client and designers;

2. brainstorming – a core of the idea-generating activity, drawing on the analysis of data gathered in the observation phase;

3. rapid prototyping – working with models helps everyone visualise and initially verify possible solutions;

4.   refining – narrowing options through iterating choices;

5.   implementation – creating the actual product or service.

Uncertainty Welcomed

Alongside uncertainty and ambiguity, designers embrace discontinuity. The term is an evocative synonym for profound change: the way things were, or the way things have been done, is suddenly ended. Discontinuity, of course, has been in existence since the dawn of man, take the examples of the discontinuity of thought and belief – the proof that the earth was round, the argument that all human beings have inherent rights; discontinuity in nature – the eruption of Mt Vesuvius and the subsequent destruction of Pompeii among many other sudden and transformative natural interruptions; discontinuity in society – the abolition of slavery, the vote for women; and discontinuity in business and commerce – the industrial age migration of farmers and artisans into the factory.

Discontinuity is nothing new, and yet it is through Clayton Christensen's concept of disruptive technology, in *The Innovator's Dilemma* and other books, that the full promise and power of discontinuity was specifically described. Christensen showed that an insurgent company with none of the advantages of the industry incumbents in size, resources, reputation or experience can still defeat all incumbents with one weapon: discontinuity, or more specifically, a different business model supported by new, disruptive technology. The term disruptive technology refers to the ability of the technology to change the rules of the game, thus disrupting the industry.

Disruptive companies completely reject the history, success and strategies of the industry that they are trying to invade. For example, Nucor invaded the steel industry by using recycled steel (a new manufacturing concept) to make rebar (bottom of the line, low-margin steel). Today, Nucor owns the steel industry. The opposite of disruptive technology is sustaining technology – sustain your competitive advantage by doing more of what you've been doing. The dilemma of Christensen's title is that to move to a disruptive technology, successful companies have to go backwards – abandoning a successful high-margin product in favour of a new, risky product. Most companies don't do this... because most companies don't have a culture infused with design attitude.

Successful companies today are those that are not afraid to build a strategy for growth based on jumping into the unknown. Organisations that adopt the design attitude behaviour of embracing discontinuity and ambiguity, and that embrace this mind-set and behaviour, are more likely to replicate the example of Nucor and other companies. As a result, they are more likely to conquer their industry by trying a new and untested strategy – the outcome of which, given the strength of the incumbent opponents, is completely uncertain.

One could argue that business is always uncertain, but that is not the point. Launching a business or a social venture is always going to carry a large measure of uncertainty, but most entrepreneurs try to reduce that uncertainty. They will make decisions – such as where to locate a new store, which customers to target, which product to sell – based on increasing their chances of success. Typically, in business, you increase your chances by emulating the successful. You determine the key success factors, key performance indicators (KSFs/KPIs) and try to replicate those factors. For example, successful retailers are located on busy shopping streets, or streets with a lot of traffic; a store on a quiet, isolated street is more likely to fail. Faced with this choice, a new retailer is not going to embrace discontinuity by opening a store on a quiet, isolated street. Instead, he is going to do what the others have done: look for a location on a busy shopping street or a street with heavy through-traffic. There is always a fine line between courage and foolishness, and that applies to the concept of embracing discontinuity as well. Those in control of companies who operate in line with design attitude don't seek out uncertainty for the sake of uncertainty. However, unlike their traditional counterparts, leaders who adopt a design attitude are comfortable with uncertainty; they will follow the uncertain path without hesitation in pursuit of greater reward rather than staying with the certain path for fewer rewards.

Except for changes in technology (vinyl records, 8-tracks, cassettes, CDs and finally MP3s), few people would have believed that one company could radically redesign the music industry. The invention of the iPod, however, started a revolution in the industry that continues to reverberate today. In one sense, the iPod is simply a record player or cassette player for the digital age; its amazing capabilities, notably the thousands of songs that can be stored on an iPod, are at its heart a side effect of digitisation, and are replicated in anything digital (imagine the contents of your laptop printed out on paper). The true revolution is not in the storage of music, but in the way that the music is distributed – song-by-song, for almost a token price per song. iTunes is a brave new world for the music industry, as are the streaming models of Pandora or Spotify.

Apple is the quintessential design attitude organisation. Design is not just a product enhancement tool; it is at the very heart of the company's mission. It's not surprising that those leading this design attitude at Apple would venture into radical new business models. Apple exemplifies the core competency behind any successfully implemented discontinuity: the ability to embrace the risk associated with uncertainty.

Embracing Risk at Apple

Embracing ambiguity and uncertainty is not possible without a certain comfort with risk. The business leaders that embrace design attitude are not reckless, but they are also not fearful. It is this comfort with risk that allows them to challenge industry-leading business models with untested models of their own. One could almost say that what makes those who run companies that are permeated by design attitude uncomfortable is the lack of risk. If there is no risk in what the company is doing, then most likely the company is not innovating, it is not pushing the boundaries or leading the market. As Robert Brunner, the former director of industrial design at Apple and author of *Design or Die: How Great Design Will Make People Love Your Company*, explains, innovation is doing something new. When you do something new, risk has to be involved, he argues.

For example, the original Mac portable was an unmitigated disaster, according to Brunner. The reason was that it was designed based on what Apple knew how to do at that time, which was to build desktop computers. The result was a large and awkward portable that weighed 16 pounds. Not surprisingly, Compaq created a portable that weighed half as much, and blew Apple out of the market.

Apple had to respond, and the product had to be quite different from the first Mac portable. That's when the innovation exploded, beginning with the track ball, a radical new way to move the cursor on the desktop. The palm rest, and even a different keyboard configuration were other features of the new portable, which was innovative, but also risky. Would customers get used to the track ball? Would they adapt to the new keyboard configuration? Apple didn't know. Apple jumped into the dark by not conducting one focus group during the product's development and launch. Apple took the risk, and it did so for a simple reason – it had no choice.

In fact, Brunner argues that no company really has a choice, given today's breakneck pace of innovation and commoditisation in any market. The real risk, he says, is not taking any risk at all. As a design consultant, he considers his best clients to be those who come to him in trouble, because they have no choice but to take risks and do things differently. Ultimately, that's what yields great outcomes.

The story of Apple's portable computer yields two important lessons. The first is that companies that embrace design attitude are willing, able and even anxious to take risks, realising that those risks lead to opportunities and breakthroughs. The second is the importance of taking the initial leap, of not waiting for the perfect moment to launch a product, an initiative, or a start-up. Apple won the portable wars because it was willing to jump into the market. Without the failure of the first portable, Apple would not have acquired the experience and knowledge that led to the successful second generation. Apple's success is a perfect illustration of the concept known as 'good enough'.

Instead of designing every product to perfection in its first iteration, company leaders will launch a product that's just good enough and see how the market reacts. They will then make adjustments and changes to the product that customer feedback dictates. This iterative approach to product development was first adopted by start-ups taking on entrenched incumbents. The 'Lean' movement introduced the concept of the MVP (minimum viable product).[4] The first iteration of the product is introduced early; by definition, it's understood that this version of the product will not be the final, perfect version. Lean methodologies reject the big-batch approach of traditional manufacturers. Before the advent of lean, manufacturers preferred to pump out products in large numbers – products that had been carefully designed and tested and thus, in the opinion of the traditional manufacturer, needed no further development. The job now was to ship as much as possible. On the other hand, lean manufacturing, as well as the Total Quality Management or TQM movement, encourage small-batch manufacturing – producing products in short bursts that not only lowers inventory level, but also helps product development spot mistakes sooner, and thus improves the product more quickly.

This iterative approach to product development and manufacturing was popularised by the Silicon Valley, which was no coincidence: by their very nature, those who first came to Silicon Valley were explorers, venturing into radical new business areas and technologies. These pioneers were comfortable with making preliminary plans and then adjusting to the shifts in circumstances and the environment that are bound to emerge in brand-new industries. Silicon Valley companies are helped by the presence in their markets of what Geoffrey Moore calls 'early adopters'. Early adopters are willing to accept glitches and less-than-perfect products, and in fact, look forward to working with high-tech manufacturers in fixing new products.

Many industries avoid having to fix products after they launch, and sometimes with good reason (one would shudder to think of an airplane manufacturer thinking that a plane is good enough). At the same time, if safety is not an issue or has been resolved, the design attitude concept of 'let's get the product out the door as soon as it's good enough' is a key differentiating factor in many industries, where prime mover advantage is so important. Ironically, the most common mistake of many technologist founders (founders of high technology companies who are first and foremost scientists or engineers) is that they are so intent on making the perfect product they hold onto the product too long; as a result, they find themselves beaten to the market by competitors who, one could argue, are led by people within the design attitude realm, who are ready to take a calculated chance on a new product that is still being developed.

It's true that the iterative process of 'good enough' involves risks, which, as we have noted, never deterred Apple from trying new things. For example, Apple's Newton was a flop, and one could consider that the revolutionary PDA was introduced into a market that, in the opinion of some experts, was completely unprepared for the product. By comparison, the iPad is not as revolutionary a product, but rather the 'capstone in a family of devices, as one analyst explained.[5]

Apple's successes, as well as its failures, demonstrate that embracing discontinuity and risk does not mean plunging recklessly ahead. Careful thinking and planning went into every one of Apple's successes ... and failures. The key, as we shall learn in the next section, is to recognise when to remain logical, and when – based on one's experience and knowledge as well as, perhaps, one's emotional senses – to take a chance on something completely different. Apple's first portable was a logical and rational extrapolation from its experience with desktops. After its failure, Apple tried radical new solutions – and the rest is history.

The Rational vs The Emotional

When asked what people are considered exceptional designers at Wolff Olins, the senior designer said, 'People who are brave, a little bit crazy, not crazy as insane but willing to say – why not! Let's do this! Let's take a chance. That's invaluable. I'd say that's the most important thing'. This sense of adventure and not being sure what is at the end of the process seems to be an important driver for designers I have met. A senior consultant, previously working for one of the major management consultancies, said the following about the positive attitude towards ambiguity and discontinuity:

> that's something I initially felt really uncomfortable with because it tends to be quite illogical. If everyone is logical you tend to come up with the same answers but designers help you think illogically almost and jump around and think about things in a completely different way and you get a different result. What you tend to get in these classically trained consultancies [can lead to] a very slow processes, and designers can come in and just say 'why don't we just do this?

Designers, in other words, bring an abductive, as opposed to inductive or deductive, approach to problem-solving. The difference between the approaches involves levels of certainty. A deduction is a guaranteed conclusion drawn from a set of factors: 2+2 = 4. Thus, if you have two oranges in your basket, and you add two more, you can deduce that you have four oranges. Induction is the most likely conclusion drawn from a set of factors. If your lawn is wet in the morning, you can induce that it rained last night. With abduction, you don't have all the facts, and you must use your creativity combined with your knowledge to determine a possible or probably conclusion. The weatherman called for rain during the night and yet your lawn is completely dry. Through abductive reasoning, you can develop some potential conclusions. For example: the weatherman was wrong; it rained, but the air is so warm and dry that the wet grass dried immediately; the rain was scattered in the region and skipped your part of town, and so on.

Applying an abductive approach to problem-solving means that you acknowledge the uncertainties in the situation, but are prepared to move forward despite those uncertainties. This ability to go to the gut and not wait for the analytical process to slowly determine a guaranteed correct response is captured in the simple phrase, 'Why don't we just try this?'

The introduction of this design attitude behaviour – 'let's just try this' – into an organisation whose culture emphasises rational thinking and careful planning of each step, and worships big batches leads to a conflict that mirrors the rational vs. emotional conflict within all of us. The rational side of us is always saying, 'Let's be careful. We don't want to eat that piece of chocolate cake because we're trying to lose weight.' The emotional side of us says, 'Cake is good, I'm hungry, let's eat!'

In their book, *Switch: How to Change Things When Change Is Hard*, Dan Heath and Chip Heath use the analogy first developed by University of Virginia Professor Jonathan Hyte, of a large elephant being ridden by a tiny human driver. The tiny human driver is the rational, analytical part of us who plans and thinks. The large elephant is the emotional side that reaches for a piece of cake. As the authors explain:

> *I love that mental imagery because it's the right mental imagery, it tells you everything you need to know in one mental image about why dieting is hard and why starting an exercise program is hard. Because the rider can think all he wants, the rider can plan all he wants, but if the elephant is not going along on that journey, the rider is not going to make it very far. The elephant has about a six-ton weight advantage.*

Dan Heath notes that the elephant is not always the bad guy, for it is the elephant that provides energy and strength and passion for any long journey of innovation. Conversely, the rational, analytical rider is not always the hero. The rider tends to overthink and over analyse. The bottom line is that both our emotional and rational sides have strengths and weaknesses. Change happens, according to Heath, when both sides are aligned.

Likewise, companies infused with a design attitude recognise the power of both the designer approach of 'let's just do this' and the traditional rational approach of careful planning and implementation. When it comes to aligning the two, however, I would reverse Professor Hyte's image. In most companies, the rational component is the elephant, stubbornly refusing to budge from the well-trodden path in the forest. The designer is the tiny rider on top, tugging at the reins with all his might, and saying, 'Let's go this way!' The challenge in creating a company with this attitude is giving the designer more opportunities and more resources to change the direction of the elephant.

IDEO, one of the subjects of the study which led to the creation of this book, is a company that exemplifies the careful balance of the rational and the emotional. IDEO is best known as an organisation that encourages, enables and inspires imagination and creativity. IDEO also has a carefully defined framework for innovation that brings structure and rigour to the company's passion. I will talk about this later in the book.

While Apple can be considered an iconic example of a design attitude corporation, one can hardly consider Steve Jobs as a letting-go leader. In fact, Jobs and other pioneers in the information technology industry were known for being extremely demanding and, yes, controlling leaders. At first glance, these examples may seems to contradict the notion of leaders in design attitude who are afraid to take the risk of letting go. However, this apparent paradox stems from a misconception about control. While much has been written about employee autonomy and the obsolescence of top-down, command-and-control leadership, this emphasis on external control misses what is one of the defining characteristics of design attitude: it focuses more on the internal rather than the external. It is less about controlling others and more about looking inside oneself and not being afraid of what a temporary lack of control entails. Jobs, who'd epitomised design attitude, was externally a control freak. Internally, however, he was incredibly freewheeling. He would allow himself to be challenged and was constantly challenging himself. Precisely because he was letting go on the inside, he had to be controlling on the outside. This is essential for embracing ambiguity at work. Many people accuse Jobs of having little empathy. I believe the reality is that he had extraordinary empathy. In fact he had massive amounts of it to the extent he had felt what other people would feel when using his products. He did not need market research to tell him what products to design. It was his incredible ability to let go of product pre-conceptions and unnecessary assumptions that set him apart. Together with his top designers, including Jonathan Ive, he was able to iterate products and services ferociously. In this sense, he was constantly on the edge of losing control, only falling on the side of control at the last minute when a design has solidified. The main points about letting go and loss of control refer to the willingness of designers to allow their aesthetics and their empathy to guide them internally rather than a set of rigid, logical rules (it has to help us hit our next quarterly figures), set product attributes (such as a physical keyboard), or market assumptions (nobody's going to pay for a $400 phone). This type of loss of control is to many managers frightening. Design professionals, on the other hand, '… have an understanding of an iterative design process that involves exploring possibilities and being open to serendipity and surprise'.[6, p. 51]

What You Need to Know

Design attitude is about embracing ambiguity and discontinuity: in short, not being afraid of the unknown and the uncertain. In the early industrial age, employees were machines and customers were automatic. The leadership of a business controlled everything and everyone. Every movement of an employee was pre-programmed and customers were expected to buy the company's product without comment.

Today, the traditions and the constraints of the industrial age have evaporated. A business no longer has control over its customers, nor even its employees. The past is meaningless. The way we have always done things is irrelevant.

As a result, the pillar of success in the 21st century is embracing ambiguity and discontinuity and the design professionals are leading the way. Clayton Christensen showed that small incumbents can rewire entire industries and send the giant incumbents tumbling from their perches simply by refusing to continue to play by the rules. Instead, spurred by their culture, they engage in disruptive strategies – new products, new customers, new business models – for which the incumbents have no adequate counterattack.

Embracing ambiguity means trusting oneself and not allowing the lack of certainty that the initiative will be successful to stifle truly disruptive innovation. The powerful message of ambiguity is illustrated through the concept of 'good enough' – instead of planning a new product launch down to the last dot on the last marketing news release, companies put a less-than-perfect product on the market without knowing how the product will fare. They do know that there are bound to be concerns, questions, and suggestions that will eventually make the product better. At launch, however, the impeding feedback is completely unknown.

Embracing ambiguity does not mean eschewing all analytics and forecasting. The key is to prepare what you can as much as you can, and then trust yourself – and to some extent your people – to handle and react appropriately to whatever lies on the horizon. Analytics, forecasting, industry assumptions, cultural precedence and any other external element are not ignored, but rather intelligently incorporated into the process without them overwhelming or limiting it.

Design attitude entails embracing ambiguity, seeking out discontinuity, and facing down risk fearlessly. Grouped together as jumping into the unknown, these attributes have the capacity to unlock the success of an organisation.

Post-it notes and penicillin are great examples of embracing ambiguity and uncertainty. In the Post-it case, 3M was trying to come up with a new type of super-strong glue. Instead, they stumbled upon a type of pressure-sensitive adhesive with particular qualities. Instead of treating the new discovery as a failure, it came up with an ingenious use of the glue in a form of a square piece of paper which can be stuck onto variety of surfaces without damaging them. In penicillin's case, it was the contamination of a petri dish with mould and the realisation that it was this which caused the bacteria to diminish, that led to the famous discovery. It wasn't directly the result of a specific hypothesis-led process focused on the antimicrobial qualities of mould's byproduct. Instead of dismissing those as flukes, the side effects of failed experiments became the main outcome. One needs to be prepared, willing and able to spot those serendipitous outcomes in what is very often a messy and unkempt process of innovation.

One could plot the various professions on a scale from loathing uncertainty through to reluctantly accepting it, to embracing it as the preferred and natural mode of operating. Designers are firmly in the latter camp. Their whole *raison d'être* is to create things and processes that are unique. From a very early stage they understand that unless they challenge themselves and others they will not be very good designers. Uncertainty is something they have to deal with constantly. For them it's not something that must be risk-managed, swept under the carpet or denied. To so many other professions it is the devil incarnated and a cause of all manner of headaches. Just think about economists, bankers or managers. Think about the terms used in relation to uncertainty: risk management (risk has to be measured, controlled and mitigated against), Black Swans (rare events with huge impact), scenario planning (attempt to pre-empt variation in what can happen). As far as designers are concerned, uncertainty and risk are a natural state of affairs and a state that can be turned to their advantage. On their best form, designers are the merchants of positive disruption; prophets of the new and different and apostles of the surprisingly delightful.

Having witnessed the convulsions of the design profession trying to normalise and describe the processes they should adhere to, I believe that what makes designers unique is that they, by definition, don't want to follow tried and tested processes. They are happy to dip in and out of some, but there is no overarching grand process that they follow. They are more interested in the flow of the project and whether they are improving the solution, rather than adhering to a process and being slaves to a particular model.

Designers' training strengthens their natural inclination that the future is not predetermined and planned. Many people, including managers, believe that we can only work within the constraints of the physical world created by somebody else. The domain of the designer is the physical world in its widest sense. Hence, their boundaries of what's possible are different to that of those who have no experience in physically shaping the world we live in.

Arguably, embracing uncertainty and ambiguity is a prerequisite for coming up with something truly original and disruptive. Incremental innovation is often practised not because it is demanded by the business but though the fear of uncertain results from bolder ideas. People who have been conditioned to value predictability over originality will naturally have an aversion to uncertainty and chaos. For designers, on the other hand, the natural inclination is to push the boundaries of the acceptable. This is inherent in their professional culture.

In the same way an architect imagines the possible shape of the building and the structural engineer who then makes it sound, the designer imagines what's possible and the Six Sigma specialist makes sure it's produced efficiently and effectively.

The designers' culture normalises ambiguity, uncertainty and discontinuity as ordinary components of everyday working life. In other words, it truly matches what we are witnessing in today's, fast-paced and ever-changing markets. As a result, it creates an environment where disruptive and brave solutions can emerge. It does not allow the team members to hide behind the deceptively attractive certainty of incremental improvement. Instead, it focuses the mind on coming up with original and bold propositions. Design attitude does not seek the false certainty of established processes, benchmarked outputs or past successes. It embraces what can be, not what was. It empowers designers and others who choose to follow in their path to be truthful to themselves – reality is messy, any results are uncertain. The only way to really make a difference is to try something out that hasn't been tried before. If we embrace ambiguity, uncertainty, rather than wish it away, we have a chance of creating breakthroughs. Otherwise we are destined for the slow lane of assured mediocrity.

Chapter 5
Engaging Deep Empathy

'Design is more about observing the world around you, than about personal creativity'. Cam Shaw.

Even without the relatively recent and important advances in human neuroscience and psychology, of the so-called mirror neurons,[1] responsible in great measure for our ability to empathise, we knew that empathy is a vitally important human characteristic. It would probably be difficult to find business professionals who would not admit to employing some degree of empathy when dealing with their clients. There is, however, a difference in degree and substance of the empathy being used within design attitude. Design attitude treats empathy not as an individual trait, predisposition or a degree of emotional sensitivity, but as a way of doing things by groups of people and organisations.

The Many Flavours of Empathy

Not all empathy is created equal. There are different flavours of empathy – from rationalist to aesthetic, from affective to cognitive.[2] There are three levels of empathy starting with the minimal level of empathy – I recognise your existence; the average level – I try to imagine how you feel in this situation; and then there's the highest level – I choose to experience the world through your basic assumptions and values, temporarily abandoning my own.

Having spent a lot of time with designers and studied the businesses where they are the dominant force, it doesn't surprise me that empathy is being talked about in a number of leading publications. This takes centre stage *Creative Confidence: Unleashing the Creative Potential within Us* by IDEO's Tom and David Kelley where it is seen as one of the most important pillars of consumer research and design thinking. In fact, one of the five attitudes that distinguishes the contribution of designers to the business world is their unmatched willingness for stepping into other's shoes, looking through their glasses or putting on their clothes, to experience what they experience. They don't do this because there is a box to tick that says, 'we must consult the consumer', rather, it is a deeply embedded cultural set of values that their professional culture adheres to.

Almost all designers (93 per cent) questioned in my survey agreed with the statement, 'Empathising with users is essential in creating best possible products and services.' When asked if 'material empathy (ability to "feel" the nature of a physical object) is very useful to innovation', 84 per cent of designers responded positively as opposed to 68 per cent non-designers.

There are a number of reasons why deep design empathy, as a part of the design attitude, is different to empathy displayed by consultants, managers, or any other professions for that matter. Some go back to the way they are taught, others stem from the nature of the problems they encounter.

For designers, a direct access to the Zeitgeist and the nuances of culture are the essential parts of their design education. An overwhelming majority of designers in the survey (70 per cent) agreed with the following, 'I must have a good connection to the Zeitgeist and the latest social trends in order to do my job properly'. This was in striking contrast to non-designers – only 45 per cent of them agreed. No matter if you are talking to a graphic, fashion or industrial designer, their work is closely linked to the current culture with its social trends, artefacts, sub-genres and particulars. There is no other group of professions whose education is this closely linked with the popular culture. None. This has an impact on how designers relate to people and objects. It is a much more visceral, direct connection. It can be called the empathy bandwidth – i.e. on how many levels and through how many different senses and platforms designers connect with the consumers. This will be discussed further in Chapter 11 when dealing with the ways designers impact organisations.

The subject matter of design requires designers to try things out, prototype experiences and products by treating themselves as an end-user. There is no escaping it; if you are a designer you are your own guinea pig. You try things out, be it a new knife handle, an attractive piece of garment or website user interface. The more engaged the designer is with the product or service as a future user, the better the outcome of their design. These incentives to engage as if one was the final customer are key to making deep empathy central to how the professional culture of designers develops.

The problems with which designers are taught to deal consist, in significant measure, of what are known as wicked problems, which require a more exploratory and open-ended stance. These problems, which defy simplification and are extremely difficult to pin down,[3, 4–6] don't lend themselves easily to a search for an optimal solution, but rather are best tackled by reflective exploration of the best-fit solution. The way in which a designer interprets a design brief is often open and fluid. The nature of the question is not entirely known until a solution presents itself. An important aspect of finding the solution is therefore empathy, which becomes a useful guide to knowing when any given proposition is right.

In the context of creativity, innovation and design attitude, empathy is the ability to see an object, and experience it through another person's eyes, to recognise and appreciate why they do what they do. It's when teams go into the field and watch users interact with products and services in real time. The Kelley brothers put it this way:

> There is nothing like observing the person you're creating something for to spark new insights. And when you specifically set out to empathize with your end user, you get your own ego out of the way. We've found that figuring out what other people actually need is what leads to the most significant innovations. In other words, empathy is a gateway to the better and sometimes surprising insights that can help distinguish your idea or approach.

In my professional consultancy work, I've seen what even a brief exposure to real consumers, rather than dry statistics and PowerPoint presentations, can do to unsuspecting managers. In the business consultancy field, one method that promises this exposure to consumers is often called 'customer closeness'. It often takes the form of a mega workshop with company executives sitting at a table with their consumers and getting a first-hand account of how their products and services are being used and have very little exposure to flesh-and-bones consumers. Design attitude puts the spotlight on what designers bring to the party, namely a very intense preference for human empathy – not because they are told to, but because they truly and deeply believe this is the key to real insights and innovation.

It is important to stress that deep empathy in the context of the design attitude isn't simply a tool, an off-the-shelf methodology or a quick-fix consumer observation. It is a deeply held belief and an embedded practice that runs through the core of how projects are carried out and how decisions are made. It is the life-blood of how design-led organisations operate.

In their book, the Kelley brothers[7] tell a story that illustrates just how deep empathy operates. It's about a team working at the d.school (a multidisciplinary design school at Stanford University) on the Design for Extreme Affordability project. The core of the project involved creating an affordable solution to premature baby deaths in the developing world. As the team iterated their prototype, they went to India to talk to potential users of their product. The insight they gained while there could not have been possible without their face-to-face interaction and willingness to really listen. It turned out that the mothers in the part of India they went to believed that Western medicines were very powerful, and often too strong. They would frequently disregard what the doctor said and instead of giving two teaspoons of medicine they would give only one. This meant that their detailed display of temperature on the mobile baby warmer they'd developed was flawed from the user point of view. It might have meant that if the mothers were told to keep the temperature at 37, they would actually heat it to well below that mark. Instead of ascribing it to user error, they changed their design to simply say 'OK' when the correct temperature was reached.

There are many tools and techniques that are designed to harness empathy. Steven New and Lucy Kimbell call them 'machinery of empathy'. These are thing such as visualisation, contextual interviews, cultural probes, other ethnographically inspired research, role-play and immersive exploration.[8–10]

There are numerous books and sources on design thinking methods, but what I would like to focus on is that designers, unlike other professions, rely heavily on a deeply held belief that empathy helps them in bringing about meaningful innovation. They put people first, not tools.

So why is deep empathy relatively rare in the business world that is not occupied by designers? Why must we turn to designers and their design attitude to seek guidance on empathy?

There are a number of reasons, but I am just going to examine some of them here. Firstly, especially in the classic management-consulting arena, the overarching concern is for numbers first then people. More worryingly, with the tyranny of Big Data, we are all meant to be worshipping at the altar of big numbers. This is clearly not the best way to innovate.[11] Big Data can show us general direction and overall trends, but it can never replace the human touch and empathy when it comes to designing products and services that connect with people's soul. The limitations of quantitative segmentation of consumers became apparent when I was working for a large electronics manufacturer client as a consultant. It turned out that product designers and product planners were unable to use quantitatively derived segmentation to design products. As often is the case, the segmentations that companies use are great for consumer targeting and communications, but are not so good when it comes to describing the real-life consumers for whom the designers can design products or services. There simply wasn't enough scope for empathy, when dealing with quantitative segmentations, for the designers to be able to create their designs. The filter of a particular segmentation in use appears to have effectively narrowed the empathy bandwidth available to the design teams. The distrust of quantitative research methods as an essential part of new product development was apparent in the survey. In fact, only 27 per cent of designers agreed with the statement, 'Quantitative consumer research is key to making, and offering, great products and services.' In contrast, half of non-designers agreed.

Secondly, there is the issue of the dominance of decision attitude over design attitude.[12] This happens when a professional jumps immediately to the end point of the process and, having listened to the problem/brief, jumps straight to best solution. It can be as a result of many factors, such as time pressure to produce instant results. This, in turn, is a direct consequence of consultants being billed on a daily rate and their subsequent need to optimise time spent on any assignment. The result of this jump to ready solutions is decisions made based on generic best practice, or reheating solutions adopted previously. User empathy might feature but only as a side issue and does not have the same gravitas. There simply is no time for what could be seen as a messy process of getting to the truth about what the users and consumers want. That kind of approach requires patience and possibly even a different incentive structure. It actually happens in some consultancies, where a proportion of their fee is linked to the additional revenue generated as a result of their work.

Thirdly, engagement with deep empathy requires suspending judgement and showing some humility. Consultants usually build their reputation on the opposite of these two attitudes in order to not only command greater respect and higher fees, but also to create a distance between themselves and their clients. Admitting that the users, in effect, know better, diminishes their professional standing and they can feel undermined. Adopting design attitude means letting go of this approach to problem-solving and start building rapport.

Finally, for deep empathy to work, it requires an open mind and a degree of naivety and playfulness (more on the latter in Chapter 7). If at the outset believes somebody that his/her point of view is better/ more legitimate/ more informed, then a deep engagement with the users/consumers may not be possible. Everybody carries their own mental models – mental structures of how our world operates. In order for us to really understand and appreciate other points of view, we need to temporarily suspend our mental models and try to adopt one which may not be that familiar.[13]

Within this framework, deep empathy can grow and thrive in an organisation. Other ingredients are also needed, such as ingenuity of method and resourcefulness.[14] In one example, in order to enable the researchers, designers and others to feel what elderly people feel when going about their daily lives, the team from MIT created AGNES, an ageing simulation suit (see Figure 5.2). It helps to experience the world in an altered way, enhancing the efforts to empathise with a distinct group of people. The core of the design attitude is not a superficial or trivial thing with which to engage. On the contrary, in order to truly empathise with the users, designers need to let go of their assumptions and expectations. The degree of humility which this act requires, is well understood and practised within the culture of designers.

Figure 5.1   I experience: Agnes (Age Gain Now Empathy System) by MIT Age
              Lab

One illuminating example of when, due to lack of user engagement and empathy, an important product prototype failed, is shared by Sam White in his TED talk.[15] He tells the story of how he and his partners were trying to create a rapid cooling system for milk in India. After several attempts at creating a viable product, and after several years of intensive R&D work, they came up with machinery that uses a 2,000-litre thermal battery. The managing director of a dairy company, who bankrolled the project, came in one day and nullified their development efforts in one sentence. He said, 'Guys, just that thermal battery, it's twice the size of any shed you'll find in our villages! What are you thinking?'

Sam White said, 'After two weeks we decided to abandon the solar power component of our solution. It was a difficult decision as we wanted the company to be a solar power company not a milk refrigerating company.' A striking technology first, user/consumer second mentality so often exists in organisations. White and his partners persevered and eventually managed to come up with rapid milk chiller that worked. He summed it up, 'I can tell you one thing with certainty, if we hadn't spent the gruelling hours applying these experiments in real-world conditions in rural India, we would never have gotten that technology out of the lab and into the village.'

Deep empathy is key to innovating everywhere, but it's most striking and visible in the developing world and on the extreme usage edges. The 'light in a bottle' is another great example of the ability to engage on a deep level with the users/consumers. Essentially, this is a 2-litre PET bottle filled with water and a drop of bleach that, at the time of writing, is giving light to 10m people. [16] It takes a special kind of attitude towards connecting to other human beings to be able to extrapolate from simple technology and people's circumstances a product so effective and yet so accessible. This is what deep empathy is all about – not projecting oneself onto the problem, but rather using oneself as a conduit of the end-users' desires, needs, means and motivations.

Figure 5.2   Illuminating empathy: Alfredo Moser and his solar lamp invention

Designers are often seen as heroes whose egos dominate in the relationships with clients and co-workers. When I was talking to a senior manager as Philips Design he acknowledged that this is generally societies' perception and that indeed 'every young designer, to a certain extent is somewhat egotistic'. However, the vast majority of designers know that the reality on the ground is very different. Many of the design executives I've talked to stressed that a lot of designers actually have an exceptional ability and natural willingness to empathise and accommodate customers' views:

> I think designers are much more tuned into people's needs and also market trends, people's lifestyle and socio-cultural trends. Designers are much more tuned to that. A lot of Philips business, research and development people come from technology background developing technologies but not necessarily knowing what they're going to do with those technologies. Designers are coming almost from the opposite end, which is people. We know about people, you know, what people want, what people need, what kind of quality of life people would like. (Senior Manager, PD)

'Whatever we're trying to design, we're always doing it from what traditionally you might have referred to as user-centred, human-centred or customer-centred point of view', a senior consultant at IDEO once told me. In order to underpin the importance of focusing on the human side of adding value to the future product, service or experience, the team at IDEO have incorporated elements from anthropology, psychology and sociology into their process.[7, 17, 18] Even though the methods and techniques are not as scientific as their academic versions, they enable IDEO to strengthen their processes in a bid to empathise with the end-users even more. IDEO is by no means alone. There are hundreds of design consultancies that espouse the same values and, broadly speaking, the same principles and method.[19] Of course, IDEO is still the pre-eminent player with a significant visibility but there are many others that espouse its values and ways of doing things.

According to Tim Brown of IDEO, empathy is at the heart of design; without it, design is a pointless task. Connecting with people on a fundamental level is what sets designers apart. He writes that, 'Empathy is the mental habit that moves us beyond thinking of people as laboratory rats or standard deviations.'[20]

The practice of engaging with deep empathy is far removed from the superficial way customers are assessed, often using the traditional method of a focus group. The latter are good for confirming minutiae and things we already know. The big stuff, big innovation, comes from deep empathy and the ability and willingness to surrender oneself entirely to the world of the end-user. The process comes with a few warnings. It could be messy, it could be unstructured, it could be unexpected – and that's why it often delivers deeper insights, and ultimately leads to some powerful solutions. Those at the forefront of design attitude practice embrace this messy, unkempt reality only to emerge at the end with a richer understanding of what is needed. If one is afraid of this messiness, if one prefers to stand on the sidelines observing from a distance, if one needs a totally structured process to feel comfortable, then one doesn't engage the design attitude to its full capacity.

One of my personal heroes, Bronisław Malinowski, the eminent Polish-born British anthropologist, emphasised the importance of detailed participant observation and argues that anthropologists must have daily contact with their informants if they are to adequately record the 'imponderabilia of everyday life' that are so important to understanding a different culture. These so aptly named the 'imponderabilia of everyday life' are the bread and butter of designers' professional life. Designers instinctively know that the only way to access to adequately respond to people's needs is to immerse oneself in their culture and be as empathetic as possible toward them. Malinowski says that the goal of the anthropologist, or ethnographer, is 'to grasp the native's point of view, his relation to life, to realize his vision of his world'.[21] That is precisely what constitutes the design attitude that I talk about in this chapter. Thanks to the way design education is structured and, in no small measure, thanks to the actual subject matter, designers are the *de facto* anthropologists in the corporate world. Often unwittingly, they study the symbols, rituals and social processes guiding various micro-cultures to respond to them with a product or a service that connects with these cultures on a deep, visceral level. Consider fashion designers and their need to understand the subtle differences in colours, textures and finishes in order to propose something that is culturally relevant and personally appealing. Even the language used by designers emphasises their fondness for empathy and applied anthropology. They often refer to customers as users first and foremost. This underscores their understanding and appreciation of the human being in every customer. Unlike business folk, myself included, who have a tendency to generalise and objectify the average consumer, designers focus on the complex human – often because they know no else. Design education simply doesn't concentrate on the consumer as a rational agent as does the business school education. This can be a virtue and a vice, the latter in relation to designers' commercial acumen (more on that in Chapter 11). In the context of connecting to the human needs hidden within every one of us, this most certainly is a virtue.

This deep empathy extends to how people see objects on a very detailed level. In an article in *Rotman Magazine*, Jane Fulton Suri and R. Michael Hendrix put it like this:

> *Designers see physical, cultural and metaphoric relationships, such as the nooks and crannies where people naturally gather and the exposed spaces that people avoid, as well as the atmospheres (welcoming vs. cold) that those tendencies create … Their own subjective awareness of how particular attributes evoke a sense of beauty, intrigue, ire, or amusement informs the choices that they make regarding how best to express those qualities in any given design. In using their sensibilities, designers connect to our sensibilities, even when we're not consciously aware of it.*[22]

This is a very fitting description of the deep empathy as part of the design attitude.

The authors describe how on one project involving designing a surgical instrument, the designer extended the understanding of what was required by engaging their deep empathy. Having spoken to surgeons about device, there was no mention of aspects beyond its function. The designer observed, by chatting to the doctors about their car purchases, that they were truly passionate about not just the look and feel of the car, but also how it made them feel about themselves. He then extrapolated that, with success, onto the materials and finishes of the device, in order to elevate the connection between the product and the surgeons.

Empathy of Communication

Designers' empathy doesn't only apply to the exploration phase of the creative process and a deeper understanding of the human needs and desires, it extends well beyond that. An important aspect of the designer's work and attitude is the need to communicate clearly and in a way that is effective. Engaging in a constructive, often visually led, dialogue is part of what makes a designer a designer. Visualising the points being made during a meeting or a workshop, creating quick mock-ups or enacting service scenarios are only a few examples of how this plays out. It's not possible to lead a fruitful conversation within a multidisciplinary team without a good understanding of how to connect with people. Producing output and communicating effectively during the design process is what sets good designers apart.

The entire infographic movement – making data beautiful and accessible – has been carried by information designers and graphic designers. Had it not been for people such as Edward Tufte, the American academic and pioneer of data visualisation, or journalist David McCandless we would still be looking at bar charts and pie charts and not compelling and highly informative designs that inspire people. It's the empathy of the designer that leads to the creation of such important graphical pieces of communication as the London Tube map and in the process saves countless hours of staring at an illegible map. It's the empathy of the designers which leads to the creation of simple, icon-based language that all cultures and nationals can understand. It's the empathy of the designer that manifests itself in the choice of fonts on which our life depends everyday as we take seconds to read these omnipresent motorway signs. To represent a piece of information in the way the human eye and brain can process instantly and without errors requires a visceral understanding of how we, as people, assimilate and respond to the world around us.

The people I've spoken to noticed that designers often let other people speak before taking part in the conversation. Perhaps a relevant concept here is the notion of 'the quiet innovation'.[23] One of the senior business consultants at design consultants Wolff Olins, the renowned brand consultancy, told me,

'I noticed in meetings that there is always a lot of doodling and scribbling by a designer. So you think that they are not tuned into a meeting, that they are in other world and they're just doodling and they're doing their thing and then at the end – boom! They'll come into the conversation having heard … but with something very relevant, so that's what I've noticed – they observe a lot and they listen a lot' (Senior Consultant, WO). This yet again underscores how important it is to allow the space for empathy to emerge.

In the famous IDEO Venn diagram (consisting of three overlapping circles), Desirability (consumers), together with Feasibility (technical) meet Viability (commercially sound). In other word, it's not enough to make something attractive to consumers that is also possible to manufacture/setup, but this something also needs to make commercial sense (or value sense in case of not-for-profit ventures).

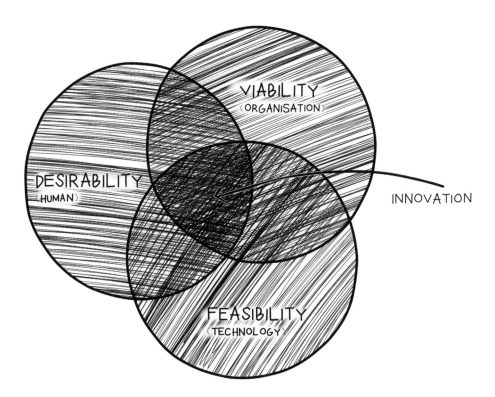

Figure 5.3   The Design Thinking 'sweet spot': Desirability, Feasibility, Viability
Source: IDEO (adapted)

It's great that IDEO popularised the Design Thinking school, but in the process they are contributing to a partial trivialising of the design attitude and deep empathy by reducing it to a set of tools and processes. Granted, they do talk about a mind-set, but that message is silenced by the significant number of tools they advertise that promise design thinking for everyone.

Empathy in the Workplace

As far as the daily life of a company is concerned, designers appear to have an additional, perhaps more subtle, role of refreshing the atmosphere and reducing tensions:

> *What design can do is inject a whole lot of excitement into their everyday experience. What we can offer people is something that is ideas and experiences that revive them, reinvigorate them and inspire them, and that's very gratifying. It often requires bravery on their part, but if they accept it and they go for it then it can be terrific. (Senior Designer, WO)*

This reinvigorating atmosphere that designers stimulate comes from their willingness to be playful. As the following passage shows, there are natural boundaries to the playful behaviour that is delineated by the sense of authenticity:

> *I think to be creative you have to be playful. If you're not playful you're probably not being creative. I think the danger is that it ends up making it harder for rational thinkers to take it seriously. So I think you have to thread here along a fairly narrow line ... I've actually seen companies make that mistake. There's a management consultancy, that claims to offer innovation consulting and very superficially think creating a wacky environment and sticking dumb toys on the wall will do it. That is just not authentic. I think people smell the inauthenticity. Playfulness is important, but it has to be done genuinely and not in a way that is just seen as a slap on. (Managing Director, IDEO, UK)*

The idea of playfulness also relates to the way in which designers structure the physical environment they work within. In the office designers display objects to stimulate their creativity, express their individuality or simply amuse the rest of their colleagues. The ubiquitous and colourful nature of their displays can seem intimidating and chaotic at first. That kind of environment sits in stark contrast to the stereotypical professional business environment. The virtual lack of emphasis placed on the visuals and individuality in the latter is instantly apparent.

In short summary, engaging deep empathy draws our attention to a rather distinct, human-centred orientation in the designers' professional culture. It relates to deep (aesthetic) listening and dialogue as a means of reaching customers' hidden needs, desires and blocks. It encompasses transparency of outcomes and aims to embed emotional reactions into products and services.

In light of what design attitude is about, I would wholeheartedly second Lucy Kimbell who, in her blog, says that we should focus on empathy as part of a culture not on individual manifestations of it:

> *This involves a move away from thinking of empathy as an individual trait, towards a collective capacity. The opportunity is to create a version of empathy that recognises its potential to constitute new configurations of people and things. So empathy becomes less about individual sensibility, and more about organisation design, culture, routines, habits, behaviours, reward systems, roles, and core assumptions about the nature of change and agency.*[8]

There is a danger of fetishising empathy as a silver bullet to cure all management related diseases. This is not the intention of this book or this chapter. What I've tried to do is to highlight the importance of deep empathy, what New and Kimbell call Aesthetic Cognitive and Aesthetic Affective empathy.

> *You often realise that you are trying to fit a new idea into an old understanding. Sometimes people choose to ignore this miss-fit and continue regardless. Sometimes people will decide to choose to do something about it. You'll acknowledge the feeling that there is something missing, that your perspective is insufficient and that a new paradigm is needed. This is very difficult or even painful. It takes humility and courage to put aside your biases and assumptions and to truly empathise. Not everybody is willing to let go of control and certainty for the sake of learning something new. When you are able to do that, you feel a profound sense of resonance, of coherence. When we empathise, we are collapsing two perspectives into one and this changes our understanding of the world and it changes the meanings associated with those two perspectives because we see a new relationship – the fancy name for this is creativity. Making is not only a process it is an*

attitude, one that embodies trust, humility, courage, integrity, honesty and dignity.[24]

Design Thinking school suggest that the adoption of empathy 'heightening' tools, techniques and methods would lead to better, more design-inspired and meaningful project outcomes. Methods such as contextual interviews, smash-and-grab ethnography, cultural probes and others are good pointers but could be misused if applied superficially. In a worst-case scenario they can be misleading and dangerous if people use them to project their own beliefs, values and agenda onto the people they are researching/designing for.

Engaging deep empathy requires humility and courage as its aim should be challenging one's mental models and learning something new. This process can be painful as one abandons the comfort of one's understanding and totally accepts the viewpoint of somebody else. Deep empathy as part of the design attitude is part of the culture and accepted within the organisation as a way of approaching challenges and projects. As it most likely puts a constraint on the scalability of the operations, it has consequences for organisations interested in adopting it. As the example of SAP (a large software company) shows, it inevitably takes the form of ready-tools and manuals that can be widely deployed. Deep empathy requires time, costs money (in the short term) and can be deeply humbling to all involved. These values need to be respected and accepted by the organisation that wants to embed design attitude.

A design attitude driven organisation, therefore, isn't for everyone. If you or your business is not ready to admit to yourselves that you really don't know the people you are catering for, if you are not willing to sacrifice efficiency of the process, if you or your bosses aren't patient, deep empathy might not work for you. If you are willing to take up the challenge, the benefits of engaging deep empathy, as present in the design culture, go well beyond creating products and services which are truly needed and appreciated. They can be deeply satisfying to all those involved on a basic, human level. Deep empathy has the capacity to feed the soul as well as the stomach. I would argue that the fact that it's effective at the highest level is beyond dispute. Possibly the best example of deep empathy at work is Apple and Jonathan Ive. He takes an enormous amount of time and patience to create products which are 'just as they should be'.

Chapter 6

Embracing the Power of the Five Senses

The third design attitude represents designers' fondness for using their innate aesthetic sense and judgement to tackle the challenges they are faced with. The philosophy which emerges allows and encourages people to use the totality of their being, not just their abstracted workplace persona as seen through flat PowerPoint presentations or 100-page reports. Following designers' lead, those applying design attitude to their projects utilise a full gamut of senses, including their tacit knowledge, to create unexpected solutions to unexpected challenges. It's not only that designers literally don't mind getting their hands dirty, they appreciate the world around us in a fuller way; you may call it the 5-D way. Using all their senses is very much a part of their training and culture.

The importance of this aspect of design attitude is not only something I've found in the design-led organisations I've studied, it was also borne out by the survey. Some 83 per cent of designers said that they '… appreciate and use the feedback provided by multiple senses to assess the efficacy of the solutions [they are] developing'. A significantly smaller proportion of non-designers (66 per cent) in the study agreed. When asked about their attitude towards sensory immersion ('I like to immerse myself in multi-sensory stimuli to do my job to best of my ability'), 71 per cent designers agreed. More than twice as many non-designers as designers, on the other hand, disagreed.

Modern managers owe it to Plato and his disciples that the act of thinking has been predominantly perceived as a logical, conscious and verbally-based process, with emotion derided as a barrier to sound thinking. Many professions, in the organisational setting, acquire the need to be pragmatic, which often translates into using this Platonic model of behaviour. They often focus on the abstracted, disembodied thought and regard, for example, 'thinking with your hands' i.e. creating physical mock-ups as a means of advancing the dialogue, as frivolous at best or counterproductive at worst. This means the accepted management culture puts the analytical mind ahead of the multidimensional and the emotional. Arguably, as this chapter will show, real business success depends on the ability to connect to consumers on those deep emotional levels that are energised by the experiences across all the five senses. The culture of designers puts extra emphasis on utilising multiple sensory inputs both in the creative process and in the form of the final product/service. This aspect of the design attitude comes naturally to designers yet is often under-appreciated by others.

Just look at the profit margins Apple is able to achieve. They are taking 72 per cent of all smartphone profits on a 9 per cent market share (as of June 2013). Their products are good (take iPhone for example) but they aren't that much better than the competition (Android-based phones). Thanks to the injection of a significant emotional component into their offering, including their brand, they are able to extract considerably more profit out of a product. While emotions form the basis of thoughts, the five senses – sight, sound, smell, taste and touch – propel those emotions. Designers know this instinctively, and what's more, they are keen to act on it. To underscore this, it's worth mentioning that the advances in brain imaging and the work done by neuroscientists[1] have placed emotion firmly in the driving seat, asserting that thinking is emotion-based, intuitive and fast.

In his book *Emotional Branding: The New Paradigm for Connecting Brands to People*, designer Marc Gobé places the consumer – not the product – at the centre. Gobé, whose clients have included AOL, Coca-Cola, Godiva, Victoria's

Secret and Estée Lauder, advocates exploring how a brand can sensitively connect with people on an emotional level.

Gobé suggested changing the Godiva's design to inject emotions into its retail brand image and took the store from elegant but austere to warm and sensuous by creating a design inspired by the Art Nouveau movement. The redesign succeeded, he says, because it communicated Godiva's 'heritage of sophisticated European pleasure in a more warm and sensuous manner that heightens the irresistible allure of chocolate'. Gobé says customers responded positively to the new design, and Godiva reported a significant increase in sales worldwide.[2]

Mark Weaver, Principal and Partner at Hnedak Bobo Group, cites the Wilderness Lodge at Walt Disney World as another example of a space where sensory design helps create a distinct brand. '[The space] incorporates sounds of frogs and crickets and the sight of lit fireflies to produce an authentic, rustic, natural park effect for its guests', he says. 'And these various sensory elements combine to create a familiarity for guests'.[2] Disney is actually one of a relatively limited number of brands that takes multi-sensory experience building seriously. If they had their way, we might soon be able to touch objects and feel their physical properties through a flat screen. It is one of several companies interested in making the ubiquitous touchscreen more tactile.[3]

At Luxembourg's Mudam, a show called Sensorium invites visitors to touch, smell, and taste the art. Revisiting the work of 1960s and 1970s installation groups such as Fluxus, the museum's light-filled atrium sets the stage for a series of interventions created by Les M, a French design office headed by Céline Merhand and Anaïs Morel. The concept behind Sensorium, explain Mudam's curators, is to 'provoke interaction and surprise'. In a screened-off corner of the atrium, a parallelogram bed and soft duvet invite spontaneous naps. Visitors can walk barefoot across a platform made of spongy wooden facets, and a 6-inch-deep bed of white brush bristles. Three hanging pendant lamps contain circular herb gardens, their domes just wide enough to comfortably smell Lamb's Ear and fragrant, rare spices. This is just one idea that shows just how designers are in tune with the five senses.[4]

What's obvious is the fascination with how designers approach the multimodal challenges expressed by business people working alongside them. People such as Claudia Kotchka, IDEO's successful change agent, who, together with Terry Leahy, a CEO of Procter & Gamble, has been injecting the design culture inside P&G. In one of her interviews Kotchka says, 'Designers speak a language that includes visual, tactile, multi-sensory elements, and [they] are able to use these elements to say something that will evoke a specific kind of response. That's what designers go to school for.'[5] Kotchka was able to use this aspect of the culture of designers to transform how innovation happens across P&G.

Barnes & Noble is as much a popular weekend destination as it is a place to buy books. The stores welcome visitors with the aroma of freshly brewed coffee and soft leather couches for reading and relaxing. Starbucks has built their entire brand on the five senses which are being bombarded through the Starbucks experiences. With the powerful aroma of coffee, the softness of the sofas and chairs, the especially composed music, the sensual lighting, small wonder it's become the so-called third space (after home and work) for many people. If we look carefully, the power of the five senses is clear to see, and feel and smell and touch. It is rather astonishing that it has been almost entirely removed from daily corporate discourse and decision-making. We are all guilty of sanitising our environments, processes and language by ignoring the full spectrum of senses so deeply embedded in us through the millennia of evolution.

Since we were school children ourselves, we've been able to name and use our five senses. 'These are sometimes called the 'far senses' because they respond to external stimuli that come from outside our bodies', according to Kranowitz.[6] Yet, even before our youngest students entered nursery, modern neuroscience had established that there are additional senses that are critical to students and teachers alike.

- Some of these additional senses are refinements of the five Far Senses, such as colour vision and temperature awareness.

- Others are among the Near Senses[6] – sensory capacities that we neither direct nor feel, such as perceiving pheromones and synchronising body rhythms to the movements of the sun (which partially explains jet-lag). Indeed, the Near Senses may be so unfamiliar that they seem baffling!

So, how many senses are there really?

'Five was obviously just not enough to account for the huge range of sensory possibilities of which the human species is capable; seventeen is probably a more accurate count'.[7] Each of our multiple senses – the Far Senses and the Near Senses – is a receiver tuned to a distinct feature of the 360-degree world around us. Regardless of how many senses there are, it is clear that the professional culture designers are surrounded by encourages their exploration and exploitation.

It is rather remarkable, given how important sensorial experiences are to us as species, that we don't pay more attention to them in our professional lives. Consider one recent study and its implications. Researchers, in one experiment, asked people to hold either a warm or a cold therapeutic pad. The subjects were led to believe that the experiment was interested in their evaluations of the products. The researchers were in fact interested in whether warmth sensations could alter people's behaviour in subsequent, unrelated investment decisions. The results showed that people invested 43 per cent more money after holding the warm pad. The physical sensation of warmth, it would seem, led people to feel psychologically safer and more trusting. It could be inferred that tactile warmth made the people on the project metaphorical warmth to others and act in warmer ways.[8]

A Sight for Sore Eyes

At the core of nearly every designer lays the ability to visualise and think through drawing. It is an essential part of their arsenal and any one at the forefront of design attitude is encouraged to take this mind-set very seriously indeed. Once, a managing director at IDEO UK told me, 'Designers at the very heart make stuff visible. They make currently invisible or unspeakable or intangible ideas visible. Suddenly something that someone wasn't able to articulate well is there, that allows a productive dialogue, to occur.' This ability to grease the cogs is an essential part of what designers bring with them. Those leading the design process need to see this as a central element rather than a side show. According to a consultant from Wolff Olins, 'You're blue in the face trying to explain a positioning or a strategy. You've analysed; you've talked about customers and then suddenly, you bring a visual and the whole room lights up. That's very special. That's what I think designers bring to the process – the ability to capture. Not only to create the ideas, but to capture them simply into something visual that people relate to.'

It is important to stress that it is not that important how things are presented, but rather that they are made visible in the first place. Sure, having an attractive-looking mock-up or a model helps our imagination even more, but this is not essential to the design attitude. What is key, however, is the willingness to engage in the visual dialogue offered by making something visible.

In the era of Big Data, it is often necessary to visualise the relationships and connections between data to decipher the meaning and stories hidden within them. We crave simple, yet beautiful and compelling, explanations to complex problems. Skilled designers are able to visualise data through beautiful and highly informative infographics.[9] These help us engage with the subject matter and move the process of understanding and engagement forward. Appreciating how to make vast amounts of data tell stories will have to be embraced by design attitude practitioners in order to communicate successfully both inside and outside their organisations. In the age of Big Data, simple bar charts no longer cut it. The information and data overload require a special design attitude approach – one that recognises not only the factual side of data presentation, but also the emotional side. It is the emotion of data that will make a difference in the over-saturated world we live in.

Even before the age of the terabit, designers helped make sense of the world and our lives easier. Consider how revolutionary the design of London Tube map was. Through its ingenious simplification of the relationships between stations by using a grid system, rather than actual distances, it made orientation infinitely simpler for ordinary commuters. It would be difficult to estimate, but the saving in time over the years must be absolutely astronomical.

Today, designers are faced with pulling off similar feats on an almost daily basis. As the amount of data generated by humanity increases exponentially – we now generate more data in two days than was generated in our history up to 2003[10] – the need to cut through the maze and present it in a way that is approachable is even more important than before. The need for cut-through representations, which work for multiple stakeholders, is essential.

What's important from design attitude viewpoint is that using the sense of sight and the practice of visualising isn't dismissed as prettifying or painting by numbers, but rather seen as vital tools in revealing the hidden structures of problems and creating compelling and elegant solutions which connect with peoples' hearts as well as minds.

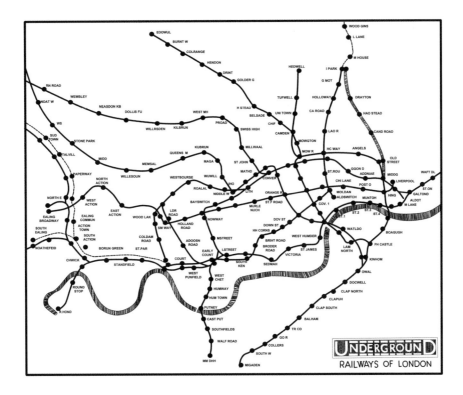

Figure 6.1   London Tube map 1932

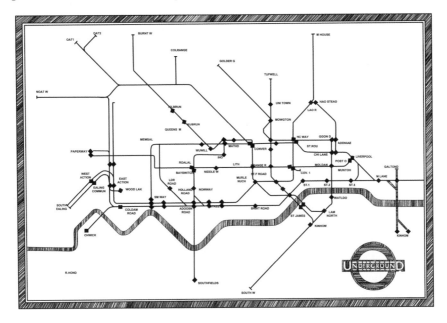

Figure 6.2   London Tube map 1933

There was an American company, which shall remain anonymous, that had an unusual idea of how to save itself from bankruptcy. With morale low, new orders drying up and cash flow seriously weakening, the general manager decided to try one last thing. He decided to spend the remaining couple of thousand dollars on painting the interior and all the machinery brilliant white. The previously tired and worn interior has been transformed, at least visually. As it turned out, the effect of this seemingly superficial intervention was dramatic. Employee morale got a massive shot in the arm and efficiency has jumped almost immediately, and slowly but surely the company started to turn around. Among many things, this shows that how what we see impacts on how we behave.

In order to investigate just how important our senses are, Martin Lindstrom initiated an experiment exploring people's reactions to an unknown brand, in relation to the type of media through which they were introduced to it.[11] The team established four different sources propagating the brand: a billboard, a storefront, a print ad and a banner ad. The made-up insurance sales brand, Insursafe, was presented in an almost identical way across all four media platforms. Subsequently, the researchers questioned 132 volunteers about which source inspired the greater impact in terms of trust and sensory impressions. What Lindstrom and his team found, using only those volunteers who had noticed the message, was quite fascinating. The more physical the media channel was, the more solid the impression it formed in the peoples' minds. As it happened, the signage on the storefront was the most trusted, followed by the billboard. Those two outperformed the print ad and banner ad. Not only was there greater trust for the fictitious insurance company when viewed on a building or a billboard, the volunteers also expressed a stronger emotional connection with it. Additionally, people also felt a stronger sensory relationship with the brand that they saw on the storefront and the billboard. When the researchers asked them what senses they linked with Insursafe, the storefront and billboard showed three times more sensory connections than the print or banner ad. The context here was that that no one had ever heard of this brand before and exactly the same logo and message appeared in all four formats. As the world becomes ever more digital, we find ourselves asked to embrace the disembodied images as we stroke their impressions on a glass surface. What this experiment, and many other similar ones, are showing is that our brains regard a physical presence as a more reliable and trustworthy conveyer of messages. It is only logical that with millennia of human evolution, we will crave those sensory impressions even more in the digital future.

Touchy-feely

Being tuned into visual stimuli and what it can achieve is important, but not sufficient to truly realise what design attitude is about. Many researchers believe that touch provides an important means of developing an emotional, or affective, connection with a product:[12]

- Skin is the largest organ of the human body, 50 receptors per 100 square millimetres each containing 640,000 micro-receptors in our brains.

- The shape of the Coke bottle – the sense of familiarity and subliminal sensuousness.

- Weight and feel of a key-fob – from the luxury glass of Aston Martin Vanquish, through solid and heavy Audi, to light and plasticky Ford.

- Every Apple product is amazing to the touch. Apple designs products that yearn to be touched. Consumers respond to that via emotion and willingness to pay a higher price.

Some 82 per cent of the Fortune 1000 brands don't take advantage of the sense of touch, according to Lindstrom. That's a lot of untapped potential.[13] This represents a significant number of people in middle and top managerial positions not truly realising the promise of their brands.

The exploration and sensitivity to what something feels like opens the doors to a more holistic approach to human experiences. Consider Starbuck's soft and welcoming furniture, inviting people to linger, or the way in which Virgin uses materials to signal its brand values – from more solid boarding passes to the materials used in its lounges. Consider the effect of how a mobile phone feels in your hand on how you perceive its value – plastic versus aluminium versus glass. These materials, when touched, have different connotations and evoke different feelings and emotions. Designers know this very well and tap into these qualities to create the desired effect and the desired emotion.

How something feels in your hand is absolutely essential to how you assess the world around you and the experiences you come across – the feel of a leather steering wheel; the weight of a Magnum ice cream, just heavy enough and balanced in such way as to evoke sensual indulgence; the texture of high-quality Egyptian linen in a good hotel; the satisfying sensation of operating the scroll wheel of the classic iPod. All these small encounters add up to engaging and memorable experiences. Those working within the design attitude framework should certainly be mindful of the power of the sense of touch and utilise it whenever possible.

Another way in which touch works is that it builds a sense of anticipation. Under Jonathan Ive, Apple products have been designed to make people yearn to physically play with them. When Steve Jobs famously briefed Jonathan on the design of the iMac, he said that it should make you want to lick it. That sort of understanding of the power of the senses and sensation on human emotion is what defines a true innovator with design attitude. In another example, around the iMac and the five sense design philosophy of Apple, Walter Isaacson reports in Jobs's biography that the handle on the iMac turned out to be a very expensive design feature but one which was exceptionally important. It meant that the computer was inviting the user to engage with it, to play with it. The concaved handle made it friendly and approachable and not necessarily more portable, considering the computer's overall weight. This subversion of function and a degree of playfulness is typical of good design sensitivity. The core premise here is reaching consumers' emotions, through the use of senses, and not simply making a technically feasible product. This is also a good example of the design attitude pushing the team to go beyond the superficial (which often is a critique levelled at design) and engage with the symbolic and deeply humane.

Think about the layout of the Apple Store, the most successful retail space as measured by $/sq meter there is. It is laid out in such a way as to encourage you, the consumers, to touch, play, stroke and fiddle with the products. Apple knows that this has the capacity to create emotional connections in our brains, which strengthen the bond with the brand and the desire to purchase things. Since they have designed the product in a way which obsesses about how the user holds it and what it feels like in one's hand, it is small wonder they want to leverage it. It is the sense of touch that elevates the experience to a whole new level.

Like all the other senses, the sense of touch informs us about our surrounding, prevents our body from direct danger and contributes to the exploration of an object but, most importantly, it can give us the feeling of safety and pleasure.[14]

Figure 6.3   Impractical yet so welcoming: iMac's concaved handle

Touch is actually a combined term for several senses.[15] This system mediates four types of perception:

- Tactile perception is defined as perception mediated solely by variations in cutaneous stimulation.

- Kinaesthetic perception is defined as perception from joints and muscles, by limb movement alone, of hardness, viscosity and shape.

- Proprioception is the sense of position of the body in relation to gravity as well as our movement through space. Receptors in the vestibular apparatus are involved.

- Haptic perception is defined as perception in which both the cutaneous sense and kinesthesis convey significant information about distal objects and events.

The haptic system unifies input from many sources, e.g. position of fingers, pressure, into a unitary experience.

Designers know that that the tactile perception is a very important part of visual aesthetic of the product and should be fully explored during the design process. The emotional effect from a tactile experience is stronger than from visual. The world of touch and textures goes beyond what we feel with our fingers. The food that we eat has textures that are an integral part of what it tastes like. We know that metal surfaces feel cold, so metal objects evoke similar feelings when we look at them – but it's really the sense of touch we are experiencing.

One reason for this is that the visual perception is connected to the tactile perception. For example, when we see a wooden surface we already know how it will feel from previous experience. Our emotional response will be triggered just by looking at the wooden object. The natural wooden surface looks good because we know it feels good. When designers engage in the design process they bring this understanding with them, be it consciously or unconsciously. This then translates into much more powerful connections that brands and products make with consumers as the various senses combine to create a chorus of memorable experiences.

What's fascinating is how what we experience with our sense of touch translates into other areas.

In one study, researchers looked into the tactile sensation of hardness. Participants in the study haggled over the price of a new car while sitting in either hard, wooden chairs or softer, cushioned ones. Those sitting in the harder, cushion-free chairs didn't feel more negative, yet they changed their offer prices less over the course of the negotiation – offering 28 per cent less than people in soft chairs. That means harder chairs made participants harder negotiators. This suggests that when people touch soft products, they may be more susceptible to outside, persuasive influences – i.e. more willing to part with their cash.[8]

Bed Bath & Beyond organises the shopping experience around touch, allowing consumers to feel their way through curtains, linens, and other home furnishings, thereby experiencing the warmth and comfort these products offer. Whole Foods is another retailer highlighting the sensory experience of consumers. Whole Foods stores strive to have an organic feel, an atmosphere aided by the use of taste stations throughout the stores. These stations provide consumers with opportunities to touch and taste, warming them up to Whole Foods' products and persuading them to put their trust in the brand.[8]

Market research by Millward Brown also confirmed the importance of touch when evaluating certain hand-held items. The research found that 35 per cent of consumers reported that the feel of a mobile phone was actually more important than how it looks.[13] The importance of touch relates to both the products themselves and the actual customer experiences. Studies have also shown that consumers prefer to select products from retailers who specifically allow their products to be touched.[16]

There is a growing body of evidence that multi-sensory (multimodal) experiences are crucial in building better brands and increasing customer loyalty. What is less well understood is the special place the designer plays in accessing, proposing and combining the multi-sensory proposition.

We know that it is key to enable the designer direct access to the user/consumer. In Chapter 11 we will look more closely at the role of how the organisation is structured.

As some researchers, including Charles Spence and Alberto Gallace, report[17] that although progress has been made toward understanding the neural correlates of tactile perception and tactile object recognition/representation, the neuroimaging approach (using magnetic resonance imaging to gain insight into what we like) to the design of products that appeal to the sense of touch (as well as to the other senses) is still not practical. It seems, replacing the designer with her instincts and attitudes isn't going to happen any time soon.

Hearing is Believing

Given that the global snack food market is set to reach $334.7bn by 2015, the humble crisp represents a rather important industry. Beloved in the UK and US, derided by health practitioners, they are extraordinarily ubiquitous and readily available. Now consider the size of the automotive manufacturing industry, including the luxury car market, which is estimated to hit $2,276.9bn in 2017. These are two chunky pieces of the global economy. What do they have in common? In both cases sound, it turns out, is absolutely key to customer experience.

There is evidence to suggest that our perception of Pringles may have a great deal to do with the sound that they make when we bite into them. [18] Research shows that 74 per cent of today's consumers associate the word 'crunch' with Kellogg's. A key component of the sensory appeal of owning a Harley-Davidson comes from the distinctive sound that its exhaust makes.[19, 20] Similarly, much of the success of Snapple in recent years can perhaps be put down to the unique sound that is elicited by opening one of their soft drinks bottles.

Lindstrom reports that an incredible 44 per cent of consumers indicate that the sound of a car is the primary factor of their choice of the brand.[13] Given the financial significance of a car purchase, it is perhaps a little bit baffling that the action of closing the door, the sound of the engine and the exhaust notes, are the things that the consumers are captivated by. Recent WV advertising makes specific references to this fact.[21] But then again, perhaps we shouldn't be that surprised, given that most cars these days are similarly reliable, are impenetrable to even most technical of minds and have similar price points across the range.

Consider the importance of sound in a supercar; here the sound of a roaring engine is not simply a byproduct of the main function of the car. To some it is THE most powerful emotional driver behind choosing and owning a supercar. The signature high notes of a Ferrari or the low grumbling noise of Maserati all create distinct personalities and enable emotional connections between the customer and the motor vehicle. Specialist sound engineers are drafted in to help with the engine and exhaust sounds. In other areas of the car, it is extraordinary to what lengths the designers and engineers go, in order to offer just the right sound package. Consider the case of BWM and the level of detail audio analysis their vehicles go through.[22] Here every detail of the car is scrutinised and inspected with the view to improving the overall auditory experience for the driver as well as for the passenger.

The point here is that those considering the importance of design attitude in the creation of products need to have the five senses on their mind, regardless of what industry they are in. They should allow themselves to be both inspired and lost in them, only to later emerge with a better final product.

Could an experience delivered by a JCB vehicle be enhanced by auditory cues, or could any gym experience be augmented by deliberate and positive olfactory signatures? Of course they could. It's a matter of opening one's mind to the possibility of engaging all the five senses in building better customer experiences.

Smell it, Taste it

Smell and taste are the shortcuts to emotions. A Brand Sense study by Lindstrom suggests that the sense of smell is the most persuasive of the senses. It is the oldest sense in evolutionary terms and has the biggest impact. The striking fact is that less than 6 per cent of the Fortune 1000 have given smell a thought as a means of differentiation.[13] Smell can shape spatial perception at least as powerfully as light or sound, producing atmosphere, narrative, and even form.

Charles Spence, Professor of Experimental Psychology at Oxford University, has amassed a substantial body of evidence demonstrating 'sensation transference', in which 'the brain uses cues from one sense – such as the music we hear – to inform another: taste'.[23]

Why are popcorn carts strategically placed at the entrance tunnels to the Magic Kingdom Vendors at Disney World, although not much popcorn is sold at 8.30 in the morning? This is because the smell of popcorn communicates the living movie message of the park. The bakery on Main Street purposely pumps the scent of fresh-baked goods into the street to support the story of America's small towns. These powerful subliminal messages combine into a multi-sensory experience where each sense reinforces the others. The memories become that much more 'hard-wired' into our brains as a result.[24]

In recognition of the role smell plays in buying and owning a Rolls-Royce, a smell is now added to new cars that mimics the distinct smell of the 1965 Rolls-Royce Silver Cloud. The smell is impossible to buy and is considered a masterpiece of sensory branding.

Tacit Knowledge to the Rescue

When compiling all the different stimuli and inputs to achieve a desirable outcome, designers use not only their rational, technical knowledge but also their implicit, hidden and multifaceted sense of knowing. Tacit knowledge, as Michael Polanyi calls it,[25] is an essential component of the daily life of a designer. Because they need to reconcile many different variables in different contexts, and they very often deal with the multidimensional 'wicked problems' I've talked about, designers are taught to depend more on this mode of knowing than are other professions. One senior designer at Wolff Olins explained how this special intuition operates, 'Often the first idea is the right one. I don't believe that's serendipity. There is something that is right about it. All your experience your knowledge and your abilities come into play in that one moment and you get something down and then you can go through endless process of trying other things but that really fresh moment when you approach something so often is right.'

Complicated, multidimensional factors of taste, integrity, tone, beauty, rhythm and meaning, which need to be addressed in the process of design, are only partially susceptible to scientific analysis. Therefore, designers are taught to use their sense of deep aesthetics to deal with them in a pragmatic way.

Designers tune into aesthetic feeling, a sense that the philosopher Charles Peirce distinguished from emotional evaluation such as pleasure and pain. The latter are secondary sensations, like symptoms and transitions, whereas aesthetic feeling is more like a disposition. It attracts or repels, according to Peirce.

When I talk about aesthetics I don't mean the commonly used term denoting superficiality. On the contrary, I mean a deeply felt appreciation. As Susan Vihma says, 'Aesthetic feeling has no representation, because it is immediate, inexplicable and un-intellectual consciousness that runs in a continuous stream through our lives.'[26] Designers not only allow themselves to tap into this mode of judging their work but embrace it wholeheartedly.

In a similar way David Gelernter, in his book on aesthetics and technology, *Machine Beauty: Elegance and the Heart of Technology*, describes aesthetics as the deep, almost poetic, fulfilment in the way products are designed and experienced. These values seem to appear in what designers themselves describe, and what I have observed while working with them. Sometimes the anticipation of the little moment of discovery is almost palpable. This cannot be reduced to asking consumers what they want in the confined environment of a feedback session or survey. Unfortunately, this it is often what happens when designing new product or services.

Engaging with this 'immediate and unconscious perception' is how Wally Olins, the co-founder of Wolff Olins, sees his work of integrating a strategic intent into a workable solution: '… we interpret the illogical thought, if you like, to make it real. So if you walk into a building, you're not talking about logic are you? What you talk about is how you feel, and you leave the building with an impression.'

Intuition and tacit knowledge has the ability to subtlety balance quantitative and qualitative aspects of decision-making. It can deal with more complex situations, than those, which could be figured out in our conscious mind:

> *This is not to say, though, that design has become entirely a question of visual representation. While it is necessary to illustrate it through photographs in a book, it must be remembered that design has many forms. Its interdisciplinary practice means that it may amalgamate a range of sensory features – of sound, smell, touch, feel, weight, movement and sight.*[27]

In his book *Brand Sense*, Martin Lindstrom makes the point that we have entered the age of 5-D branding, but what is clear from what I have observed is that designers have the right attitude and culture to make this work. Designers are often either in charge directly or have a lot of say in how the experience is delivered physically. Instead of being shielded from the five senses reality, by the flattening managerial processes and culture, designers have a much more direct input in how the brand reality is created.

Chapter 11 will look more closely at the issue of marketers controlling the flow of information to and from consumers, often effectively narrowing the bandwidth of that information available to designers.

Sound of Silence

Only 9 per cent of all brands utilise the strengths of audio in making their brand more distinct, clearer, consistent, and memorable across a majority of their channels:[13]

> *Perfect visuals, perfect audio – this is where the brand-building process traditionally stops. It stops despite the fact that a total sensory experience would at least double, if not triple, the consumers' ability to memorise the brand. If you decided to examine any of today's Fortune*

500 brands, you would quickly realise that decades concentrating on the audio-visual dimensions has narrowed the focus to only these two dimensions, neglecting the other senses as if they do not exist or even go so far as to say that the perfect utilization of audio has not yet been achieved. So many brands focus their energies on strong visuals, often to the detriment of the audio component.[13]

Less than 3 per cent of Fortune 1000 companies have even given smell a thought.[13]

The reason for this poor performance is that those who are in charge of products, services and the companies have been desensitised by years spent in rather sterile corporate cultures not paying too much attention to ideas about multi-sensory experiences. Designers, on the other hand, live and breathe the five senses, as it's the canvas they work with on a daily basis.

The enemy of the 5-D approach to innovation and brand building are culture and process inertia – it is often about small experiences and cultural permission to engage all the senses in the process of creating new offerings.

If it's so important for every brand to use all five senses, why are so few brands doing it? The answer is that those in charge of these businesses and brands have been taught and acculturated to focus on logic, limited dimensions (usually beginning with profit) and benchmarking against competitors rather than against the full spectrum of human experience.

All our senses are interconnected; we hear with our eyes – check out the McGurk Effect;[28] we taste with our nose, as 90 per cent of what we perceive as taste is actually smell;[29] we feel with our eyes – see the recent experiments in neuroplasticity;[30] we can also see with our hands – braille is a good example of that.

Despite what the consultants from IBM seem to be saying, which is that five years from now Cognitive Computing will enable computers to use the five senses to understand and act upon their surroundings,[31] the role for the five senses in developing truly compelling and ultimately profitable products and services will not be diminished. The messy, conflated and multifaceted landscape of the senses will have to be tackled head-on. The design attitude influenced designers will know that, and will take full advantage of the power of the five senses. Their attitude will be one of total multi-sensory commitment and deep aesthetic appreciation.

Lindstrom advocates a methodology he calls Smash Your Brand, where brand is instantly recognisable based on even the tiniest of its components. For example, the brief for the original Coca-Cola bottle was that it has to be recognisable even after it was smashed. Other examples include Micky Mouse's ears, the Golden Arches of McDonalds, the smell of Play-Doh, the smell of Rolls-Royce or Microsoft Windows' opening tune. The methodology is a kind of an audit, a critique and assessment. What Lindstrom fails to note is who ultimately delivers these signature ingredients that make the brands smashable. By now it should be obvious that it's the designers with their ability to tap into the power of the five senses and human emotions. The right colours or brush strokes on a logo, the right scent, the right kind of interior, all have the capacity to create lasting connections with consumers. The marketers and managers can brief the designer, but ultimately finding the right formula will be, to a large extent, in the hands of the designer.

Designers are trained and acculturated to use all five senses. They are comfortable in the conflicted world of multimodal stimuli and, unlike many managers, they use different senses for inspiration. The most successful brands utilise multiple senses to create powerful human connections. They are fully aware that emotions and memories are heightened by the simultaneous use of multiple senses. Through their skills, attitudes and training, designers have access to the consumers' emotions and have the capacity to create signature brand elements that make the brand instantly recognisable. Managers must learn to embrace the multimodality of experiences and expand their list of criteria when it comes to creating and assessing new products, services and brands. In the world dominated by computer software and the touchscreen, both designers and managers must actively seek out other means of engaging users/consumers across multiple senses. They must also retain the sensitivities and skills required to manipulate and utilise all five senses effectively.

Chapter 7
Playfully Bringing Things to Life

'The opposite of play is not work. The opposite of play is depression'.
Steve Keil[1]

As a species, we play a lot. We engage in sports – for fun, as Olympians or as professional athletes. We play instruments, we dance, we sing or we mess about. It's been shown that play stimulates growth of the amygdala, which is responsible for emotions.[2] It boosts pre-frontal cortex development – in other words it stimulates cognition. The benefits of being playful are many: heightened creativity, increased openness to change, improved ability to learn, and a sense of purpose and mastery.

Play has evolved as an advantageous and necessary aspect of behaviour. Why is it then that we so often leave it on the other side of the office door? We are banishing an extraordinarily successful and useful developmental mechanism in favour of seriousness? However, there appears to have emerged one group that refuses to subscribe to the seriously depressed school of professional behaviour – the designers.

The Serious Jester

It goes without saying that designers visualise and bring things to life. It's very much at the core of what the profession stands for. However, the way in which they are doing this rarely finds the spotlight. It is very much a part of designers' way of doing things to challenge and subvert the status quo. That is how they test what's possible and what's not. In fact, 70 per cent of designers in my online study said that '[they] see [their] role as somewhat subversive and aimed at challenging the received wisdom'. Being the archetype jesters of the corporate world gives them permission to be playful, joyful – more human. It also allows designers to criticise established methods and stances because their approach is seen as non-threatening. There is a parallel to this role in Poland, where I originally come from. We all know of Stańczyk, the most famous court jester in Polish history, who was employed by three sixteenth-century Polish kings. Unlike jesters of other European courts, Stańczyk was considered to have been much more than a mere entertainer. He is remembered as a man of great intelligence and a political philosopher gifted with formidable insight into Poland's contemporary and future situation. He used his job to criticise and challenge his contemporaries through satire. His witty jokes often pertained to current political or court matters. This is the version of jester that I believe many designers choose to emulate these days.

This permission to be playful is often granted to designers under the cover of creativity. When managers say 'we are not the creative type' they often mean 'I'm not willing to appear not in control' or 'I don't want to be playful because that might be interpreted as being weak'. Designers are seen as the creative types, giving them more scope and cultural permission to behave and think differently. Working within these permissible cultural boundaries, their culture encourages playful experimentation, pushing the boundaries, and adopting unorthodox and ungrounded methods. By the virtue of their position, they will have more freedom to explore unexpected avenues and novel solutions. This is not because they are inherently more creative, but because they've been given more cultural space to be creative. This is how design attitude works. It's not about the ability but about the cultural, attitudinal and behavioural framework within which we operate.

It's quite remarkable how stepping outside this invisible creative ring becomes culturally less acceptable even in the adjacent field of marketing. Here some playfulness is tolerated, but it never feels entirely native to the discipline. After all, marketing as a domain has spent a long time trying to boost its serious, scientific credentials in order to become more powerful in the boardroom. This process has meant that it's less capable, or willing, to appear playful or naive.

In contrast, the permission to be playful bestowed upon designers has acted to increase its prevalence in the profession. Designers see it as something normal and ordinary. It only becomes extraordinary when somebody from outside design lands in the middle of it (as in my case) or when designers are trying to extrapolate their playfulness onto often rigid, managerial cultures.

In the survey, 87 per cent of designers agree that being playful at work is very important (40 per cent completely agree). Additionally, 88 per cent of designers agree that 'playfulness is key to successful exploration of ideas' as opposed to 75 per cent of non-designers. This difference is even more visible when we look at only those who completely agreed (top box on a 7pt on the scale). Here we find that 44 per cent of designers are committed to it entirely, versus 21 per cent of others.

Playfulness encourages unexpected experimentation and exploration. After all, if something falters, it's not the end of the world and a designer may say, 'we are only messing about a bit'. This attitude is inherently linked with another design attitude, embracing uncertainty and ambiguity. If somebody is uncomfortable with uncertainty, she would most certainly be uncomfortable with being playful as a means of professional engagement.

Importance of Professional Humility

It is worth asking what cultural norms are dominant in design culture. Is it more appropriate to appear infallible or humble, detached or involved, objective or values-driven, human-centric or metrics-focused? In the world of design the latter is almost always how things actually work. Designers have a tendency to take on a lot of the challenges with scepticism and a natural subversion. They project a certain naivety in order to get under the skin of the user. They also often don't take themselves too seriously. This allows them to be playful and appear silly, which is one of the secret weapons of getting to truly transformational solutions.

One great example of professional humility was when an obstetrics consultant from Buenos Aires allowed himself to be persuaded by a seemingly silly idea behind a party trick involving a wine bottle and a cork. Jorge Odon, an Argentinian car mechanic, had no experience of obstetrics but had an ingenious idea. Having seen a party trick that involved extracting a cork from an empty bottle using only a plastic bag, he came up with a novel way of delivering a baby in complex births. 'The Odon device imitates the bottle trick. A double layer of plastic is inserted via the birth canal to surround the baby's head. Some air is then pumped into the bag, inflating a plastic chamber that gently grips the head around the chin. Then the baby can be pulled out through the birth canal, without causing damage or bleeding.'[3]

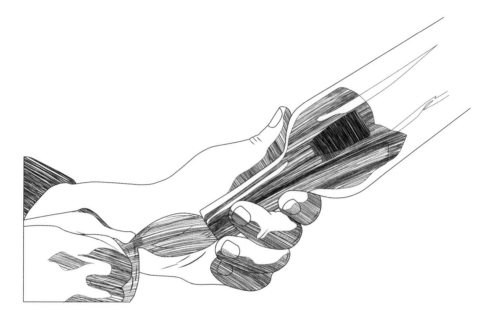

Figure 7.1   A hell of a party trick

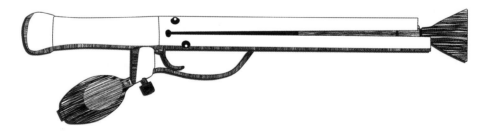

Figure 7.2   The Odon device

Considering the last viable invention in this area happened hundreds of years ago, it was rather remarkable that Odon was given time and resources to develop his idea, which has the potential to revolutionise complex births in both developing and developed nations. It would not have been possible had professional rigidity prevailed. It was the open-mindedness, humility and embracing uncertainty that allowed this invention to take place. Even though neither the obstetrician nor Odon were professional designers, they displayed the design attitude that I've been describing.

When traditional management consultants are involved, playfulness and professional humility is often restricted. This sits in contrast with how the design profession and design consultancies operate. New and Kimbell[4] tell of consultants being seen as spies due to the power imbalances in the relationship between them and the client. As the authors note, there is a need to offer something more than *only* process, empathy or visualisation in the context of the higher fees present in traditional, management-led consultancies when compared to those of design-led ones. Consultants are expected, therefore, to offer a degree of assurance combined with a convincing performance. The authors say that, 'The presumed expertise of consultants perhaps eliminates the humility and acceptance of ignorance required for empathy.'[4, p. 9]

Empowering the Kid within You

Playfulness in the design domain is the core theme of IDEO's Tim Brown. In his TED talk he stresses that playfulness is not used instead of seriousness but alongside it.[5] They must coexist in an environment that is good at fostering innovation he says. 'It's not an "either/or", it's an "and". You can be serious and play.'[5]

Brown says that our fear and embarrassment at being judged by our peers prevents us from being playful. We impose on ourselves a ban. 'What if I try and embarrass myself. What if my prototype is rubbish and everybody then thinks I'm rubbish?' The decision attitude prevalent in business schools and management circles wants to jump over the messy, unfinished and often serendipitous world of the early prototype and go straight to choosing which one of the options is best.

It is often the fear of being judged that stops us from being playful and experimental. Frequently, as a result of a remark by somebody close to us, be it a parent or a teacher, we stop seeing ourselves as capable of creativity. Author and vulnerability researcher Brené Brown calls it the 'creativity scar'. We then tend to go into 'lockdown' and not think of ourselves as creative any more.

The Kelley brothers devote their entire book *Creative Confidence*[6] to the notion that everybody can be, with the right attitude and tools, creative. They talk about how the fear of being judged is imprinted on us at a very early age. As kids we are allowed to come up with less than perfect drawings, without being dismissed as lacking in talent or ability. As we grow older there are situations when others judge what we've produced as insufficient or not good enough. This is when our creative confidence takes a knock and we become less and less free to experiment. Limited by our own projection of what others think of us, we often stop being playful. Educational systems don't help here either. The recent focus on STEM subjects (Science, Technology, Engineering and Maths), both in the UK and USA, and the continued importance of standardised tests, which stress existence of ideal answers and emphasise ways of thinking that are clear-cut, also implicitly suggest that multifaceted, playful design thinking is less worthy. In fact, one of the significant voices of the design world, the former dean of the *Rhode Island School of Design (RISD)*, John Maeda, suggests that the insertion of Art and Design into STEM (making it STEAM) would make much more sense for the twenty-first century.[7] Moreover, classic education doesn't tolerate mistakes. It banishes them as the worst thing that can happen. This is contrary to the heart of what design attitude is about, where playful experimentation enables people to surprise their colleagues and even themselves with unexpectedly great solutions.

I'm sure you have seen, or experienced, this fear of being judged first-hand in your organisation. There are very few companies beyond the start-up world that actively encourage controlled failure. Once a business or an institution reaches a certain critical mass, the fear of failure then becomes greater than the joy of experimentation. That is why so many of them get outmanoeuvred by small and nimble units that know how to fail quickly and effectively to ultimately create better solutions. In a world where Facebook is the Internet giant, Snapchat, which promises 'no trace' conversations, is a great example of a playful experimentation that took hold. On the face of it, why would anybody in their right mind want to use a messaging system that deletes your posts soon after the recipient views them? At the time of writing, Facebook has valued what seems like a ludicrous idea at $3bn. A start-up that was willing to be playful and experiment with the notion of non-permanent messages has become a serious contender.

There are also lessons on what type of artificial playfulness to avoid. Managers are often forced to fiddle with plasticine during creative exercises or creative away-days and are told to 'just have some fun'. It's likely you've witnessed those situations when a moderator struggles to convince the sceptical manager or consultant to 'give it a go'. We all know the game, and we soon come back to our keyboards, screens and words and boring PowerPoint presentations after the cringe-worthy activities are over. This is definitely not what design attitude is about. It's about a heartfelt desire to experiment, be playful and creative.

Playful Reinterpretation of Meaning and the Injection of Emotions

There is a certain quality encapsulated by objects and experiences done well. It's sometimes difficult to pinpoint exactly why they move us, yet moved we are. There are things that stop us in our tracks and things that gently lodge themselves into our subconsciousness. Think, for example, about the embossed titles and texture of some books. How about your car keys – do they feel substantial or light and flimsy? Behind all these objects are conscious, design decisions that have a significant bearing on how we feel about the world in which we live. Most of the things we come into contact with are unremarkable and often blend into the background of our day, and this may well be their purpose. Take road signs for example; they are masterfully designed to guide us in a split second and then to disappear from our memory. Other things, however, stir our emotions.

In 1991 Alessi, an Italian company specialising in household items, started a project called Family Follows Fiction. It would revolutionise consumer goods well beyond Alessi's industry and result in the company growing in double-digits annually. The project led to a new family of playful plastic objects, most with anthropomorphic or metaphoric shape. One of these objects was Allessandro Mendini's 'dancing' Anna G. corkscrew, which features twisting head and arm-like levers, and Mattia Di Rosa's pressure plastic bottle cap, whose name says it all, Egidio. The little man has lost something.[8, p. 40). This is an exquisite example of designerly playfulness taken right down to the market level of a successful product family. Alessi's inspiration came from the concept of transitional objects – in effect those things, such as toys, teddy bears, and safety blankets that represent the happy world when children were still with their mothers. These objects help children become autonomous and in the process the objects become indispensable irrespective of their actual function (ibid. p. 41). The researcher behind these findings, Donald Winnicott, a paediatrician and psychoanalyst, also showed that adults have transitional objects that they take from their childhood to adulthood. A recent study actually claimed that as many as 30 per cent adults took their teddy bear with them to bed.[9]

In the process of designing the Family Follows Fiction range, Alessi have mischievously altered the meaning of everyday objects. From purely functional pieces they became transitional objects full of emotion and personal significance. By being playful, the designers in this case achieved a real human connection via a set of seemingly ordinary, household objects. Alberto Alessi captures the sentiment in this way:

> There is no difference, at heart, between a coffee pot or a kettle and a teddy bear … We know very well that our activity has not as much the purpose to satisfy a primary need: we know that one can light up a burner, boil water, make a coffee or serve tea, dose salt and pepper, crack nuts and clean toilets with tools that are more 'normal' than those created by us. What we do is to try to answer to a desire of happiness of people.[8]

This is an accurate representation of the sentiment behind the design attitude of playfully bringing to life. The designers' love to be playful not only as part of the process of designing but also look to the playful possibilities within the things they create. However, their domain isn't limited to just objects, it extends to services and experiences as well. Increasingly designers influence policy with the flavour of all of their attitudes and values.[10]

Figure 7.3   Alessi, form follows fiction

Playful is Who Playful Does

There is a real affection for creating things and bringing solutions to life in a way that is unexpected, original and playful. Throughout the interviews I've conducted for this book, it's not only been strongly echoed by designers themselves, but also by non-designers working with them. Wally Olins, the co-founder of Wolff Olins, has expressed his delight at something special being created in front of his eyes:

> *I like seeing things that are new and different. I get a genuine shock of delight to see something that I've never ever seen before work ... And this is what designers often do.*

During the time I spent with designers this attitude has been very visible on many different levels. I would observe designers engaging in activities where they would be rapidly create small mock-up models of a very early design idea. They would then show it to their friends and colleagues to seek feedback, and in this process physical interaction becomes a pretext for continued dialogue. This would often result in an increased intensity of communication among the people in the group alongside a positive change in the dynamics of the group.

A senior designer at WO described it to me:

> *Design delights people. Good design is exciting and makes people feel great. You're never going to do that with a PowerPoint presentation or charts or graphs. It can be interesting, it can be intelligent and it can be inspiring in a way that you're projecting into the future, but when you look at something that's just wonderful and it makes you smile or makes you laugh, or just excites you – that transcends that kind of rational thinking. And it's the hardest thing to achieve but it's the most gratifying.*

Designers love the tangible world of objects. Whatever is said about their impact on the design of processes, it's often the tangible things that most excite them. Certainly, there is a growing group of service designers that take equal pleasure in seeing systems work perfectly, but even those people, coming from the traditional design professions, cannot do without physical manifestations in their work. The urge to use all five senses' aesthetic appreciation is very strong (see Chapter 6). It's no surprise, as many designers say, that it's extremely rewarding having something physical as a result of one's work.

Playfulness is one of the cornerstones of many service design methodologies. Role-play and acting out scenarios are a perfect example of how design-inspired discipline embraces being playful in a meaningful and productive way. It takes professional courage to take on a persona and improvise how a service case might unfold in front of others. Many adults are reluctant to engage in role-play. Some of their reluctance is due to embarrassment, but some of it is based on not believing in the solutions that eventually emerge. This sort of practice is very common among the professional design community and not only embodies the capacity and willingness for playfulness but also designers' deep empathy. The willingness to play is admired and celebrated at many design-led organisations.

Fuelling the Creative Dialogue

Prototyping provides a different mode of dialogue for the solution to emerge. Prototyping enables a dialogue which focuses on the iterative process around a solution rather than the abstracted planning phase upfront.

In the business world it is often the case that there is a certain fear of seeing the potential solution too quickly. It needs to be 'properly' researched and investigated before being revealed. This is being challenged by the MVP (minimum viable product) and agile methodologies, but it's still the prevailing culturally-accepted mode of operating. 'Don't show it to me before you are ready' is the typical stance in business schools. In the design setting it is accepted and understood, and indeed normal, that the first solution is as much a representation of testing the boundary conditions of the brief as an attempt to move the process of action research forward:

> Designers use observation and prototyping methods of different kinds to help them figure out the best ways to express certain sensibilities. With sketches and models, they try things out to explore their effects, experimenting with physical elements (finishes, forms, fonts, materials) and control sensory inputs (contrast, rhythm, sound, space, pattern, pace) to determine what works and what doesn't. And, ultimately, they discover how to deliberately evoke particular feelings to support the desired experience.[11]

Creating models (of absolutely anything) is absolutely essential in a successful design process. In an interview for the *Wired* magazine, Jonathan Ive makes this point. He says, 'When you make a 3D model, however crude, you bring form to a nebulous idea, and everything changes – the entire process shifts.'[12]

This attitude is very much present in the results of the survey. A striking difference in how designers and non-designers see the role of rapid prototyping emerged from the study. Forty-five per cent of designers totally agreed (top box) with the statement, 'Fast, iterative prototyping as early as possible in the product development process is preferable' versus only 4 per cent of others – a × 10 difference at the top of the scale. Furthermore, 88 per cent of designers said that 'Making ideas tangible is essential to moving the process forward' (44 per cent ticked the top box 'completely agree'). Only 15 per cent of non-designers completely agreed with this statement suggesting a much lower commitment to prototyping as a way to developing ideas.

Thinking with one's hands, creating multiple low-resolution prototypes quickly is also a form of playfulness at work. Giving team members permission to think with their hands enables quite complex ideas to be visualised and explored. Having simple prototypes in one's hand enables us to talk about our ideas and it lets others into our thinking space. At IDEO top management admires employees' willingness to play. In other words, they admire their attitude to playfulness at work.

Playful exploration, playful building and role-play are the modes in which IDEO's culture engages serious playfulness. Play is not anarchy. Play has rules that need to be followed for it to work in a business setting.

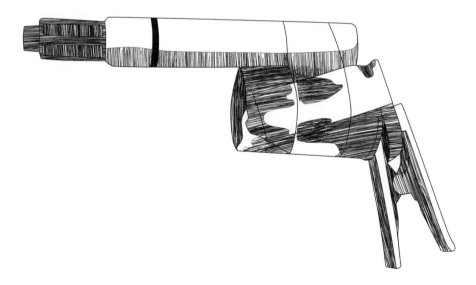

Figure 7.4   An early and playful prototype for the Gyrus ENT Diego, a surgical tool

The beginning of the design process is really about dealing with an enormous amount of intangibles. It's more about developing understanding, observing and acquiring new knowledge, and then [engaging] the analytical process.[This is about] applying creativity and being able to make rational judgement about the various concepts, the various ideas and then quickly steering them into the process of product creation. There is this ability to rapidly go from very broad, subjective project into something that is rational and tangible, something that is discussable and debatable with our clients. (Senior Consultant, PD)

According to a senior figure at IDEO, among the three essential things that designers bring with them is the ability and drive to make '… currently invisible or unspeakable or intangible ideas visible' (General Manager IDEO).

Infographics as a Means of Playful Visualisation of Hard Data

Playfulness and light-heartedness have an increasingly important role in an area traditionally dominated by lifeless charts. Infographics is a way of showing often heavy and impenetrable pieces of information in a way that makes an impact and cuts through complexity. When access to data and statistics becomes ever easier, we strive for simplicity and the human touch when it comes to their presentation. A quick look at today's newspapers, blogs and books reveals that funny, playful, surprising and beautiful infographic visualisations have become the norm. The key individuals making it happen are non-other than graphic and data visualisation designers. Apart from their skills, we rely on their attitudes and preferences when it comes to bringing these things to life. It's often the case that a playful/and or imaginative depiction of a dry piece of information makes a difference between it being ignored or understood and appreciated.

It has the capacity to move the debate or enlighten people. To underscore that this is an attitude not a skill you need to see Hans Rosling's presentation from TED.[13] He's a data scientist but he understands that unless the data are wrapped into a playful and compelling narrative, not many people will notice or care. He's particularly well known for his animated charts. Even though they are clearly not beautifully designed (as they would have been by a competent graphic designer) they are very evocative and entertaining because there is a certain underlying playfulness in them.

Essentially, we all have a choice – be playful/engaging/emotive/funny or be serious/drab/dry. It is up to us which of these we choose to endorse in what circumstances. It so happens that designers, through their professional training and practice, have chosen the former group more often. That is not to say that others don't do so too. It is simply to highlight that they are significantly more into playfulness as a professional stance than others.

We often self-edit ourselves as we don't want to appear as non-original or boring. This is something that children don't do. They are uninhibited in their ways of coming up with ideas. Sometimes our desire for convergence kills the very creativity we are trying to espouse.

Creating Conditions for Play

Designers as a professional group are immersed in the tangible world full of symbols, talismans, textures and artefacts. This is not only the effect of their playfulness but also the fuel for it. These are all 'play signals' as Stuart Brown calls them – in effect cultural markers that play is allowed and trust is encouraged.[5] Enter design working spaces and studios and you'll understand immediately.

In order for playfulness to flourish, there needs to be a safe environment that enables adults to feel they are not being judged as soon as a thought leaves their mouth. It's about creating a permissive environment that is filled with symbols that remind people that it's good to be playful, that it's good to be inquisitive. In IDEO's case a meeting room in a shape of a VW minibus is just one such example. Pixar offices have wooden sheds, while at Google, it is a giant skeleton of a dinosaur covered in pink flamingos. Those symbols play a role in how people relate to each other, how they approach new ideas being generated, how they pass judgement. Using artefacts and office spaces to encourage playfulness is totally within the arsenal of the methods available to leaders involved in cultivating design attitude. Symbols such as these have the capacity to be one of the ingredients of a culture that is playful and welcoming.

Playfulness gets people to better creative solutions, helps them feel better and work better. Play is particularly important in the phase of a project that involves exploration. As kids we tend to ask a question 'what can I do with it?' of almost any new object or substance we encounter. As we become adults we tend to gravitate towards making snap judgements and categorisations – 'This is this, not that.' Play doesn't just happen by accident. Nor can it be sanctioned in an organisational culture which is not permissive and where trust is at a premium. In order to have playfulness at the heart of the business, the top management must value it as a business tool rather than a gimmicky Friday dress code or a so-called creative away day.

Since we are adults and not kids, IDEO has created rules for creative brainstorm sessions. It seems a bit counterproductive to have rules in order to break rules, but they insist these actually work.

An atmosphere of trust allows people to take creative risks that are inherent in a design process.

'Really important is this bringing things to life, being able to build prototypes, do it fast so that you don't invest a lot of time and money into something that's not what you want it to be.' (Senior Manager IDEO)

At IDEO's offices, every conceivable medium for prototyping is readily available – from plasticine, Lego bricks, all manner of canisters and boxes, everything is there. The importance of these materials being available so readily is that that the designers don't need to go into formal brainstorming or prototyping sessions to make low-fidelity prototypes. They can just do them whenever they feel they want to make a point, want to move the conversation forward or are seeking feedback on an early idea. By contrast, in a typical office, the best construction tool might be the Post-it note. This not only reduces our propensity to be playful but it also removes a cultural code that says that being playful and experimental is allowed or encouraged.

The playful experimentation and bringing things to life also allows for an iterative process of developing product ideas with consumers which is much more effective than otherwise would have been possible. This, of course, is a very different mode from the one that encourages the company to design and build the object and only in the last possible phase test it with consumers.

Play and the state of being playful is a basic human predisposition created by evolution as massively advantageous to our species. It helps our brains develop correctly and makes us who we are. It is impossible to imagine a life without play: no music, theatre, sports, dance, games, etc. Yet we deprive ourselves of it when we step in the realm of work. We confuse playfulness with frivolity.

Designers are a professional group that proudly embraces playfulness and bringing things to life. They demonstrate that seriousness and playfulness can coexist in an organisation and can lead to great outcomes and satisfied employees. Designers see playfulness as a lubricant for creativity and as a prerequisite of joyful exploration of ideas and a huge boost to creativity.

Symbols, be they a slide inside an office building, superhero figurines on your desk, pink flamingos on a dinosaur or a casual dress code, all serve to set the scene for play to take place. They are not merely expressions of our creativity. They are essential tokens creating an environment where playfulness is encouraged and expected.

When we are playful we open up and become vulnerable. We enter a state where we are no longer bound by certain rules and behaviours. Generative and open-ended play requires permission for moments of suspended judgement. Therefore, an environment that supports it needs to engender trust and be a safe environment for goofing around. Only when such conditions exist, can playfulness truly take hold.

Fast, joyful and playful prototyping of both products and services is one of the key behaviours in a design culture. It is made possible by an attitude of openness towards play and exploration. By bringing ideas to life in such way, a more productive and humane dialogue can occur between members of the project team.

In the world of Big Data it is even more important to be playful and exploratory with how we present information. Infographics, as a way of making data easier to understand, beautiful and impactful, is one of the ways in which designers' professional attitude of playfulness manifests itself.

Chapter 8
Creating New Meaning from Complexity

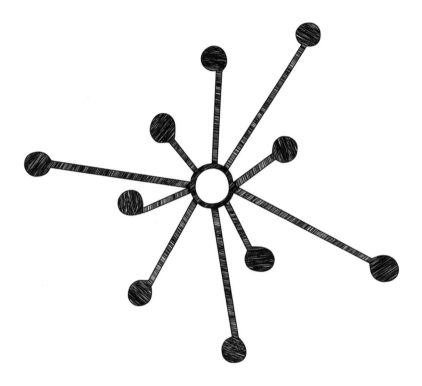

*'We are searching for some kind of harmony between two intangibles:
a form which we have not yet designed and a context which we cannot
properly describe'. Christopher Alexander*

Wicked Problems: Designers' Bread and Butter

Designers often deal with what have been described as wicked problems. These
are problems that are difficult, or impossible, to solve because of incomplete,
contradictory and changing requirements that are often difficult to recognise.
Additionally, because of complex interdependencies, the effort to solve one
aspect of a wicked problem may reveal or create other problems.[1]

These multifaceted challenges, often with missing boundary parameters and with multiple possible outcomes, are very slippery concepts to grasp. When designing for wicked problems, there are multiple possible scenarios for solving them and multiple possible outcomes, which have various degrees of satisfaction attached to them. The outcome of a wicked problem is never optimal; it's always as good as the recipients judge it to be.

The characteristics of a wicked problem according to Jeffrey Conklin[2] are:

1.   The problem is not understood until after the formulation of a solution.

2.   Wicked problems have no stopping rule – i.e. there is no clear and objective end point.

3.   Solutions to wicked problems are not right or wrong.

4.   Every wicked problem is essentially novel and unique.

5.   Every solution to a wicked problem is a one shot operation.

6.   Wicked problems have no alternative solutions.

There are high-level wicked problems such as climate change, nuclear proliferation, AIDS, pandemic influenza or economic, environmental and political issues. These problems are of a systemic nature and as such a single person or even a group of individuals are not expected to solve them. Furthermore, the constituent components of these problems can often be reduced to simpler, non-wicked problem sets. The expectation is that these problems take time to get resolved and require the consorted effort of a number of institutions and governments. On the other hand, there are basic-level wicked problems; such as designing hospital services, designing a product and service package, creating a new company or bringing a completely new product to market.

Whereas high-level wicked problems work over long cycles, we encounter the basic-level wicked problems much more often. Designers, in particular, are exposed more than others by virtue of being on the frontline of dealing with these most common of wicked problems. The intersection of people, technology, aesthetics, processes, politics, ecology and economy make many design problems wicked, and designers live with them on a daily basis.

To designers these are just another set of problems to be solved; they are used to being bombarded by stimuli and are expected to cater to numerous, often conflicting, agendas. It's part of their culture to see these challenges as ordinary. This gives them a certain attitude towards these problems that acknowledges their very unstructured nature as a given. This, in turn, enables them to deal with these problems, recognising that they are not merely optimisation challenges, that is to say focus on juggling known pieces within a known problem space. Other professions, such as marketers or engineers, start from a position of trying to find the optimal solution. They are taught in the tradition of reliability, are usually pointed to a finite number of best solutions and are told to find benchmarked, best-in-class case studies to apply to any given problem. The culture, in this case, focuses more on trying to avoid making mistakes rather than on creating surprising, coherent and beautiful solutions. That is not to say that these professions don't use creativity to solve their problems or don't come across wicked problems, because they do. It's rather to focus on the predominant mind-set and a mental model of how the world around us works.

Bolland and Collopy[3] call this 'decision attitude' whereby, upon being given a challenge, managers almost immediately jump to the best, and often only, conclusion.[4] Their attitude is one of attempting to reduce anxiety caused by the unknown, uncertain and unresolved problem in front of them. Designers, on the other hand, happily embrace ambiguity because they know it is a normal state to be in when dealing with problems. They don't try to hide the fact that they don't have the right answer. Instead, they concentrate on how to first maximise access to as many sources of solutions as possible, before trying to investigate their efficacy in a complex, often messy, back-and-forth process. In my survey, two attitudinal statements stood out as being differently received by designers and other professionals. In response to the statement, 'I seek out as many varied points of view as possible to find the right solution', 81 per cent of designers agreed versus 77 per cent of others. Another statement, 'The best project results are always achieved in a diverse, multi-disciplinary teams', was supported by similar shares of designers and others professionals.

There is nowhere for designers to hide, no ultimate processes and rules, and no industry bibles – their professional culture isn't one that is fundamentally based on finding somebody to blame when things go wrong. It's based on proposing better and new solutions, trying them out and seeing if they connect with the people they are designed for. It is a fundamentally different way of doing business that advocates lengthy planning, followed by artificial evaluation, followed by a big-bang launch. It also stands in contrast to the we-know-best attitude displayed by many professionals who view designers' deep user empathy as a wishy-washy concept.

According to graphic designer, Leo Lionni:

> *The good designer aims at a perfect fusion of the various considerations which enter into his design. He aims at an untortured unity – a direct whole. He arranges his levels consciously or subconsciously, adhering to the requisites of the problem he is asked to solve or to his own inclination. Some designers see total act through a disc of aesthetic considerations – others, more practical minded, may put economic considerations at top level.*[5]

In the absence of firm rules and guidelines, it's up to designers to make the leap of faith and jump from a seemingly boundless plethora of options and variables to one single, coherent solution. Other people can judge, evaluate and critique, but it is the designer who makes this leap of faith and postulates the future through an object or a service. It is not so much the ability to do this as the belief in the power of such leaps that is interesting from the point of view of the design attitude. Designers know that the only way to reconcile the conflict between the constituent elements of the problem is to try out an actual solution. It is this working through a series of potential solutions (sometimes referred to as rapid prototyping) rather than a series of plans which distinguishes their preferred ways of working from those of other professions. The abductive process of probing reality by proposing specific designs enables designers to hack complexity by, in effect, cutting through it. Where others often get bogged down in the detail of the analytical process, designers jump to the potential end result to test the practical boundaries of complexity. Only through physical testing and dialogue can complexity be cracked more effectively. The series of physical manifestations of the design output – be it products, services or experiences – enables designers to use their deep aesthetic sense of judgement and tacit knowledge to evaluate and iterate the solution to the 'wicked' problem at hand.

Reconciling Contradictory Objectives: Mastery of Comparing Apples and Pears

> *Designers are skilled at harmonizing disparate elements into a whole, without sacrificing each item's individuality. (John Maeda, former Dean of RISD)*

The interviewees I've spoken to have drawn a lot of attention to the role of a designer as a person who brings a variety of resources and pieces of information together. The designer weighs and reconfigures meanings and reconciles contradictory objectives. 'The designers appear to be willing to look at a situation from a great variety of perspectives, bringing together a humanistic standpoint, deep, emphatic understanding and technical limitations' (Senior Commercial Partner IDEO). Their role in organisations is to make connections and pull together different threads:

> *Designers themselves are actually managing all the constituent parts,*
> *and therefore managing the connection and the connected contribution*
> *of all the constituent disciplines in solving any problem or creating*
> *a landscape for exploring further problems or further opportunities,*
> *further possibilities of growth. (Senior Director, PD)*

It seemed that many of the designers I interviewed were willing to engage not only their sense of aesthetics and logic, but were also aware of other aspects of their projects. They were very charged with making trade-off decisions about aspects of a product or service they were designing. The art of seeing parts and the whole appears to be an essential part of their daily work. This, of course, is also something that other people in other organisations are asked to do, but it struck me just how important ability and willingness are to bringing together very different and often contradicting elements of a solution. Where others would perhaps shy away from asking questions about how it all fits together – including colours, shapes, textures and so forth – with the manufacturability requirements or the strategic message, designers are fully engaged in finding actionable solutions to these questions.

This design attitude has very strong connections to a number of other attitudes highlighted in this book, but particularly to deep empathy and the power of the five senses. In this respect, designers appear to have an advantage in consolidating different parts of the analytic-synthetic equation when it comes to linking both very tangible and intangible elements of a product, service or strategy.

Swinging between Synthesis and Analysis

It seems that, contrary to popular belief, whereas designers are predominantly seen as engaged in synthesising[6–8] their strength actually lies in utilising both – 'putting things together' and 'taking them apart' simultaneously. Walker[6] juxtaposed managers and designers, by saying that designers' predominant thinking style is 'synthesis'. This is how an experienced manager from IDEO talked about the designers' contribution to their organisational culture:

> *There are only a few things that designers [distinctively] bring to the party and the first is this way of looking at the world that is at the same time analytical and synthetic ... (General Manager, IDEO)*

In his book *The Art Firm: Aesthetic Management and Metaphysical Marketing*,[9] Pierre Guillet de Monthoux introduced the concept of *Schwung*. *Schwung* comes from a German word meaning to swing between poles and he uses it to explain the dynamic balance of 'aesthetic energy'. He uses it in relation to swinging between extremes such as 'the everyday and universal'; objective and subjective'; and 'the sensual and reasonable'. This term appears to capture what designers stand for. Designers are both synthesising and analysing when working. This process often happens in very tight loops making it difficult to pinpoint what is synthesis and what is analysis-driven. Perhaps that is why designers are seen by some as willing and able to cut through a complex situation in order to pragmatically infuse it with actionable clarity. As one senior consultant as Wolff Olins puts it:

> *Designers bring the cut-through. If you had just lots and lots of thinkers thinking in one way you'd never get that 'cut-through', that's the difference. If it's complex on the inside and extremely complex on the outside, they [designers] will try and help you simplify things.*

We find this sentiment elsewhere, too. Goldschmidt[10] says, '... [the designer] oscillates between overviews and technical details between functional aspects of the design product and issues related to human factors. He thinks of features, product identity and aesthetics along with stiffness, strength and ease of production' (ibid.: 90). That's why designers are so used to this mode of existing in several states of mind simultaneously – at the same time clarifying the solution and exploring other potential avenues.

Another prominent design scholar, Bryan Lawson,[11] showed, through experiments on architectural and science students, the differences in the way they approached solving a design problem. Although inconclusive with respect to the origin of the differences (whether they were created as a result of socialising by the educational system or were dispositional in nature and only became reinforced by education), the results showed that in relation to science students, architecture students were more solution-focused rather than problem-focused. What is important from the point of view of the design attitude is that the experiments demonstrated that final year architecture students consistently used the strategy of analysis through synthesis. They '… learned about the problem through attempts to create solutions rather than through a deliberate and separate study of the problem itself'.[12]

Connecting Multiple Languages and Media

Looking at what viewpoints designers actually connect to in an organisation, Wally Olins explains, '… we are talking about branding, we were talking about the way in which an organisation projected an idea of what it was, through its buildings, through its environment, through its people, through its behaviour, through its advertising, literature and everything else'. Designers are engaging with all of these so that they all work on an individual level and as a combined, cohesive whole.

Talking about the role designers played in the development of WO, Olins raises two issues – their ability to visualise and their close integration into the culture of WO. 'Designers were much more important in WO than you would think, because although WO was very much a strategically based consultancy business, hugely relied on designers to give … to show, to visualise this stuff and very often it was led by designers, not by consultants'.

We find this view reflected by Guy Julier, 'Design is about concepts, relationships, ideas and processes. It is also a collaborative venture which is supremely interdisciplinary in that it unites specialists in two- and three-dimensional communication, visual and material culture, and it is interdisciplinary in that it brings different professional domains together'.[13]

Essentially, the concept of creating new meaning from complexity emphasises the designer's role in reconciling multiple, operational and strategic objectives. It points to the ability to operate in an analytical-synthetical loop in order to achieve a balance between internal cohesion and meeting practical constraints. In other words, designers master '… the comprehensive design process [that] is a rich, complex integration of the scientific and the sensual, the intellectual and the intuitive'.[14]

Co-founder of Bauhaus, Laszlo Moholy Nagy, offers this eloquent summary:

Design has many connotations. It is the organization of materials and processes in the most productive way, in a harmonious balance of all elements necessary for a certain function. It is the integration of technological, social, and economical requirements, biological necessities, and the psychological effects of materials, shape, color, volume and space. Thinking in relationships.

Designers as Radical Researchers

In his book *Design-Driven Innovation*, Roberto Verganti argues that designers have a unique capacity to radically challenge the meaning of objects and services. He notes that user-centred design organisations seek out radical researchers who 'envision and investigate new product meanings through a broader, in-depth exploration of the evolution of society, culture, and technology'.[15] He also suggests that designers could be putting themselves at a disadvantage through their attempts to become more science-based, arguing that:

> *In presenting design as a codified, predictable and mandatory process-making it more digestible for executives educated in traditional management theories-designers risk losing their ability to do such forward-looking research ... In attempting to mimic the language of business, design seems to have followed the pattern noted among executives: it values methods more than designers' personal culture, thus losing the capability to harness this precious asset.*[15]

This is what appears to be happening in certain parts of the design thinking debate. Here designers, preoccupied with attempts to create more legitimacy in the eyes of the more established professions, are seeking to firm up the way in which they are perceived.

The conditions for creating truly radical innovations, innovations in meaning, require adopting a culture that nurtures those that embrace ambiguity, strive to cut through complexity, and are willing to use all available sensory and emotional bandwidths. The transformation of meaning, as Verganti argues, must be based on culturally-specific context. In opposition to analytical, benchmarking and codified processes, that are often culturally neutral or a-cultural, creation of radical new meanings demands seeing beyond these right to the fabric of what it means to be human and living in a specific culture.

Reinventing the Meaning of Products and Services

Products [and services too] embody notions of identity that are socially recognized and thus become tokens in the symbolic exchange of meaning.[16]

When service design consultancies say they want to create 'service envy' instead of 'ownership envy' they are innovating what service means to people. The focus shifts from having to using. This is already having a profound impact on how we live our lives. When Elon Musk created Tesla, a very attractive electric car with a great range, he changed what it means to own an electric car. It's no longer about government-led coercion to buy low-emissions vehicles, but about personal preferences and desires. When Alfredo Moser (see Chapter 5) designed his solar lamp – effectively a plastic bottle filled with water – he radically changed the meaning of a piece of consumer waste. When two design students set up Airbnb – a peer-to-peer accommodation renting service – they changed the meaning of how we travel. Instead of going from one uniform hotel to another, people visit unique, interesting personal spaces and enjoy their stories and histories. When Swedish designers some up with an 'invisible' bike helmet – essentially a really fashionable airbag (see Chapter 10), they radically altered the meaning of an object. Instead of focusing on its current form, they ask what it would take to protect cyclists' heads in case of an accident. The result is not so much a new product as a new meaning of what it entails to wear a helmet.

These are only some of the examples of how designers challenge complexity, context and the status quo to come up with new, often radical, changes in what services and things mean. Ultimately it is the people/users/consumers who make their own meaning based on the products they buy and experiences they share. However, it is the designers who offer them the scope to create new meanings. By combining, reconfiguring, mashing-up cultural, technical, aesthetic and other elements of a product or a service together, the designer creates the conditions for the new meaning to emerge.

Mihalyi Csikszentmihalyi and Eugenie Rochberg-Halton explain how people assimilate objects into their lives and infuse them with symbolic meaning as expressions of their experiences, 'Things embody goals, make skills manifest, and shape the identity of their users. His self is to a large extent a reflection of things with which he interacts. Thus objects also make and use their makers and users.'[17]

To create new meaning from complexity, or create the conditions for such outcomes to occur, designers need to propose future scenarios, through an object or an object-service system. They need to assemble all the ingredients and make a leap of faith into the unknown. This requires a degree of audacity and conviction, as there often isn't a reference point for the new meaning. It's either adopted by the public or it isn't.

In Chapter 11, I write about Segway, a product that failed due to its social meaning being rejected by the public. Despite the product's technical innovation and strong usage case in the city – it was meant to revolutionise the way we commute within cities – it failed because of what it represented in a contemporary society. There a numerous examples of propositions that were technically very good, but they did not succeed because they did not offer what people wanted at the time.

As Jonathan Ive noted, it is unfair to expect consumers to envisage the future.[18] This is the role of the designer. He or she needs to put forward a coherent solution, having assimilated and weighted a variety of sources.

There are certain attitudes and preferences that are forged in the context of creating new meaning from complexity.

- The way in which designers approach problem-solving shows a preference for abductive methodology. This essentially means trying things out to see how to define a problem as well as simultaneously test how a problem can be answered.

- Ongoing exposure to complexity and contexts with multiple dimensions – across senses, physical manifestations, and meanings of objects – moulds designers in a way that creates an expectation that this varied and chaotic environment is something that needs to be embraced rather than dismissed or swept under the carpet.

- The deep aesthetic gauge for sensing if the solution is providing the expected new meaning has two dimensions. Firstly, it is a tool designers use to assess the efficacy of the idea in the face of enormous complexity and 'wickedness' of the problem. Secondly, it is their preferred means of operating.

- Tendency to gravitate towards simplicity as the preferred design outcome. It often seems that the ultimate goal of many designers is to tame complexity by creating something simple and approachable. I don't think that the fact that many prominent design outputs (think iPhone for example) or schools of thought (think Bauhaus), embrace the notion of simplicity and clarity is accidental. It's part of the designer's make-up to try to give order to things. This act forces designers to commit their values and personal preferences to a solution. There are no objective or value-free design outputs. They are all informed by who the designers are, their background and personal motivations.

Bounded Rationality

Another aspect of the process of approaching the creation of new meaning from complexity is the limit on how many things we can hold in our minds. Research has shown that the average person can think of seven things – give or take two – at the same time. This is as true for a designer as anyone else. Herbert Simon[19] writes about bounded rationality that limits us as to how many independent pieces of information we can process at any given moment. We are all limited by this, so we all need to take shortcuts in our thinking – an objective or optimal thinking process is not possible.

Whether we like it or not we all make cognitive shortcuts. Brands are a prime example of how we depend on simplified messages. We can't analyse the world afresh every time we go to the supermarket, so, we only we re-evaluate our choices occasionally, otherwise we stick to the signposts we know work for us – such as going for the brands we liked before.

We all have an internal mechanism that means decisions are emotional and not rational – the difference is that designers embrace the process instead of searching for culturally-convenient excuses that would prove they decide using logic alone. There is more about tacit knowledge and aesthetic decision-making in Chapter 6 (*Embracing the Power of The Five Senses*).

Cutting through complexity requires cognitive and heuristic shortcuts. There is no other way around it. The question is which shortcuts do we choose and whether we openly admit to them. If we choose to hide behind the façade of infinite rationality, tick-box optimisation, and infallible processes, we are in danger of missing out on the great opportunities that come with tackling complexity head-on.

From Faster Horses to iPhones: Market Research and the Creation of New Meanings

If I had asked people what they wanted, they would have said faster horses. (Henry Ford)

Nobody understands the sentiment captured by Henry Ford better than designers. In my role as a strategic marketing consultant, I've organised and sat through my fair share of focus groups, workshops and similar market research arrangements. What they all have in common is a focus on what the consumers, usually belonging to a specified target groups, think of a concept, product or a piece of advertising. What I've found over the years is that these market research tools are great at confirming or criticising. They are very rarely, if ever, good methods for coming up with something new and different. As marketers we are aware of their limitation, for example through the use of a framework called Johari windows. It essentially acknowledges that there are different types of insights – ones that are known to self and others that are beyond our conscious understanding – thus beyond reach of traditional market research methods. As we also recognise, these tried-and-tested methods of generating consumer insights have their role and place, but the creation of a new meaning simply isn't one of them. Similarly, quantitative market research tools are great at painting the big picture and summarising people's explicit concerns, but they are practically useless when it comes to creating breakthroughs. This has consequences in so far as it infuses the professional culture of sellers of these methods with a certain vocabulary and framework set. Subsequently, that informs how ideas are created, judged, evaluated and put forward for approval. In the light of Chapter 11, where we examine the impact of designers themselves, it is likely that radical new meanings will have difficulty getting though the marketing-driven development and approval process.

Radically new meaning, in the shape of radically new products or services, doesn't stand a chance in traditional market research testing. It has to be proposed to the public by its designer, based on their best-guess assessment and gut feeling. I would go as far as to say that the only way in which it's possible to test a new and radical meaning is to put it on the market. This, I believe, is the reason Kickstarter (a community funding website) is so useful to many entrepreneurs, designers and artists. It gives them a real-life, market-testing experience. By putting their products and services out there, they have a chance to show their vision to the public. The public, in this case, is a somewhat less risk-averse community of early adopters who are not afraid to get their fingers burnt.

In the absence of Kickstarter and similar websites, which aren't frequented by the large organisations, the only way to test radical meaning is to launch on the open market. There are plenty of examples of design-led organisations that explicitly state that traditional market research in the new product development process is not very helpful. Perhaps the most prominent of them all is Apple. When Jobs was as its helm he openly derided market research as a means of coming up with radical solutions. He and Apple are known for seemingly going 'against' the wishes of the consumer, only to be proven to be trendsetters – introduction of a mouse when nobody has been asking for it; removal of floppy disc drives when everybody was using them; introduction of the USB when nobody knew what it was; removal of the CD-Rom drive from MacBook Air when wireless data speeds weren't impressive; removal of a physical keyboard on a phone when everybody was expecting it ... the list goes on. If any of these were put in front of the average, specially-selected consumer, she would have rejected these ideas outright. However, because they were put forward as propositions for the future, with the clout and endorsement of a known and loved brand, they were given the airtime and subsequently became not only major hits, but sometimes even changed entire industries.

It is clear that even the great Steve Jobs wasn't the one to actually distil the complexity into a product. He would do that on the level of a vision or a concept, but actual groundwork was down to Jonathan Ive and his design team. 'If Jobs didn't like something, he'd say so, but that was the only direction he gave. His feedback was always non-directive. He never suggested how something should be changed, but rather pushed Jony and his designers to come up with a better solution.'[18] This is what I'm referring to when I say that designers are really good at creating new meaning from complexity. They assimilate and mash-up the extraordinarily varied and multifaceted inputs to come up with a product or a service that actually has the capacity to offer the new meaning to consumers. When so much actually depends on execution these days, rather than on the concept alone, it is essential to appreciate just how important this is for the overall success of the venture.

Verganti quotes the famous Alberto Alessi, 'There is a way of doing design that is giving people what they ask [for], which is never something innovative. And there is a way of doing design that is more artistic and poetic. It is like commercial art ('commercial' because it needs to be approved by the audience; eventually people need to love it).'[15] Looking at designers as commercial artists is actually a good way of expressing it. They need to propose what they believe will create a new meaning for people, for which they will be willing to pay.

User-centred and human-centred research cannot be dismissed, however. When talking about deep empathy (see Chapter 5), an intimate connection with the user is a very important component of design attitude. It is crucial to be able to empathise meaningfully with the very people for whom the products and services are being created. This can be seen as a very special case of consumer research.

Designers' natural territory is wicked problems – ones without clear parameters or optimal solutions. Their instinctively adopted attitude is one of acceptance of ambiguity and uncertainty that is part and parcel of the daily challenges they face. This makes them more at ease in situations that are less structured and less defined with a greater number of competing agendas. Designers are used to embracing complexity in all its forms (from systems and macro-level considerations to senses and micro-level considerations) rather than ignoring it. Unlike managers who often employ a reductionist approach fuelled by decision attitude, designers thrive on the existence of multiple stimuli and multiple exploratory paths. This design attitude positions them well in situations that require the creation of new meaning.

Designers often focus on taming complexity through simplicity and aesthetic appreciation of the potential solutions. They embrace abductive iteration of solutions as the best way to deal with wicked problems. Embracing creative leaps, as opposed to meticulous and exhaustive planning, is seen as a useful way of tackling complexity. Innovating the meaning of products and services is what designers often aspire to do. By interrogating complexity and questioning basic assumptions surrounding current solutions, designers open up the possibility of new meanings to emerge. Traditional market research methods are inadequate tools in creating new and radical product and service meanings. They focus too much on the current understanding and reference points. User-centred research should concentrate on deep empathy and allow the design teams the option to iterate multiple solutions in a bit to create a great consumer fit.

PART III
Design Attitude in Action

Chapter 9

How Design Attitude Influences Frameworks

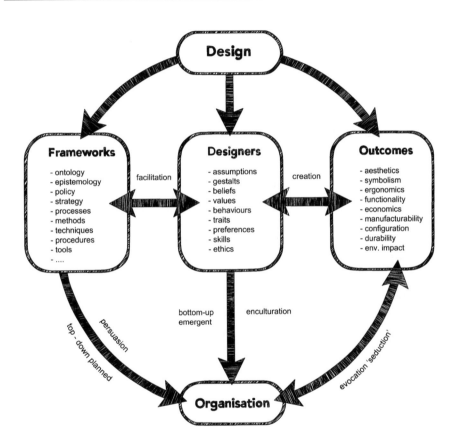

Figure 9.1   Channels of design's impact on organisations

As concepts, design attitude and design thinking are part of what I call design-inspired frameworks. Philosophical, methodological and practical, the thing that they all share is that they are all conceptual constructs that have to be adopted, or at least discussed, in order to be effective or to have an impact.

There are many ways to address design's impact on organisations. There's the financial impact of investment in industrial design,[1–3] the strategic importance of design,[4–8] design's own knowledge and impact,[9–12] design's impact on innovation,[13–15] political, ethical and social implications of design,[16–18] implications of design thinking in management and the importance of service design.[19]

There are many different interpretations of what design is, and often instead of clarifying definitions, commentators, scholars and practitioners blur it even further. Some authors, for example, use design as signifying particular processes, epistemology or the ethical and social consequences of designing. To illustrate how this works in practice, let me introduce a design management example. It is not to my intention to criticise its author, Brigitte Borja de Mozota, who has contributed greatly to the understanding of design in managerial context, but rather to show how the design-related discourse can be perceived by somebody from outside the field.

When discussing the role of design in an organisation, Borja de Mozota's[5] looked into 33 companies that took part in the European Design Prize competition (2003). The author argues that design plays three major roles in an organisation: it helps to differentiate product offering (design as differentiator); coordinate innovative activities (design as coordinator) and transform organisations (design as transformer) (ibid.: vi). While these roles would undoubtedly be recognised by designers in the organisations studied – design as differentiator, coordinator and so forth – may not be entirely clear to outsiders. Bearing in mind the large number of meanings of the word design (i.e. process, product, function, plan, conception, intent, pattern, blueprint, art, activity, creativity, industry, etc.) we can hardly expect that people grasp what is meant by design's impact.

Framing design as strategy also does not resolve the issue. Using such a broad and ambiguous term arguably clouds the picture of what is meant by design, especially when it is thought that design is what we all do[20] and that designing is simply changing current situations into preferred ones. [21] Are we talking about the design process that is doing the differentiation and coordination, or is it the outcome of it? Or perhaps it is the design as a business function at work? What follows is the list of Borja de Mozota's (ibid.) conclusions summing up the exploration of design as differentiator:

1.   Design creates a differentiation of the form that has an impact on consumer behaviour.

2.   The design-form encompasses cognition, emotion, message and the social relationship with the consumer.

3.   The consumer has aesthetic preferences that come from design principles but vary accordingly to the context and her or his experience with design.

4.   Design creates differentiation through brand identity development, building brand equity and through architecture (ibid.: 113).

In points 1 and 4 the word design is used as if it was an intelligent agent. The form 'design creates' suggests that. The usage of design as an actor capable of creating, affecting and acting is rather common adding, in my opinion, to potential misinterpretation and misrepresentation of design and designers. It can compound audience's perplexity when the message of the professional community of designers is being communicated to the outside world. Instead of making an abstract and all-encompassing word *design* the centre of attention, wouldn't it be better to use a more focused terms such as design process as practised by professional designers; design method(s) as used by professional designers or indeed professional design culture? It would clarify what precisely is being argued when describing design's role and its qualities.

Thus, taking into account the lack of a broad framework addressing the inconsistencies and the problematic framing of design's impact on organisations; outcomes and conclusions stemming from the research on the professional design culture; and reading of mainstream interpretation of design, I propose a model for viewing the ways in which design affects organisations (see Figure 9.1).

The model is based on the assertion that all design has to offer, both to an enterprise and through it to a broader economy, is channelled in essentially three ways: *frameworks* informed and inspired by designers and design thinkers, *outputs* produced during the design process, and *professional designers* as direct carriers of their values and values, attitudes, believes and behaviours.

Frameworks

Firstly, we've got frameworks inspired by professional designers or design thinkers. These include theories, methods and tools that often take the form of such things as books (such as the one you are reading), articles, blogs, lectures, conferences, Internet-based discussion groups, and Twitter hash-tags. Their primary function is to lay down an argument or engage in a dialogue to persuade the public or learn something from it. These frameworks inform the way we think about design methods and their general usefulness. They help us to get familiar with the topic, convince us of its merits and sometimes seduce us with the clarity of their arguments. Their nature is very much cognitive, grounded in an ability to logically put forward a case of the design approach. These frameworks are planned and purposeful and have a diverse range of proponents ready to stand behind them. Accidental or subliminal impact on us is rather unlikely, as they all need to be explained and directed at somebody or something.

The design-inspired frameworks are a means of spreading the message about design. Below is a selection of frameworks that have made an impact.

Design Thinking

The first one is Design Thinking. It's as a set of approaches, methods, tools and techniques for a design-inspired, human-centric creativity advocated by design thinkers.[19, 22–5] Increasing innovative powers of companies through the design process.[4, 15, 26, 27]

Here, over a number of years, the focus has been on popularising a method of solving problems using what is also known as a human-centric approach. IDEO and the Stanford d.school, are not the only ones to fly the flag of design thinking, but they are some of the earlier proponents and remain a strong voice in the debate. A host of other design consultancies are following a very similar trajectory in bringing the message of design thinking frameworks to the mainstream. The debate has progressed significantly in recent years, with increasing numbers of organisations and institutions adopting the principles of design thinking. There are a rich array of tools, methods and processes advocated by the design thinking approach.[28, 29] Among those are things such as shadowing, customer journey mapping, contextual interviews and co-creation. Some of these tools are not inherently linked to design thinking but practiced and available elsewhere (e.g. marketing-led initiatives). The differentiation of design thinking is based on the genuine and deep-felt focus on the human perspective instead of commercial perspective as the ultimate gauge.

Frameworks within design thinking also focus on persuading organisations that following the design process enables them to unlock their innovation pipeline. The authors propose that an exploratory, human-centric and pragmatic approach employed by designers is an excellent model to follow to achieve meaningful and rich innovation objectives inside companies and organisations.

Service Design

Service design is a way of looking at designing services in a way advocated by designers as opposed to other professions. It is a sub-genre of design thinking and is sometimes quoted in the same breath.

Service design, apart from being a set of tools and techniques, is also a way of thinking about what is important when it comes to creating services. Services were being designed well before the term service design was proposed. The difference is that the services were mainly arranged, assembled and put together by professions such as design-engineers, marketers, business people and public officials. With the specific design attitudes carried by the design profession, the nature of services design, within the service design framework, have a different quality to those that are designed outside it. Here service design can be seen as a school of thought, which concentrates first and foremost on the human-centred aspect of the service. The attitude of deep empathy, which is enhanced by tools such as service mapping, service enactment and cultural probes, is only one of the key differences in how service design operates as a framework. The main difference between service design and other formats offering the creation of services is that it provides a human-centred approach which is integral to the way the professional design culture functions.

Managing as Designing and Design in Business Schools

Despite the occasional flirtation, schools of design and business schools managed to avoid each other for many years. This is not surprising, given my arguments about the art-based nature of the design professional project, which is at odds with the mainstream management education that is predominantly science-based. The design management movement has mostly been orchestrated from within the design profession with design being trivialised outside the field. Only relatively recently has design rhetoric reached a critical mass and been picked more vigorously in management education. Not only do top international outlets such as Harvard Business School feel comfortable talking about design as a robust concept, but some are also aligning their positioning with design. Take, for example, Rotman School of Management or Weatherhead Business School, both of which have been consciously creating brands distinct from the rest of the field with a strong emphasis on design.

Rotman's Roger Martin, a vocal proponent of Design Thinking inside business education, has been named as one of the top 50 most influential business thinkers of 2013.[30] Case Western Reserve, Weatherhead Business School went through a transformative experience with the design and creation of their Frang Gehry building. This, in turn, has sparked interest and started a debate on how to incorporate design into the mainstream business school curriculum and business thinking.[31, 32]

The focus of design-inspired frameworks is firmly on the benefits of design-inspired thinking and concepts on business practice and research. In this case, design methods, philosophies and ways of doing things are being studied as potentially game changers in the ways in which business conducts itself. The authors active in this field acknowledge and appreciate design-led ideas and processes as different in style and substance to traditional business teaching and theory. They recognise the qualities of 'abductive' thinking practiced by the design professionals and suggest paying more attention to the unorthodox and human-centric practices adopted by the design-led school of thought.

Design approach is undoubtedly starting to have an impact on business education. It's far from being widely adopted framework, though. It must be said, however, design is still on the margins of interest of most business schools.

Design, Public Services and Policy

Design rhetoric and ideas are starting to significantly inform public service provision and polices.[16, 33, 34] The UK government has been looking to design methodologies to enhance the way in which public services are delivered to the public. The Danish Government has been involved in embedding design throughout public services for some time now. Government officials have also implemented initiatives such as 'Design against crime'. NGOs, including Participle and UNDP, have been working within the design framework. In the USA, IDEO has been involved in creating a Design Thinking K12 schools' map and directory. More recently, the EU has been pursuing design-inspired innovation policies.

As the impact of design frameworks moves up the decision hierarchy in organisations, it reaches the levels of policy and public service provision. It is not only that policymakers need to see a tangible value in design, but they also need to see the wider context. This includes the environmental, ecological, legal and strategic propositions carried by design theorists and practitioners. The influence of design here is concentrated on policy-level input and tangible public services. Some great examples of the impact of design-inspired framework include the excellent gov.uk initiative and team. It is essentially a UK government digital service setup, run remarkably like a service design consultancy with full focus on the user, which has great aesthetic dimension to the services it provides. The Policy Lab – UK government's unit for prototyping new initiatives where designers and design methods play a significant part – is also a good case study. The Circle Movement by Participle and Hilary Cottam and their innovative service for the elderly have been created on the basis of the human-centred design approach (see Chapter 10). Another example of a design-led public service provision comes in the firm of MindLab – the Danish Government's cross-governmental innovation unit that involves citizens and businesses in creating new solutions for society.

Tangible Benefits of the Design-Driven Approach

Design has also been talked about as making a significant economic contribution to businesses, organisations and economies.[1, 2, 35] It shows that design-inspired thinking and business models are definitely not skin-deep and provide a good return on investment. Institutions such as the Design Council in the UK, the Design Innovation Research Centre and the Design Management Institute are serious about making sure the economic case for design is put to organisations, funding bodies and to the public.[36]

These examples highlight the power of design-inspired frameworks, which, when adopted, have the capacity to transform their new domain. In business school settings, they are creating a new mind-set and new methodologies. They empower managers and business people to think more laterally, creatively and openly. By shining a light on what's possible rather than what's proven, they release individuals and organisations to experiment and iterate solutions in the environment where ambiguity and error are not only tolerated but also encouraged. In public service provision, design frameworks offer a safe and politically neutral common ground by focusing all efforts on the needs of the users – not customers, not constituents, not voters – but actual people who use those public services. Design frameworks have the human-centric model at their heart – hence they are uniquely positioned to assist public officials and governments in delivering their services. No other framework is so politically non-threatening. It's not inherently connected to cost-cutting and job losses, as in the case of management consulting, and it's not inherently connected to selling ideas, as it the case marketing consulting. The primary objective of design framework and design thinking or design-led consultancies is to create something functionally flawless and aesthetically engaging. The relentless focus on the user makes these frameworks very attractive to policy makers and designers of public services. As a result, I can foresee the role of design frameworks growing significantly within the public domain. In organisations and businesses, design frameworks call for a bigger, more prominent role of the designer. The debate centres around the return on investment in design. Study after study shows that it is a good idea economically to look to design for a competitive advantage and increased profits.

All these frameworks share a common method of influencing actions in and outside organisations, namely persuasion. In order for these frameworks to have an impact there needs to be somebody who argues their case. Convincing rhetoric, supported by fashions and trends, receptive audience and big names propagating the message, all contribute to helping these frameworks achieve the desired recognition and influence. Those efforts contribute to making design and designers more visible and help them achieve a more professional standing in society (their professional project). Institutions such as the Design Council in the UK, the Design Management Institute in the US, and numerous consultancies, NGOs and individuals, work to promote design-inspired policies, theories and tools in society.

The process of proposing those frameworks to the public and players inside organisations is, to use Mintzberg's[37] terminology, mostly top-down and planned. Consequently, the impact is felt only after a significant time when the frameworks had the time to bed-in. Very often the adoption of these frameworks is related to a process of peer verification and will depend on its outcome. Essentially, whatever is proposed in the name of design by design scholars, practitioners or those inspired by design, is not immediately felt or translated into action. It has taken several years for design thinking methods to be more widely used and recognised, for example. The conditions need to be right for the ideas carried by these frameworks to make their way into general consciousness.

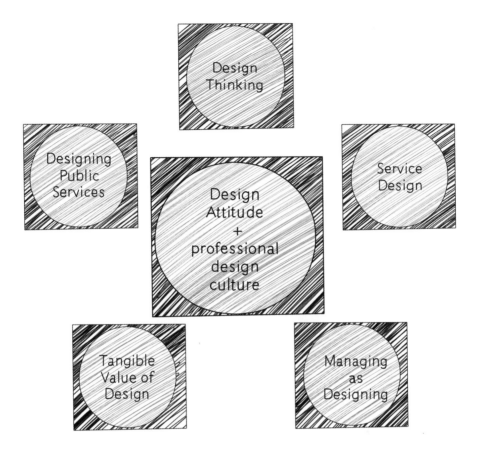

Figure 9.2   Design-inspired frameworks

The Spectrum of Design-Inspired Frameworks

Design-informed frameworks are one of the channels through which design rhetoric imprints itself onto organisations. Those frameworks, theories, methods and tools could be attributed to different kinds of professional values and motivations. Their characteristics and overall message rely, to a certain degree, on who the authors are, what their chosen field of practice is and their personal agenda. Broadly speaking, and for the sake of clarity, the work can be mapped onto a continuum between two extremes: the first driven by practical concerns and usually advocated by professional designers, the second driven by knowledge creation, usually driven by non-professional designers (see Table 9.1). The Ideal Type descriptions of the frameworks proposed by those two extremes suggest that the former is more concerned with practical advice that concentrates on achieving particular results, is usually heuristic and unstructured, and uses evocative and emphatic rhetoric. The latter, on the other hand, is engaged in more philosophical debate that seeks structure, methodical tools and uses logical-descriptive rhetoric.

Table 9.1   Continuum of design-inspired frameworks

Frameworks, including: epistemologies, theories, methods, processes, techniques, tools, etc.		
Driven mainly by *practical* concerns (professional designers, business practitioners)		**Driven mainly by *epistemic* concerns (usually by philosophers, design critics, economists and scholars)**
• practical and immediate • concentrated on achieving particular results • heuristic • evocative and emphatic rhetoric		• philosophical • concentrated on achieving understanding and conceptual distinctiveness • methodical • logical and descriptive rhetoric
Kelly[27] Kelley and Kelley[23] Brown (IDEO) • design process often flexible and open-ended • design tools: brainstorming, rapid prototyping, shadowing, observation etc. • creativity confidence framework for everyone	Schön[38] • reflection in action • conversation with materials and situations	Simon[21] • natural and design sciences • bounded rationality
Marzano[39] (Philips) • ambient intelligence	Papanek[18] and Manzini[40] • ethical conduct of designers • environmental consequences of designers' work	Romme and Van Aken[41–3] • epistemology and research methods informed by design
This is Design Thinking (add ref) • service design methods, tools and processes	Alexander[44] • pattern language	Weick[26] • organisation design
Peto[45] • random nature of design • importance of 'accidents' and errors in design process	Cross[46, 47] • design thinking and design intelligence • design methods	Csikszentmihalyi[48, 49] • self-identity and designing
	Cooper and Press[33, 34] • policies informed by design • design's role in economy	Dewey[50, 51] • design, culture, experience, learning
	Verganti[52] • innovation as a radical change in meaning	
	Martin[25] • Design Thinking as a source of competitive advantage	

The aim of this book is not to discuss the frameworks listed in the table comprehensively, nor is it to create an exhaustive list of design-inspired sources. These cover a wide range of separate conversations and debates. Here I aim to illustrate how the discussion regarding the design-inspired approaches is being played out by bringing forward an example related to the publications and frameworks proposed by California-based design consultancy IDEO, which is considered 'the world's most successful design firm, according to a number of commentators.[25, 53, 54] It is aimed at practitioners focused on creating environments that support and encourage innovation.

Tools, Methods, Ways of Thinking and Creativity Manifestos

Design practitioners from IDEO proposed a set of frameworks inspired by design. Here we find a source of practical inspiration on how to create a culture in which innovation flourishes and product and process boundaries are being rewritten. Instead of focusing their attention on epistemological clarity and academic soundness, authors such as Kelly[27] introduce ways in which designers at IDEO successfully collaborate and inspire. Since it is mainly a case study it remains a framework that could be advocated, argued, persuaded and eventually adopted by practitioners with greater or lesser enthusiasm. Judging by the take up of design thinking by NGO's; governments (see Francis Maude and gov.uk); the business press, such as *Forbes*; HBR and others, it is gaining popularity and followers.

A major part of the IDEO storyline is the ubiquity of their design process (see Figure 9.3). It has not only been highlighted by the founders and managers of the company but also discussed by various commentators.[54, 55] In itself, the process creates the backbone for the innovation mechanisms and is used to focus project leaders' attention. Myerson[54] reports one of the founders of IDEO as saying, 'At IDEO we have steadily moved away from a sequential idea of design process towards a set of values which contribute to a rich design & innovation culture. These values provide a framework within which chaos, risk, experimentation, innovation and vision can thrive' (ibid.: 91).

However, as the Managing Director of IDEO London acknowledged in my interview, this process is an important galvanising tool for designers and other professionals working on projects.

The process, or as Kelly[27] calls it 'methodology', has five basic steps or parts: (a) understand, (b) observe, (c) visualise, (d) evaluate and refine, (e) implement (ibid.: 6–7). It is also presented as: (a) observation, (b) brainstorming, (c) rapid prototyping, (d) refining, (e) implementation.[55]

There are a number of variations of this process across the industry, but the core essentially stays the same.

Observation: Understanding

Usually the first step in the process is aimed at trying to understand the situation. Here designers utilise one of the most effective customer research tools, namely observation (for more in-depth discussion on anthropological methods and design, see[15]). Instead of asking the customers what they want, IDEO use empathy while engaging directly in a number of ways. Together with cognitive psychologists, anthropologists, sociologists they use a number of techniques to aid the process. These, for example, include:

- shadowing – whereby people are observed while using products, going to hospitals or shopping;

- behavioural mapping – which involves recording peoples' movement and behaviour in a given space over a couple of days;

- unfocus groups – interviewing diverse groups and studying their reactions to the existing products (adapted from[55]).

In a turbulent business environment there usually is no time to conduct a fully-fledged ethnographic study. Instead IDEO, as well as other design consultancies, use simplified design-ethnography to rapidly achieve its aims in a quick and dirty process feeding into the product development. 'We have no time for detailed scientific studies at IDEO, nor does most of the rest of the business world. We aren't interested in hundreds of carefully qualified users filling out detailed forms or sitting in focus groups.'[27]

The realisation that we live in an experience economy[56, 57] does not surprise ethnographers who have been making this point for many years.[58] However, it took professional designers such as those in IDEO to reinterpret this academic and commercially alien specialism into a useful business tool. They provide a bridge between the culture and the company like no other profession within a firm's framework.[59] Designers embrace deep empathy in order to gauge users' reactions and create a counter weight to treating 'customers like statistics'.[27]

Brainstorming 101

At IDEO, brainstorming follows observation and understanding as the first step in generating potential avenues for exploration. It is thought that brainstorming '… is not just a valuable creative tool at the fuzzy front end of projects' (ibid.: 5), but also an important cultural engine.[60] The skill of brainstorming is evidently an important ingredient, but what perhaps is more important is the intensity, playfulness and pervasiveness with which brainstorming is practised at IDEO: 'Brainstorming is practically a religion', says Kelly.[27]

There are a number of rules of brainstorming which the members must adhere to. These are:

a)   defer judgement and do not dismiss any ideas;

b)   build on the ideas of others;

c)   encourage wild ideas / be playful;

d)   be visual / get physical;

e)   stay focused on the topic;

f)   one conversation at a time (adapted from[55]).

These brainstorming rules instil values and attitudes, which align with design attitudes. The most visible connections are between: embracing uncertainty and ambiguity (a, c), where freedom to think and behave differently is encouraged and the power of five senses (d), where visual and tactile discourse is valued and expected.

Kelly's rules with regard to what kills brainstorming sessions are: (i) the boss gets to speak first, (ii) everybody gets a turn, (iii) experts only please, (iv) do it off-site, (v) no silly stuff, (vi) write down everything.[27]

An ethnographic study carried out by Sutton and Hargadon[60] showed six consequences of brainstorming at IDEO:

- supporting the organisational memory of design solutions;

- providing skill variety for designers;

- supporting an attitude of wisdom (acting with knowledge while doubting what one knows);

- creating status auction (a competition for status-based on technical skill);

- impressing clients;

- providing income for the firm (ibid.: 685).

Rapid Prototyping: Visualising

Prototyping and physically making things has a special place in IDEO's culture. I also observe this to be the case in other design-intensive organisations. Therefore, one of the categories identified in the professional design culture is called playfully bringing to life, and includes rapid prototyping, preference for working with tangibles and willingness to creatively manifest ideas.

Kelly[27] writes that prototyping is 'both a step in the innovation process and philosophy about moving continuously forward, even when some variables are still undefined' (ibid.: 5). In this respect, it gives a sort of visual and tactile guidance in the mode of action based on acceptance of ambiguity and uncertainty. It is clearly an encouragement of reflecting in action and 'listening to the situation back-talk'.[38] In my study, prototyping was thought of highly by the designers with 87 per cent agreeing with the statement: 'Fast, iterative prototyping as early as possible in the product development process is preferable.' Some 68 per cent of those from other professions agreed.

Kelly says, 'Quick prototyping is about acting before you've got the answers …'.[27] In fact, it creates answers and new questions at the same time by helping to crystallise the solution step-by-step. It is more evocative than pictures (ibid.: 112) and helps in decision-making.[55] The activity of prototyping is as much about solving already known problems as it is about making accidental discoveries.

The process usually does not follow a predetermined pattern. 'We don't care if we sometimes go down the wrong routes, so long as we eventually arrive at the right product', emphasises Kelley.[54] This again links closely with the design attitude of embracing ambiguity and uncertainty. In this case the fear of not knowing what or how to reach it gives way to an eager acceptance of the likelihood of blind alleys and mistakes. The (temporary) loss of control is acknowledged and embedded in the culture.

According to Kelly, those three elements – observation, brainstorming and prototyping – are 'the fundamentals, the reading, writing, and arithmetic of innovation' (ibid.: 121). The remaining parts of the process such as evaluating – refining and implementation – borrow from the three basic elements and are more instrumental. Nevertheless, these are also of great significance since the final outcome depends on the quality of input during those phases.

In addition, IDEO studios subscribe to the set of underlying principles known as FLOSS where 'F stands for Failure, meaning don't be afraid to take risks; L stands for Left-handed – remember that not all users are like you; O stands for Out there – don't just sit at your desk; S stands for Sloppy – prototypes don't need to be perfect; and the final S for Stupid – don't try to be too clever or presume you know it all'.[54]

Figure 9.3   Design process at IDEO (adapted)

Both examples of design-inspired frameworks – the former academically-driven and the latter aimed at practitioners – attempt to persuade the audience to pay more attention to methods and tools put forward by designers. Yet both do so differently and send different messages as to what constitutes the design approach and how to go about implementing it. Arguably IDEO's approach is more closely linked with the professional design culture, whereas the other, more theoretical, example lies further away from it. Hence one of the ways in which to judge and analyse the frameworks that subscribe to design as their focal point might be on the basis of their relationship with the professional design culture and its members. The attitudes of embracing ambiguity and uncertainty, playfully bringing things to life, the power of five senses, creating meaning from complexity and deep empathy will most likely be displayed and encouraged by those who have been a part of this particular professional culture.

David Kelley says, 'Design, as a methodology, is non-threatening because it's human-centred.'[23] It's a glue that allows multidisciplinary dialogue to occur. This is also witnessed by MindLab and various governmental organisations.[61] They see that it's less intimidating dealing with consultancies that are focused on the user/human, than the consumer/customer. It is the process expression of the pervasive empathy among designers, which allows them to engage in a non-threatening way with the problem matter.

> *For a long time companies that wanted to shrink went to consultants for help. Consulting groups did a pretty good job in helping them. But the people who can tell you how to shrink are not the people who can tell you how to grow. They may be good at helping you to control the number but not at helping you to expand and create new ideas. For top-line growth, you have to sell something. For that you need design. Design innovation will provide the new products. Designers can tell you how to grow, how to innovate, how to change your culture.*[55]

When designers and design-inspired commentators and scholars propose a theory, a method, a tool or a way of thinking – in fact design thinking and design attitude belong to that category – they are making an attempt at persuading the public of the virtues of the design-informed approach. Collectively, I suggest describing them as frameworks. They form one way in which design propagates itself indirectly. It necessarily takes time for these frameworks to be adopted. Through conferences, publications, public announcements, research papers and policies, these frameworks sometimes more, sometimes less successfully filter through and become part of the mainstream. In fact we are seeing an increase pick-up of design-inspired frameworks by governments (UK and Denmark are good examples); established businesses (SAP, Google, Facebook are waking up to the importance of design and are only the latest examples); NGOs (MindLab); schools (K12 design thinking movement in US); international organisations (UNDP Europe and Central Asia).

There are differences between frameworks advocated by professional designers and other authors. The former usually concentrates on practical concerns, and uses evocative and rich examples. In contrast, the latter group of non-professional designers focuses more on epistemic and philosophical implications of the design approach.

Chapter 10
How Design Attitude Influences Outputs

The second channel by which design makes its mark is through the actual things that designers create. The nature of these outputs is manifold, including aesthetic, symbolic, physical and experiential manifestations of their work. Those include the visible and tangible artefacts such as products, logos, spaces and environments, as well as the less tangible things such as brands, services, experiences and fashions.[1, 2] This is where the designer's sensitivity becomes relevant. Physical and experiential outputs have substantial evocative powers and, in a very direct way, influence all consumers, users, co-workers and stakeholders – essentially all those external recipients of the work of designers. [3, 4, 5] Unlike frameworks, which I discussed in Chapter 9, the impact on the outputs is instantaneous. Just imagine our reactions to a beautiful piece of jewellery, a particularly attractive car or a gorgeous evening dress. Now picture a very welcoming hotel room or a very friendly working environment. All these outputs created by designers have the capacity to imprint themselves onto popular culture or shape the inner workings of an organisation. As Pasquale Gagliardi[5] argued, artefacts and spaces that surround us are not just an expression of deep underlying assumptions – as in Schein's[6] view – but, rather, equally shape how cultures are carrying deeply symbolic meaning. For example, a particularly configured workplace, such as the one at IDEO, Google or Pixar, is not only an expression of the creativity of the people working there but is also the catalyst for innovation.[7, 8] There are considerable gains available if the quality of the ergonomics of a workplace are carefully attended to by designers.[9, 10] Steelcase, the parent company of IDEO, knows this very well.

There are a number of sub-fields dealing with how the products interact with customers and culture. There are areas such as product semantics, product semiotics, product interaction, interface design and communication design. [11–14] An extensive literature on evocative and culturally significant products can also be referred to.[15, 16–18] It is important to illustrate how design and design attitude moderates the production of those outcomes.

Design Outputs: Products, Services and Environments

PRODUCTS

In the era when design professionals are working hard to shake off the reputation that they are only interested in shiny products by focusing their efforts on designing services and complex systems, there remains a significant domain where their impact is being felt particularly strongly; namely physical products. These physical and digital objects form the fabric of the cultures we live in. These are the symbols and artefacts that help us navigate our twenty-first century life. The Facebook app on our phones that we open in the morning, the journey to work in a space designed by industrial designers, to the buildings we inhibit are all manifestations of the work of designers with which we interact constantly. In fact, so prevalent are those experiences across a multitude of touchpoints, that we often do not pay enough attention to the people and processes that made them possible. We notice when things don't work because they jar with our expectations and our daily flow. It is often that the objects and things that surround us are not designed but instead they are put together by people who don't give enough attention to how their creations impact on those who use their products. We all can recall a product or a thing that was either impractical, ugly or both. By the same token we remember products that delighted us with their intent, fluidity of application, humour or beauty. Designers, as a professional group, are equipped with sensitivity and values that mean they are more likely to put the human at the heart of the design process. They don't have exclusivity for being human-centric in the realm of product and service creation but, as a professional group, they are the most in tune with this type of approach.

There is a certain mindfulness and approach to creating things that are displayed by designers. To those who are unfamiliar with this project aesthetic, it might not be as clearly recognisable. There are certain markers that help to distinguish these product aesthetics:

- Is the intent of the product/service clear; does it communicate its purpose well?

- Is the usability of the product/service spot-on?

- Is there certain playfulness of form and function?

- Is there a visual balance and a harmony? Do the shapes, colours and fonts work in unison to create a coherent whole?

- Is there an attempt to innovate the meaning of an object?

Figure 10.1   Designing out medical error at College of Art Helen Hamlyn Centre for Design

During a project that ran from 2008 to 2011, a research team in England approached the problem of preventable hospital errors. The diverse group consisted of designers, clinicians, psychologists and human factors experts. As part of a project called DOME – designing out medical error – they studied medical mistakes with an eye towards designing devices that could reduce them. Led by Jonathan West, of the Helen Hamlyn Centre for Design in London, the team initially thought there would be one or two glaring areas for improvement that could be tackled with a few significant design interventions. While shadowing doctors and nurses at the hospital at Imperial College, London, it soon became apparent that what makes the problem so persistent is its extreme complexity. After long hours of observation, the team identified high-risk health care processes and analysed them for critical points of failure. They then created design briefs and enhanced them during focus groups with various experts. The end result was a suite of prototypes meant for real-world testing. One of these prototypes eventually became a device called the CareCentre (see Figure 10.1). When observing patients, the DOME team noticed medical staff often had to hunt for hand sanitiser, gloves and aprons. Medication cabinets were located far from the bedside and many had to carry around bins to dispose of needles. What's more, there wasn't always an easy place to scribble notes into a patient chart. Each of these problems present a potential trigger for a preventable medical error. The CareCentre showed measureable improvements in hand hygiene, fresh glove and apron use, and old glove and apron disposal and contributed to reducing medical errors.[19]

This is an example of how design intervention, through a thoughtfully designed object, managed to directly impact on patient care and reduce human error in a hospital setting. There are countless examples of how design impacts our lives through physical objects. The point I wanted to make here is that this is one of the ways that design attitude impacts our daily lives. It is difficult not to be affected by the world of objects that surround us. Design sensitivity and design attitude have a particular way of impacting on the nature of these outputs and subsequently the nature of the culture we are part of.

The degree of mindfulness among designers about how to design objects and experiences is on a different plane to other professions. Who else would collect – and pay attention to – the hundreds of design principles?[20]

As a result, these principles, to a greater or lesser extent, have been incorporated into the products and services that come out at the other end of the design process. Without these principles and the impact the family of design professions has on them, what we are left with, more often than not, are substandard products that are not satisfactory.

Whether we like it or not, people's first conscious experience with design is often through the physical objects they interact with and admire. There is nothing wrong with the joyful exploration and appreciation of the objects present in our cultures. A significant amount of pleasure and delight is delivered through the things with which we surround ourselves with. Despite the protestations of today's professional designers (particularly design theorists and service designers) regarding the scope of their domain, in particular their dislike of physical products as the focus of their professional attention, the reality is that this is still how the vast majority of society views and interacts with design. Accepting that this is a crucially important path of design's influence allows us to focus on it constructively. We should no longer shamefully turn our heads away from the products that seriously compromise the health of our planet but rather focus and acknowledge that the things that we make should deliver the right kind of meaning to the cultures they enrich. With the renewed focus on the crafts traditions, with the growth of viable 3D printing techniques enabling people to make production batches of one, the focus on the nature of the objects we design and manufacture is becoming even more intense.

The fact that the physically designed world is so prevalent means we often forget about the agents who made this world possible. We hardly ever examine or debate their values, attitudes, assumptions, mental models and morals. These, however, have a tremendous bearing on what our world, cultures and daily lives look like. Our happiness and mental well-being so often depend on small interactions with physical and digital objects. Think about how many times you ended up frustrated because there was something annoying in the way an object or an interface was designed: trying to charge a tablet only to find you're always inserting the plug the wrong way round; trying to find seemingly obvious information on a website and failing; having to remember dozens of passwords and pins only to be reminded at the till that your card is blocked or having to fill out impenetrable official forms many times over.

The way in which designers approach designing physical and digital objects depends, to a significant degree, on their attitudes and ways of doing things. Design attitude points to what we can expect from such an engagement. We can expect that things designed with these values will be more multilayered and purposeful (creating new meaning from complexity; the power of the five senses), will have in mind the human being and the user firmly at their core (embracing deep empathy), and will be challenging the status quo and the meaning of objects more often (embracing uncertainty and ambiguity).

The examples below demonstrate what is possible if design attitude is at play – but not necessarily the tools and techniques advocated by Design Thinking.

Industrial design students from Lund, Sweden, have developed an entirely new product to protect the head of a cyclist.[21] Instead of focusing on what helmets look like today and getting hung-up on their age-old form factor, the designers decided to use their deep empathy and have certainly embraced uncertainty and ambiguity to come up with something that challenges the meaning of what it means to wear a helmet. By hacking existing airbag technology, adding a dash of fashion and a good understanding of women's dislike of getting their hair messed up, they've devised a product that is unlike anything else out there. In many ways it perfectly captures how design attitude present in the professional design culture operates. It instils in designers values and attributes that enable them to make practical, imaginative and commercially relevant leaps of imagination. It pushes them to challenge the status quo and not to submit to an incremental conveyor belt of incremental improvements.

Figure 10.2   Invisible helmet: Deep empathy at play

Figure 10.3   Ode: The power of the five senses and deep empathy

Figure 10.4   Original 2007 iPhone: The result of deep empathy, embracing uncertainty, creating new meaning from complexity and the power of the five senses

Ode is an innovative product with dementia sufferers as its target audience. A team of British designers has focused their deep empathy and observed that weight loss is common to most people with late-stage dementia and can also be an early indicator of the condition's onset. They've identified that malnutrition costs the NHS around £13 billion a year compared to £5.1 billion for obesity, yet there were no products specifically focused on using scent to stimulate appetite in people with dementia. Their design attitude, to focus on an underused sense, together with the willingness to create a new meaning in a complex set of circumstances, enabled them to create this product.[22]

The *New York Times* writes:

> *The impact has been not only economic but also cultural. Apple's innovations have set off an entire rethinking of how humans interact with machines. It's not simply that we use our fingers now instead of a mouse. Smartphones, in particular, have become extensions of our brains. They have fundamentally changed the way people receive and process information. Ponder the individual impacts of the book, the newspaper, the telephone, the radio, the tape recorder, the camera, the video camera, the compass, the television, the VCR and the DVD, the personal computer, the cellphone, the video game and the iPod. The smartphone is all those things, and it fits into your pocket. Its technology is changing the way we learn in school, the way doctors treat patients, the way we travel and explore. Entertainment and media are accessed and experienced in entirely new ways.[23]*

Jonathan Ive's team was instrumental in bringing the iPhone to fruition. The iPhone is an exquisite example of design attitude at work. Apple and Ive have a history of creating products that appeal to many senses simultaneously (including taste through our inherent synaesthesia). From 'lick-able' iMacs to 'stroke-able' iPods, Apple and Ive have always appreciated the power of the senses on our emotions and preferences. Ive deliberately toyed with handles that served a metaphorical and not an actual function, or materials that create a closer, human connection. Leander Kahney quoted Ive as saying, 'The iBook has been designed to encourage users to touch it. The use of curved surfaces and rubberized materials an intimate, tactile feel.'[24] The iPhone not only created a new industry but also created a new meaning associated with hand-held communication device. The term 'mobile phone' has been totally transformed because of how the iPhone re-defined the parameters of a traditional phone. To all intents and purposes this is a highly mobile personal computer – a twenty-first century extension of our brains. The creation of such a device did not require a lot of traditional market research – Ive said that it is 'unfair to ask consumers to create the future'.[24] Instead, it required a deep and obsessive use of empathy on the part of everybody involved, but in particular by Ive and Jobs.

Another good example of an output produced by designers inspired by design attitude is the Nest thermostat.[25] Through the elegant, graceful and intelligent product, inspired in no small way by the design-infused culture of Apple, this product is already changing how America is saving power. Making energy efficiency sexy is how this object changes the game, and it opened up the possibility that other devices, seen purely through their utility and mainly put together by engineers, may have the Nest treatment one day. Like the iPhone before it, it has the potential to shift the focus of an entire industry. By the looks

Figure 10.5   Nest learning thermostat: Embracing ambiguity and uncertainty, creating new meaning from complexity

of things, it's already doing that as the industrial $70b behemoth Honeywell has developed a competitor to Nest which draws on its ideas and aesthetic. The acquisition of the company by Google also signalled the recognition of the importance of the technology and the ideas and people behind it.

SERVICES AND EXPERIENCES

Another way in which design and designers influence the world around us is through the direct impact services and experiences have on us. From the innovative and award-winning online First Direct bank service, through Virgin Atlantic Upper Class experience, to the integrated Apple Store and Genius Bar experience, services which have been designed with care and an attention toward the user have not only an extraordinary positive bearing on the brand, but also make us feel special as people.

Design as a profession has been transforming particularly vigorously in the last decade. Many designers have grown into their new roles as service and system consultants. Most have the traditional design human-centred background and are making use of this in their new expansive domain. We've seen a rapid growth of service design consultancies such as Live|Work, Fjord, IDEO, Continuum and Engine.

With a vast majority of the economy consisting of services (services now account for around 78 per cent of UK Gross Value-Added according to the ONS report from 2009), it is unsurprising that there is a big interest in designing services and the viewpoint proposed by the design profession. As explained in Chapter 8, design attitude encourages bringing disparate elements together into a coherent whole. It so happens that services consist of multiple touchpoints, interfaces, journeys and interactions all of which lend themselves to human-centred, design intervention. In the past, services have been, more often than not, put together without sufficient interest in the feelings and views of the users. They've been created around a capability, technical constraints or particular legal and health and safety regulations. Practices such as detailed, ethnographic analysis of customer journeys and user views were often secondary to the process of developing those services.

As things stand, the service design movement, which originated with the design professions, is growing in stature and an increasing number of organisations are turning to it for advice and help. It is developing its own style of intervention, which is different to the one offered by the traditional management and marketing consultancies. To give you a flavour of its worth, it is useful to illustrate how one prominent service design consultancy, live|work, has tackled a service challenge.

A collaboration between a London-based car sharing company, Streetcar, and live|work is a case of how an ambitious, design-driven team is shaping and reframing the challenges we face. The way the live|work team set the brief was to 'shift desirability of owning a car to desirability of using it'. Streetcar is a membership-based service with cars for rent by the hour, day, week or month. The cars can be booked for as little as 30 minutes to as long as six months. At the end of each month, members receive a monthly bill for their usage. In order to make this proposition appealing to consumers, live|work have worked with Streetcar to create a service which could rival car ownership itself. The service design consultants identified that two major obstacles to mass-market adoption of Streetcar were the complicated PIN code-driven way to start the car and inability to compare the offer to anything else in the consumers' experience. live|work helped to redesign the entire service from the joining process to the printed information, as well as the web and car booking interface. By creating a compelling, cohesive and human-centred experience, they helped Streetcar achieve its ambitious goal of taking car sharing into the mass market. In 2010, the company merged with Zipcar.

Other noteworthy examples of the impact of the service design method of intervention are Circle Network by Participle, Egg banking and Apple stores.

When designers and design attitude are involved, there is a particularly significant focus on making experiences more pleasurable and satisfying for people than is otherwise the case. The practice of employing designers and their methods and attitudes leads to the creation of some impressive public sector solutions. One such example is The Circle Movement by Participle.[26]

Figure 10.6   Zipcar logo

Figure 10.7   Circle Movement – Participle – engaging deep empathy, creating
                new meaning from complexity

    The Circle's approach to care and ageing, firstly, expands the definition of
resources to combine public, private and voluntary resources and, secondly,
creates a radical change in the way services and systems are configured so that
they focus on all the different aspects of quality of life and well-being that are
important to older people, particularly participation and relationships. The
question is not just, 'What can public services do to improve quality of life and
well-being for older people?' but rather 'How can a locality mobilise public,
private, voluntary and community resources to help all older people define
and create quality of life and well-being for themselves?' In Circle's case, the
two most prominent design attitudes are deep empathy and creating new
meaning from complexity. By focusing relentlessly on the more vulnerable,
older citizens and getting deep under their skin over time, Participle was
able to identify their most pressing needs and not just the ones immediately
visible externally. Through a great awareness of attention to multiple
viewpoints, stakeholders and agendas, combined with deep empathy, they
were able to propose a new framing of the central issue and thus created a
new understanding and a new meaning. This sort of empathy-driven strategic
consulting is made possible by the attitudes and believes embedded in the
organisation that does it.

Figure 10.8   Gov.uk: The most useful and best-looking government website in the world?

Another great example of design attitude in action is the gov.uk public information platform. Here government used the methodologies and ethos of a service design consultancy to come up with an award-winning solution. [27] It incorporated a vast array of previously impenetrable official information and displayed it in a user-friendly and attractive way, saving the government significant resources and simplifying things for the public. It is admired internationally and is thought to be one of the best government websites in the world. The difference that design attitude has made in creating this output was the sheer focus on the usefulness from the end-user point of view. The creators didn't just use a one-off ethnographic study to fulfil external requirements placed on them. They've embedded the culture of the design profession into the organisation that produced gov.uk. Through deep empathy and a willingness to iterate and experiment with possible solutions, within the context of ambiguity and uncertainty around the exact shape of the final outcome, the team was able to produce something that both the public appreciates and government is praising. According to Francis Maude, a senior UK government minister, and Mike Bracken, Executive Director of Government Digital Service, the gov.uk team did not follow standard procurement procedures and instead adopted the agile processes advocated by the design-led and start-up methodologies.

'We've really taken on the language and the cultural behaviour of many of the web-based companies and adopted it to government services. At the heart of the Internet generation is that you try something, you get user to use the services and then you iterate really quickly. That is very different from how government services worked in the past', Bracken said. Creating new meaning from complexity also played a significant part as a mode of operating. From literally thousands of government websites that had nothing in common, the digital team were able to distil the essence and organise it and present it in such a way as to empower the individual member of the public instead of bamboozle them into confusion.

The brief for what was to become giffgaff was to design and launch a new brand and business for O2/Telefonica in the UK – one that would be significantly different to any other mobile network.

Figure 10.9   giffgaff: Anything but a gaffe

The idea was put forward by O2's Head of Brand Strategy, Gav Thompson, who envisaged a mobile network run on the principle of mutuality – a mobile network that rewarded its community of customers for doing much of the work normally done by paid employees. Albion was the integrated agency that won the project. Armed with a business plan, they went to work. The brief was to define and name the brand, identify and understand the target audience, design and build the web interface, help develop the business strategy and process, create the launch communications and to get involved in everything required to turn the business plan into a fully fledged and profitable business. The proposition evolved into giffgaff, 'an operator that does things differently to the big mobile networks because it's run by its members'.[28] giffgaff's members get rewarded (with payback) for answering customer service questions, recruiting new members or helping to make the brand famous. This meant the brand could keep its costs low and pass the savings back to members. After defining the brand proposition and personality, creating the name, and helping to develop the identity, Albion opted for a launch strategy not unlike the one used by start-ups. In the beta phase, an audience of young, tech-savvy, digitally native people became the focus. Albion created Tool Hire – a series of unusual marketing tools that people could use for free. They then had to make a video, using the tool that would demonstrate the principal of mutuality that lies at the heart of the brand. For the full brand launch, the challenge was about creating instant brand awareness by cutting through to the brand's broader target audience of value-seekers, and igniting word of mouth in social media to drive low-cost acquisition of new customers. Thus, giffgaff is now recognised as a novel way to design and bring to fruition a new service proposition. From the socially-led business model, to NPD, to customer service, to marketing, giffgaff is a platform for its members to create the service they want.

Figure 10.10   Airbnb: A new way to travel the world – creating new meaning from complexity, embracing ambiguity and uncertainty

Created by two designers from Rhode Island School of Design, this innovative peer-to-peer accommodation booking service is transforming how people around the world book their stay when travelling. The service allows renting anything from a night on a couch to a castle for a month. It is built around a community of people who want to share their experiences as well as actual, physical spaces. It is not an accident that industrial designers conceived it. Their values attitudes and beliefs informed the novel and human-centred way in which service is designed. Deep empathy, playfulness, the creation of new meaning is visible in this particular design output. The strap-line captures it quite neatly: 'travel like a human'. Additionally, as renting your own flat is a regulatory minefield, the pair of designers who embarked on the journey of creating Airbnb must have embraced uncertainty and ambiguity. Rather than focusing on the many obstacles, they focused on the potential disruptive opportunities. In the process of creating the service, the pair of designers helped to create what is being called the sharing economy. An article in *Fastcompany* summed Airbnb up by saying, 'Airbnb's primary influence may be in changing the way techies think about design'.[29]

'Design used to be an afterthought', according to business designer Carlton Gebbia. 'Startups wouldn't hire designers for months or a year after funding. Now, start-ups as varied as Square, Flipboard, and Instagram count design as crucial to their success.'[29]

Refining Existing Experiences

Continuum, the US design consultancy, worked with a global medical diagnostic firm to create a new service experience for blood testing. They found the test itself took only a few moments. Customers, however, perceived their wait time as being incredibly long. This was due to the anxieties they had about the blood-drawing process, potential outcomes, time away from their job and paying for the test. By focusing on anxiety as the key experience driver, the company worked to minimise anxieties by altering the layout of the space, the information available and the intake form, as well as installing an electronic queue that would allow patients to know where they stood in line. In order to capture the emotional aspects of the experience, they implemented a touchscreen survey at the end with a series of simple questions to understand how the wait time matched the patient's expectations. Using that data, they were able to help the company make subtle changes in how representatives greeted people or seated patients, monitoring the effects on the experience in real time to improve the experience overall.[30] The approach Continuum took was similar to the one described by IDEO when they talked about reframing the brief from 'how to shorten waiting time in a hospital' to 'how to shorten the perceived waiting time in a hospital'.[31]

Work Environment as a Design Output

There's no shortage of beautifully designed and amazingly realised offices around the world.[32] The physical environment in which we work in has a significant impact on how we feel and how we live. After all, most of us spend more of our waking hours at work than we do at our own homes. As the debate about the positives and negatives of open office rages on,[33] we should focus on how the intent and attitudes espoused by the people who are responsible for imposing those environments upon us impacts these spaces – and us in the process.

Ask yourself a question, 'Would I rather work in this environment?'

Figure 10.11   Office cubicles

'… or this environment?'

Figure 10.12   Google offices

Considering that built environment and office space are designed by people and not simply manufactured by robots, it is difficult to understand why so many offices are so unbearably dull and soul-destroying. Enter into a space where designers work and you'll immediately see that they can't help but make the environment more personal, playful and inviting. They simply can't stop themselves from embellishing with quirky, unusual or impactful items. There is something playful and deeply humane in their professional culture, which encourages them to use their office space as a means of expression and creativity.

It means that the spaces they occupy tell dozens of stories and bring an element of surprise and delight to daily work. It's not possible to escape the influence of these arrangements, as they imprint themselves onto everybody that comes in contact with them.

Pixar, a company teaming with designers, is very well known for its eclectic offices inspired and designed in great measure by Steve Jobs. Brad Bird, Pixar designer and Academy Award-winning director of *The Incredibles* and *Ratatouille*, does a good job of describing the Pixar building that Jobs created:

> *If you walk around downstairs in the animation area, you'll see that it is unhinged. People are allowed to create whatever front to their office they want. One guy might build a front that's like a Western town. Someone else might do something that looks like Hawaii ... John [Lasseter – Pixar's Chief Creative Officer] believes that if you have a loose, free kind of atmosphere, it helps creativity.*[8]

In an interview with Jobs towards the end of his life, his biographer Walter Isaacson quotes the Pixar leader as saying, 'There's a temptation in our networked age to think that ideas can be developed by email and iChat. That's crazy. Creativity comes from spontaneous meetings, from random discussions. You run into someone, you ask what they're doing, you say "Wow", and soon you're cooking up all sorts of ideas.'

Jobs said about the Pixar building, 'The building was designed so that people could meet and talk in the central atrium.' John Lasseter said, 'I kept running into people that I hadn't seen for months. I've never seen a building that promoted collaboration and creativity as well as this one.'[8]

The way places look and feel has a profound impact on how we behave, how we relate to each other and our work, how creative we think we are and what expectations business places on us. Picture the typical offices of a bank or an insurance broker; now the typical decor of a toy shop – and ask yourself a question – given that we are all creative (for a very convincing argument see Kelley brothers' *Creative Confidence* book), which environment do you think would promote joyful, unabashed creativity? Which would promote making prototypes and product or service prototype? Which would make you want to try something new and different? Which would allow you to fail and try again? Above all, which one would inspire you to embrace the playful and exploratory part of your psyche? This is essentially the difference that design attitude outputs can make, when it comes to the physical world we surround ourselves with. Design attitude does not allow for a de-humanised work environment where people feel oppressed rather than empowered.

Of course, I choose to focus here on the work environment, but it equally relates to home environment and its impact on our well-being, architecture and urban planning.

We could put forward a series of tests to check if product/output have been designed by somebody who espouses design attitude:

> *Is the output challenging the received wisdom in terms of what the thing, product or service is supposed to be? A helmet should be on someone's head not their neck; services for the elderly offered by the taxpayer vs. empowering community to organise itself; iPhone consisting of several, seamlessly interwoven capabilities vs. a traditional mobile phone.*

Is the output designed to primarily meet the demands of a stage-gate process or has it been designed to connect with real people? Was meeting the deadlines more important than creating a product that stirs the human soul? Apple was never really the first to innovate. They were the best at innovating around human needs and desires. This is a direct effect of the design attitude being at the heart of the company via Ive's design team.

Is the product/service uni-dimensional or is it multilayered including the use of multiple senses? Does the product or thing tap into our innate sense of perceiving and translating from one sense to another? Something that is designed to look sharp in order to feel sharp is an example (plastic spikes, that look like metal ones, on top of a wall preventing it from being climbed). Are the experiences or products engaging our sense of smell and touch to multiply the power of the message they carry?

Is the output the result of carefully considered and skilfully reconciled points of view (e.g. personal comfort and usability, economic impact, environmental impact, social impact, emotional connection etc.), or does the nature of the output point to a one-sided or a random viewpoint skew?

Does the product, service or experience connect to the user on a meaningful and deeply satisfying level, or does it leave us unaffected and unmoved? When deep empathy is truly in use in the development process, the potential for creating something that addresses some fundamental human needs exists.

I believe that it is useful to look at how design and design attitude influence the world around us and, in particular, the inner workings of organisations. There are essentially three ways in which design impacts businesses:

frameworks, outputs (products and services) and designers themselves. Whenever we hear that design is used as a mediator or as an influencing force, we can understand how it is being applied.

Outputs have a very direct impact on how we relate to and perceive the world around us. They take the form of physical objects that we use and touch such as the smartphone; or they can be complex services which interwove many discrete touch points, such as computer interfaces, communications channels, spaces or modes of transport.

Designers, through their professional culture and design attitude, have a way of shaping outcomes which is more user and human-centric than other professions. Their influence is felt via the everyday objects that we come across.

Chapter 11
How Designers Directly Impact Organisations

'A business person has been trained to do, what I call analytical thinking
– analysing the past to provide reliability. Training of a designer, what
they're interested in isn't consistent, replicable outcomes as much as an
outcome that they love.' Roger Martin[1]

Design Culture as Mediator in the Product Development Process

Products, brands, services, and experiences are symbolic, aesthetic and physical mediators between designers, organisations and internal and external customers. Taking those constituent elements apart is a standard procedure in virtually any design process; however, it appears that professional designers are uniquely positioned to be able to bring those elements together in a unified and coherent package. By engaging design attitude in connecting multiple viewpoints and using deep empathy, designers come up with an interconnected web of objects and experiences which make cultures and organisations what they are. Because of the ubiquity of the process, we sometimes forget that it is one of the most powerful and important ways in which they impact our lives from the phone we touch and stroke multiple times a day, the computers we type on, to the steering wheels we touch and the clothes we wear. These are all designed with a purpose and intent and have a quiet, yet profound impact on how we feel, how happy we are, how safe we are and how we relate to other people and ourselves.

It is the professional designers' ability and willingness to engage on these immediate and culturally relevant levels that make them arguably the most adequate agents to connect the firm's internal and external customers and the things designed for them. According to Buchanan, 'Designers construct objects to satisfy fundamental human needs that are susceptible to some level of scientific or engineering analysis. However, the constructions are inevitably complicated by arbitrary factors of taste and preference which the designer is often able to address only by emotional sensitivity and intuitive understanding.'[2]

The way in which professional design culture mediates, through designers themselves –in the creation of results inside an organisation – can be explained by reviewing two models of the product development process (PDP). In Model I (see Figure 11.1 – Model I), design and designers are seen as tools in managers' hands. Their assigned (or assumed) cultural role is to act upon a design brief, usually created and provided by the engineers or marketing teams, or other functional part of an organisation.[3] In Model II (see Figure Model 11.4 – Model II), they are integrated into the process in the early stages, as well as the later stages, of the PDP. The former arrangement inserts a cultural filter, or what can be seen as sensory and aesthetic bottleneck, in the form of manager's

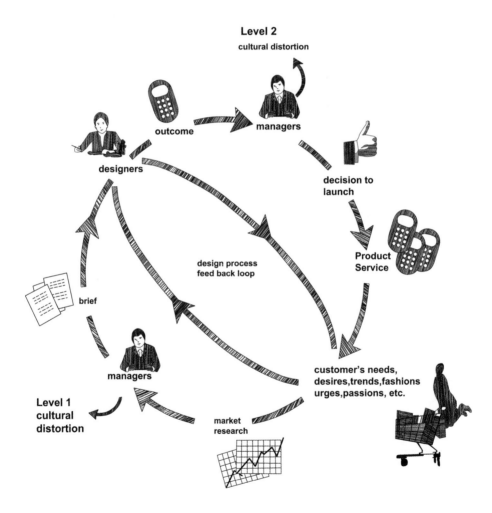

Figure 11.1   Model I product development process: Professional design culture organisationally subordinate

perceptions of the culture and the customers' multidimensional needs. Here the primary means of accessing users' needs, preferences and desires is through a brief created by non-designers. Such briefs have the potential to significantly reduce the empathy bandwidth available to designers. The latter case brings designers closer to the users, thus enabling their professional culture to have a more immediate and effective relationship with them.

In order to explain the key differences between the two models, I propose to include a concept of the levels of cultural distortion. The role of designers' professional culture in addressing *operational* (level I) and *strategic* (level II) cultural distortions is explained below.

LEVEL I CULTURAL DISTORTION: THROTTLING THE EMPATHY BANDWIDTH

The nature of Level I *cultural distortion* is operational. It is involved in the early stages of the product development process and sits where the company meets its customers. Here the professional design culture and design attitude provide more cultural points of contact with users, broadening the base for potential innovation. James Peto says, 'First we desire then we rationalize.'[4] Designers, who are used to using deep empathy and reconciling multiple viewpoints, may find their empathy bandwidth throttled if they are not given direct access to consumers. Designers mash-up layers of product and service and put forward a new and modified piece of culture. In these ways, such as various observations described in IDEO's practices, the culture and customers' experiences are being deciphered and acted upon. As observed in the chapter on deep empathy (Chapter 5), designers give this process more depth and ground it more in what human beings actually feel and need. Instead of seeing people and customers through the often obscured and distorted lens of market research or abstract concepts such as socio-economic groups,[5] they connect with human needs and desires on a more direct, personal and emphatic level.

Augusto Morello[6] juxtaposes two categories of users and consumers. The former is the subject who uses and the latter is the subject who chooses for use. On the basis of a deeper understanding of the needs of consumers and users he calls for a rethink and redefining of market research methods to incorporate the attitudes of both.

Morello argues, 'If "design" is defined as a complex of projectual acts intended to conceive products and services as a whole, the only way to design properly is to have the user in mind; and the role of marketing (a new marketing) is to have in mind the true project of the consumer, which, paradoxically, is not to consume but to be put in the condition to use properly' (ibid.: 70).

In the process of designing, designers use cognitive, sensory and emotional probing to gauge the situation.[7] By acting in this way they perform the role of organisation's ethnographers. Indeed, it can be said that designers are the de facto ethnographers in the corporate world. However, their focus is not to describe cultures, as it is in ethnographers' case, but rather on creating elements of new ones.[8] If the link between the company's intent, on the one hand, and its designers' ability to directly access consumers, on the other, is hampered, the resulting innovations might suffer. When discussing the connections between designers and marketers, Margaret Bruce and John Bessant,[3] write, 'Often project failure … is the result of the failure to provide design with adequate information about the target market' (ibid.: 83). Consequently, this results in designers being briefed 'second hand', where it becomes a case of Chinese whispers (ibid.). This scenario is presented in Model I (Figure 11.1). In many organisations, especially those that have heavily relied on technology, market research tends to be presented in quantitative form. Even if it is presented in a more contextually sensitive way, the important detail and nuances may be lost if designers are not directly involved.

There are countless examples where tech-obsessed engineers or entrepreneurs stumbled because they did not make full use of the access to what users and consumers feel and want. By limiting designers' access to empathy, they came up with products that were possible to make technically, but not necessarily that desirable. Let's look at two examples.

Segway – the self-balancing two-wheeled scooter hasn't delivered on its hype, to put it mildly. It was to revolutionise the way we move in the cities. In fact, Segway has become a by-word for failed innovation and bad taste. Health and safety issues notwithstanding, as demonstrated by some famous people falling off them, the general public simply don't want to be seen riding one. As one commentator noted, 'Someone riding a motorcycle isn't working any harder [than someone riding a Segway]. But because he's sitting astride it, he seems to be making an effort. When you're riding a Segway you're just standing there.' Segway was a technical innovation (very precise, digital gyroscopes) looking for a problem to solve. In the end, it delivered a specific product that jarred with the popular culture, becoming an object of ridicule in the process.

Figure 11.2   Segway: A cultural misfit

Another example of a product that failed miserably due to the lack of emphatic and designerly intervention in its inception was the Sinclair C5. Created by electronics engineer Sir Clive Sinclair, it was a battery-driven electric tricycle steered by handlebar beneath driver's knees. It became an object of media ridicule shortly after it was put on sale in Britain in the 1980s. The C5 suffered from a few, not so minor, problems: cold British weather significantly shortened battery life; the driver was exposed to the elements and, because it was sitting only inches above the ground, doubts were raised about its safety in traffic. According to Sinclair C5 Enthusiasts website, via *Wikipedia*, 'The problems were addressed with a second battery, side screens for bad weather and a reflector on tall poles, all available as extras from the launch.'

These are some of the most visible and famous examples of such failure, but there are countless ones we have not heard about, because they didn't make it into popular consciousness. In fact, if one observes the world around them while walking the streets, these products and services can be seen quite easily. Through looking consciously at the objects that you touch or experience, you could become a design attitude product fail spotter. All you need to be asking yourself is, 'If there had been somebody, at the inception of this object/service, who empathised deeply with the ultimate user, would it still be designed the way it is now?' Whenever one looks, one sees examples of products and services 'cobbled together' rather than designed with consciousness and awareness of the real human beings who are meant to be using them.

The fault often lies in the organisational structures, which prevent designers' direct access to the Zeitgeist. In fact, when asked directly through the survey I conducted for this book, there were significant differences between designers and non-designers. The former agree more often with the statement, 'I must have a good connection to the zeitgeist and the latest social trends in order to do my job properly' – 70 per cent versus 45 per cent for non-designers. I would argue that the issue here is not with individuals, but with organisational structures that filter and screen off what is really bothering actual human beings. Organisations can, inadvertently, obscure the clarity of human needs by focusing on an artificial concept of a consumer. Businesses invent the language, which they think helps them sell to consumers but in the process they tend to forget the language that helps them design for real people.

In my survey, designers' frustration over their place in organisational structures is clear; 70 per cent of them say that 'Design should constitute a

Figure 11.3   Sinclair C5: We've got you covered …

separate business function just as Human Resources, Finance, Marketing or Operations' as opposed to other professionals (55 per cent). What's also apparent is the distrust of marketing as the function which should be in charge of designers: 72 per cent designers disagree with the statement 'Design belongs inside Marketing as a business function' (46 per cent completely disagree). Even among the non-design professionals, who albeit hold positive views towards design, the disagreement with the above statement is high at 60 per cent (26 per cent completely disagree). This shows that designers, in their view, would prefer to be emancipated from marketing to do their job properly. I pick up this point later in the chapter.

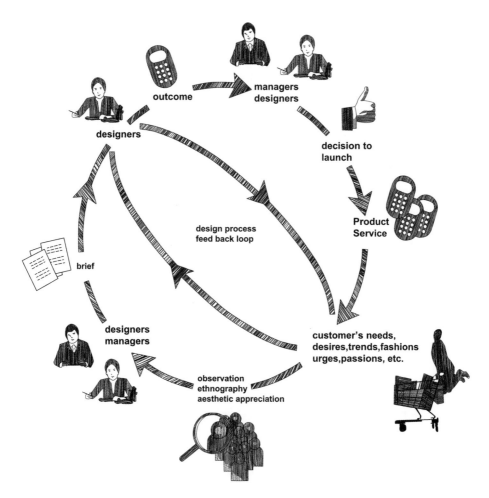

Figure 11.4   Model II product development process: Professional design culture integrated

Design culture and design values injected directly into the space between the customer, and organisation, stimulate a more profound way of looking at innovation. Roberto Verganti calls it designing 'meaning'.[9] It is directly linked to what I describe as design attitude. For example, designers, by truly appreciating the power of all the five senses and deep empathy, are able to achieve an intimate and multilayered sense of what the user/client wants, needs and, above all, desires. Being able and willing to use Gestalts and images of the experiences, designers can connect with users on a profoundly human level. Their positive attitude towards ambiguity and uncertainty prevents them from jumping too quickly to conclusions and creating too narrow a set of choices, thus limiting the creative process.

LEVEL II CULTURAL DISTORTION

Level II cultural distortion is of a strategic nature. It involves resource allocation, organisational design, product and service launch decisions and general strategic direction. On the strategic decision-making level, where issues such as which products to support and which to drop are considered, there exists a danger of missing the outcome-culture fit once again. Instead of delivering product, service or experience that connects with the user, the decision-makers often follow a purely quantitative and metrics-driven approach to launching new products. This in turn might produce an outcome that looks great on paper but fails to attract people, as it fails to appeal to human emotions. The opposite appears to be true when professional designers and their culture are directly involved in making those strategic choices. Two examples I have come across in my research suggest strongly that such involvement can have far-reaching and positive consequences on an organisation's performance through producing culturally compatible outcomes.

One example of what happens if the two cultural distortions are absent involves a product launch decision at Apple. When, in 2007, I asked Jonathan Ive how decisions on the strategic level are made at Apple, he responded by describing the story of a then recent product launch. At a certain point after a lengthy and costly product development process, a team consisting of senior executives, including top designers, was faced with deciding whether to launch or not. According to Ive, there was no one identifiable figure who was making the decision –common wisdom would have us believe that CEO Steve Jobs would do that. With considerable pressure on time and resources, the team made the decision not to launch the product. In Ive's own words, the reason given was simple yet profound, 'The team didn't feel the product connected with the audience'. Such aesthetic criteria are known to be the basis of major investment decisions,[10] but in this case highlight the involvement of designers in making a strategic contribution. It would simply have not been possible for Apple to launch extraordinarily successful products such as iPod, iPhone or the iPad, had it not been for the involvement of designers at the highest level of the organisation. Who designs and who gathers customer insights, on the one hand, and who decides to launch based on what criteria are of key importance to how a design-inspired organisation works. In the case of Apple neither cultural distortion I nor II exist, which makes creating products that connect with users on a visceral level more likely.

The second example concerns Nissan. Here two pieces of evidence suggest that integration of designers and design attitude into organisational culture may be a very significant element in producing better-than-average products, which translate into significant financial gains. In an interview, Nissan's senior designer stated that after establishing the partnership with Renault, the internal position of design and designers has been steadily rising to reach the current high level. What follows is an excerpt from my interview with him. It illustrates the shift from Model I to Model II that took place in Nissan after it was merged with Renault. It also demonstrates how the professional design culture and design attitude present inside Nissan.

KM: Is design taken seriously at Nissan?

Nissan: Very much so, more than ever because since the alliance with Renault there's been a drastic shift from a more engineering-oriented company to a more design-oriented company. Everything that we communicate in the media, motor shows, through the products we launch, wants to convey the message that it's about strong innovative design, but with thoughtfulness behind it. We always keep in mind the customer and the impact on customer expectations.

KM: What about internally, has it [the merger with Renault] changed anything in terms of people's behaviours and attitudes?

Nissan: Absolutely, I was with Nissan 10 years ago and have been with Nissan since the alliance and I've seen a drastic change. The fact that we are here in the heart of London is one. There is no other carmaker today who has a facility in the heart of such a major European city and it's not just coming up with the ideas, we are bringing cars into production … the mentality has changed … an awareness. I would say that the previous brand identity and the design we were communicating to the market was inadequate. There was a gap between the trends and were we were.

KM: Are you saying that Renault brought more design awareness to Nissan?

Nissan: Definitely, I think right from the top managers. The CEO, Carlos Ghosn, and the Executive Vice President clearly set goals relating to devoting a lot of attention to the design, aesthetic of the car, but not just aesthetic, the quality involved. Now we have the perceived quality department in our studio ... We are working much closer with the engineers. Engineers used to dominate designers in a way, psychologically and intellectually. They would impose some solutions that were non-negotiable. But now it's different. We have to sit down together.

This excerpt provides an example of transition from a PDP driven by technical parameters and engineers to a process driven by potential solutions and with much higher involvement of design attitude and the design profession. It also demonstrates a shift of internal influence, from power being concentrated with engineers to more power being given to designers. This move has been supported by establishing a Senior Vice President role with a separate budget for design activities. As I see it, there has been a major cultural change, whereby professional design culture has been given a much more significant, strategic position within the business.

The same can be said of the relationship between other professions and design within organisations. My experience and interviews directly contradicts the authors of *This is Service Design Thinking* who claim, 'It probably does not matter whether service design is part of marketing, or vice versa.'[11] What Nissan design executives told me, and what Steve Jobs says in his biography, is that design has to be given equal weight organisationally in order to have the desired impact on business, products and the bottom line. In case of the latter, it couldn't be more emphatically put than in this extract from Jobs' biography:

At most [tech] companies, engineering tends to drive design. The engineers set forth their specifications and requirements, and the designers then come up with cases and shells that will accommodate them. For Jobs, the process tended to work the other way. In the early days of Apple, Jobs had approved the design of the case of the original Mackintosh, and the engineers had to make their boards and components fit. After he was forced out, the process at Apple reverted to being engineers-driven. 'Before Steve came back, engineers would say "Here are the guts" – processor, hard drive-and then it would go to the designers to put in a box', said Apple's marketing chief Phil Schiller. 'When you do it that way, you come up with awful products'. But when Jobs returned and forged his bond with Ive, the balance was again tilted towards the designers. 'Steve kept impressing on us that the design was integral to what would make us great', said Schiller. 'Design once again dictated the engineering, not vice versa.'[12]

Designers as a professional group provide a channel through which design makes a direct (social integration and enculturation) and indirect (frameworks and outputs) impact on organisations. They do so by interacting with other professionals in an organisation on a social and decision-making level. Two issues seem of particular importance here: firstly, the relationship between marketers and designers needs to be looked at. The reason to include it is two-pronged (a) designers are often subcontracted by the marketing function, hence are in close cultural contact with them, and (b) design in an organisation is, from a manager's point of view, often interpreted through the prism of marketing. Secondly, it is the strategic dimension of incorporating a professional design culture into an organisation.

Seeing Design as Subordinate to Marketing

The fact that design is in close proximity to and in a symbiotic relationship with marketing[3] suggests analysing the relationship between professional design culture and marketers is a good starting point to investigate its impact on other professions within an organisation. Probing this close connection can give us insights into how designers fit into a wider organisational culture.

As far back as 1984, marketing guru Philip Kotler said that design is misunderstood and under-appreciated as a strategic marketing tool. Many design management publications since have cited his article when discussing the strategic implications of design.[13–17] In Kotler and Rath's[18] article *Design: A powerful but neglected strategic tool*, design is seen as a device in marketing's hands with the unique capability to differentiate the product offering.

According to Kotler, benefits of well-managed, high-quality design according are the (a) creation of corporate distinctiveness, (b) creation of personality for a newly launched product, (c) reinvigoration of product interest for mature products, (d) communication of value to the consumer, and (e) entertainment and highlighting visual impact (ibid.: 17). The designers' role here is to 'blend creatively major elements of the design mix' (ibid). These components include: performance, quality, durability, appearance and cost. This heavily marketing-centric approach has far-reaching consequences in relation to the place and status of design in an organisation.

Design is still a relatively niche topic in the business domain, despite the efforts of people such as Roger Martin (former Dean of Rotman Business School), who have recently been named among the top 50 most influential business thinkers,[19] the top IDEO executives, including Tim Brown, David and Tom Kelley and the late Bill Moggridge, and a host of commentators, including Bruce Nussbaum.

The progress and pick-up of design in the business domain, however, seems to have accelerated recently. With dedicated publications and websites such as FastCompany and FastCoDesign, the proliferation of blogs, business schools positioning themselves differently – as with Rotman and Case Western Reserve Weatherhead Business School – business schools starting to include dedicated electives – as at the Saïd Business School, Oxford University – the momentum seems to be building. There is, however, still a significant gap between these efforts and the mainstream appreciation of design, design thinking and creativity in the business setting. Borrowing from the Danish model of design ladder,[20] which ranks businesses on the level of design integration (see illustration), I would venture a guess that the majority of businesses globally sit somewhere between stages 1 and 2. It would actually be fascinating to repeat the study on a wider, international sample of companies. Sure, there will be those modern and dynamic start-ups sitting squarely on level 4 where, 'Design is integral to a company's continuous renewal of their business concept as a means of encouraging innovation. The design process is fused with the company's key objectives and plays a role at every stage of development'.[20] However, the vast majority of even the most interesting companies are nowhere near level 3.

Based on my research and a decade in business consultancy positions, I would argue that the single most important reason why design has failed to effectively communicate its message and true identity has been the extensive curatorship of design in organisations exercised by the marketing function. Design as part of marketing has no separate voice and is a subject to the governing values and rules created and interpreted by marketers. For the last 50 years this interpretation has been heavily influenced by marketing's utopian quest to become 'truly scientific' as Stephen Brown[21] admits in self-flagellating fashion,

'... the heroic but utterly wrongheaded attempt to acquire the unnecessary trappings of "science", a self-abusive orgy of mathematical masturbation which rendered us [marketers] philosophically blind, intellectually deaf and spiritually debilitated' (ibid.: 260). Here, while describing design the use of words such as 'optimisation of consumer satisfaction', 'design-tool' and even the form 'to manage design' denotes a high degree of control and predictability. Design seen through the eyes of marketers is simply a utilitarian device that should be managed to increase the visibility of the product or differentiation of the brand. It also must be accountable and predictable along the lines of the 'scientific' expectations. If it is not, then it is dismissed or deemed flimsy or fuzzy by the marketing establishment.

Augusto Morello,[6] while discussing the drawbacks of a marketing approach in addressing users' needs, points to consequences of maintaining competitiveness mainly through product differentiation (the primary mode in which marketing uses design). These are:

- an over-complication of performances;

- the dominant idea that design is mainly a way to communicate;

- the separation of product form from structure and the reduction of design to styling, an over-decoration of products (ibid.: 72).

Seeing design as subordinate to marketing is so pervasive it has even penetrated the work of the key proponents of design as a unique contributor to corporations' success.[16] The function of design, as stipulated by Kotler, has been recognised as one of the three ways in which design inputs into an organisation. Instead of being 'strategic' as the author suggests, the approach could be better described as operational. Borja De Mozota outlined those three ways: design as *differentiator* (here Kotlers' view fits best), design as *coordinator* and design as *transformer*.

The problem with the power imbalance between marketing and design in organisations is this: when looking at designing and designers through the prism of the marketing 'science quest' they do not appear as predictable, controllable, accountable, quantifiable and hence are deemed inadequate or subsequently seen as highly problematic. Taking them seriously also does not contribute to making marketing look more predictable and scientific. This in turn brands design as whimsical or unscientific. It consequently puts designers and design managers in the position where they have to defend themselves by coming up with excuses, or better still, refutations regarding their methodological flimsiness. They feel the need to argue their case and to show evidence of accountable process, controlled tools and respectable behaviour. It is not, in my view, because they want to, in order to do their job properly, but because of their struggle for recognition and reward with the people who historically have had more to say in organisations. This trend is seen in over-reliance on the design thinking as a set of tools and methods that can be defined and almost automatically deployed by anybody. Verganti says, 'In presenting design as a codified, predictable, and mandatory process – making it more digestible for executives educated in traditional management theories – designers risk losing their ability to do such forward-looking research.'[9]

In order to contribute and create value, designers often need to go through the marketing gatekeepers (as those shown in Model I in previous section) who are influenced by values only partially compatible with those of designers. As it has been pointed out, the relationship between marketers and designers can be conflictual and problematic.[22–27] Bruce and Docherty[25] list the following problems which may exist between designers and marketers:

a)   differences in goals and objectives;

b)   misunderstandings and lack of agreement which leads to the rejection of each other's ideas;

c)   lack of trust, respect and cooperation;

d)   different educational backgrounds;

e)   different methods of working and the lack of common language;

f)   lack of personal chemistry;

g)   reluctance to be directed by someone outside their area of expertise.

This long list of sources of conflict is indicative of the deep, underlying differences between these groups, differences that stem from different training backgrounds and different value sets. Calls for more understanding and appreciation of each other by researchers, such as Bruce and Cooper and Kotler, still fall largely on deaf ears.

The reason does not lie with the lack of willingness to learn from each other, but from polarised political and cultural positions of the two groups. Design and marketing have two different evolutionary routes. Design, after the Industrial Revolution, followed the more art-oriented values in its quest for identity and relevance in society. Marketing, on the other hand, as part of the 'scientific management' tradition which was initiated by the likes of Taylor, Fayol, Bernard, followed the route of the 'scientific' values.[21, 28] Values, beliefs and ways of thinking change slowly. One can assume that the old character of marketing will be showing for years to come. Indeed, with fixation on Big Data, ROI and KPIs it seems that the scientific quest has only just started to accelerate. This is not so say the quest is not important to many people or indeed organisations. It is to point out that it diverges from the path chosen by design as a family of professions.

Marketers can arguably be considered the closest representatives of the management camp to designers. The similarities between design and marketing have even prompted some authors to state that they are the same thing.[22] This appears to be in stark contrast to what I have observed in professional practice. Marketers, in many cases, still play the role of the interpreters of designers to the rest of the organisation. By attaching their own interpretation they often misrepresent designers as a professional group. This only heightens the need for movements such as design thinking or service design, which try to emancipate design from the marketing umbrella. It also creates separate conferences and debates. Bruce and Bessant[3] describe barriers to integrating design expertise. One of them is 'design illiteracy' whereby managers do not know what is involved in design activities, and do not have the experience to appreciate designers' contribution. The authors note that this may, in many cases, be led by 'design segregation [which] occurs in companies which repeatedly outsource design expertise and therefore may have a tunnel view of what the design function is' (ibid.: 50). The outsourcing of the design function may have consequences going far beyond simple misunderstanding of designers by managers, which we will look at in more detail in the next section. Other barriers to integrating design include the high risk associated with design by managers, failing to acknowledge the potential benefits for strategy and growth, and under-appreciation of the value of creativity (ibid.).

The ownership of design in organisations where professional design culture is not the dominant force will most likely belong to the marketing function. If this is the case, design is filtered through a different set of professional values instilled during formal education and on-the-job training and enculturation. If design attitude is to reach its full potential as a useful concept in organisations' success, their voice needs to be liberated from marketers and reclaimed by designers themselves.

Design, Designers and Strategy: A Potent Mix

Bruce and Bessant[3] say, 'Designers play a key role in providing firms with raw materials for making decisions. If they are performing their proper function, they open 'doors of opportunity'. They help 'decision-makers to explore alternative futures'. (ibid.: 65) What is hidden in this statement, and which highlights positive contribution of designers to strategy formation, is that designers are 'helpers' to somebody who is their superior and who makes strategic decisions. This view places designers as useful but somewhat lesser members of the strategic team. Borja de Mozota[16] notes that design has an 'identity problem' when it comes to being successfully integrated into some companies. Despite these words being written a decade ago, they still have resonance today. She writes that designers are often to blame for the opposition design meets in organisations (ibid.: 51). In their view, some designers want to create perfectly designed objects for markets where 'bad taste' does not exist. Moreover, Borja de Mozota criticises designers for being too eager to claim their strategic role, 'Designers are sometimes tempted to confound the strategic character of certain design projects with conviction that they can be strategists of the firm' (ibid.: 51). Her view is that the objective of the design profession is to make the strategy visible and to 'help the firm conceptualise [its] fundamental values' (ibid.), not to take a leadership role in the company.

Furthermore, designers are not prepared to work with management despite the fact that design education is changing to include marketing and strategy courses. Borja de Mozota remarks that 'creative' staff often cultivate an 'ego', but lack confidence and communicate badly (ibid.: 51). This is borne out by the fact that even now there are very few management-focused courses at design schools. Her assessment of the reasons why design struggles to be fully integrated into a company mentions such factors as: a lack of design management courses and research policies with long-term mission; young age of the design profession; small library of references; poor communication of methodologies by designers which creates a 'fuzzy' working environment (ibid.). In order to embrace design, 'Managers need strong reference marks, reliable information and assurance that they will be able to finance design with security' (ibid.: 66). This statement demonstrates what, in my view, is the somewhat deficient thinking of managers rather than the inadequacies of designers. Firstly, 'strong reference marks' in a constantly changing market place do not exist, 'reliable information and security' of investment are as rare in managers' output as they are in designers'. The difference is in the style and rhetoric of presenting the security and reliability. In the designers' case, this will most likely be dressed up in rather colourful clothes and playfulness (signifying to managers qualities such as flimsiness and unreliability). In the managers' case it will be much more professional looking (signifying reliability, stability and security). These culturally ascribed symbols of reliability and security are one of the issues that prevent both groups from effectively engaging in a productive, strategically anchored dialogue. This is changing, as I said, but not fast enough for the demands and expectations placed on a modern twenty-first century organisation.

Designers as Agents of Change

One of the most significant roles of designers in organisations is their influence as agents of change, enabling the process of transformation of value to take place. This has partially been explained in the case of designers making joint strategic decisions in the product development process. In addition, an important adjusting factor is the pervasiveness of the professional designers who need to establish critical mass that would enable them to leverage their cultural significance and strategic integration.

When looking at the effects of numbers of designers in an organisation and the strategic integration of design, Johansson and Svengren[29] conducted qualitative research in a company which attempted to turn design into a strategic resource. Initially this job was assigned to only one designer. This person was the personification of the design profession to the rest of the company's employees. She struggled to be adequately understood and was trying to build up a 'critical mass' (a sufficient number of in-house designers) to have 'more influence' (ibid.: 9–10). As she was able to bring more full-time designers on board, the appreciation of design increased and became richer. When a core team came into existence and a design laboratory was established, the level of design involvement into the operational and strategic decision-making process became more central. As this was happening, other groups, such as engineers and managers, started to benefit from the more transparent and effective communication. Learning became a collaborative venture drawing especially on designers' experimental nature. There was a marked improvement of the position of design in the company after creating the 'critical mass'. Not only did the rest of the organisation find out for themselves how designers work and what design is about, but the designers' own professional development was also stimulated. What could be said about this case is that a single designer with her professional design values has not been able to culturally connect to others in the organisation. Managers and engineers were not able to comprehend and adequately respond to the challenges of a lone designer. Johansson and Svengren[29] reported her saying, after she was finally in a group of designers, 'Now I have others to talk with' (ibid.: 14). This is indicative of the different language and values designers as a professional group use in their corporate life. The authors conclude that in order to stimulate establishing design as a strategic resource, companies should consider the critical mass of designers in their staff. This observation, although as Johansson and Svengren admit is only based on one single case, adds to the debate about the role and place of designers as a professional group in an organisation. At this stage it cannot be safely inferred that a considerable group presence of in-house designers is a *sine qua non* precondition to successful integration of design on a strategic level; but given other findings discussed here, it constitutes strong grounds for a working hypothesis for further exploration.

IDEO: Evangelists of the Design Culture

Another case of integration of designers into an organisation is associated with IDEO. The consultancy is now globally recognised and continues to spread design thinking methodologies and philosophies. Even though this example is as much about the systems and methods developed by a company as about the people, it illustrates quite well the reactions of people not familiar with the professional design culture.

IDEO claim that as a result of customers' requests, they have launched a service that they call IDEO 'U' (for University) whereby they teach others their way of innovating. This began with IDEO engaging its corporate clients in their five-stage design process. Firms experienced (a) observation and the input of cognitive psychologists and anthropologists; (b) brainstorming, the cultural engine of IDEO, with heavily visual and tactile content; (c) rapid prototyping and speedy creation of simple mock-ups; (d) trial-and-error refining within strict time and specification constraints; and (e) implementation.[30, 31, 32]

After being exposed to such a visually rich and tactile process, which is something most designers would quickly recognise, clients of IDEO became convinced of the merits and benefits of such an approach to innovation (including strategic innovation).

One of their customers is Procter & Gamble, a FMCG giant and one of the oldest companies in the world.[33] The CEO, Alan Lafley, is reported to have teamed up with IDEO to create 'a more innovative culture'.[30] This statement is nothing unusual in the business world in itself, but when expressed by the head of one of the most innovative companies it signifies the appreciation of the corporate executive of the IDEO approach. In the process of learning how to innovate the IDEO way, Lafley took his Global Leaders Council of 40 strategic business unit heads to the company's headquarters in San Francisco for a one-day immersion in IDEO's culture. The result was astonishment and praise for the approach. This showed what results can be gained through exposure to the culture of designers by managers.

As part of the IDEO 'U' programme, more permanent and long-term relationships were in place. During weekly workshops and monthly stays in IDEO, P&G managers were taught the techniques that go with observation, brainstorming, prototyping and fast implementation (ibid.: 92). Additionally, IDEO built an innovation centre for P&G where employees are enculturated into the process and arguably design culture as well. Claudia Kotchka, former Vice President for Design Innovation and Strategy at P&G, said that 'they [IDEO] opened our eyes to new ways of working' and 'they solved problems in ways we would never have thought' (ibid.: 92). Her statements can also be read from the viewpoint that she is an accountant by training and she has been made responsible for making design part of P&G's DNA, i.e. organisational culture.[34] Kotchka is reported to have said, 'Design used to be soiled at P&G, viewed by most as peripheral and unimportant. Now most designers work directly with researchers within each unit. This sparks new sorts of innovation and makes it easier for non-designers to understand what design is.'[35] This statement reiterates an earlier suggestion regarding the importance of physical presence of designers if design is to be understood and acknowledged.

The new ways of working to which Kotchka is referring, in my view, comprise the professional design culture which essence I was hopefully able to capture throughout this book, but particularly in the chapters on the five aspects of design attitude. Instead of being unique to IDEO, it is present in environments where considerable groups of designers work. There are a number of companies that could be seen in a very similar light to IDEO, with regards to the prevalence of the design culture within them. These include Continuum, Frog design, Fjord, Designit, Adaptive Path, Experientia, STBY, live|work, Method Design, Punchcut, Jump Associates and Moment design, among others.

The General Manager of IDEO London has himself admitted in an interview that what they do is not unique in the design world (interview with General Manager, IDEO London). It is conceivable that 'the culture of designers', which spans professional, design-intensive organisations, possesses qualities recognised and appreciated by management executives. It is quite likely that, unknowingly, the managers recognise designers' values and beliefs that are more widely present.

Hence, the problem might not reside solely on the designers' side (as unable to sell the qualities of design to managers) but might also stem from managers who fail to appreciate design for what it is. Managers, taking myself and my colleagues as examples, are conditioned by their education to mistrust, to certain extent, the colourful, serendipitous and open-minded, yet this is how they themselves need to behave in order to respond to the unexpected problems they face in a turbulent business environment. The reason why design and designers are not seen as 'business-like' is of a cultural rather than a content-based nature.

The March of the Designers

This chapter explored the way in which designers impact organisations directly. Here designers have been identified as being the closest group between the company and both its internal and external consumers. Their professional culture makes them particularly willing and capable of tapping into the desires, needs and multidimensional messages communicated by the users. I have described the dangers of removing designers from directly inputting on operational and strategic levels. I have shown two examples of companies (Nissan, Apple) that have embraced designers as contributors at all levels of the process.

Designers themselves impact on organisations by the means of socialisation and enculturation – meaning they transmit their ways of doing things, their thinking and crucially, their attitudes to the people that they work with. This is happening on two levels: (a) the level of cultural interfaces between arguably the closest professional group to designers, namely marketers; and (b) the strategic level of integrating designers as significant change agents who are transforming broader organisational cultures.

It is clearly necessary to re-examine the culturally subordinate role of designers freeing them from contextual and political grip of other professions.

Examples of 'teaching' companies' design culture indicate the realisation, on the part of the commercial world, of the benefits of the professional design culture as a catalyst for innovation and organisational transformation.

Finally, it is important to appreciate just how far design and designers have come in the last decade. In order to do that we just need to look at a headline from Forbes, *Design Is Eating Silicon Valley*.[36] It's not the hyperbolic title that is important but what is actually being written. The article points out that it is almost impossible to compete today without great design. It suggests that if eBay or Amazon launched in the ugly and not so user-friendly format they had originally, they wouldn't stand a chance in the marketplace today. With companies such as Pintrest, Airbnb, Instagram, Square, Flipboard design has become an integral part of their appeal and ultimate success.

By now it should be very clear that when I say design I don't only mean attractive graphics. It is the whole way in which these companies are run, how decisions are made and the impact and power of designers inside them that counts. Even Google and Facebook, two giants of the Internet founded by engineers and techies, cannot afford to dismiss the importance of design. Both have been relatively late to acknowledge the power of design. This is not surprising, since neither had designers in positions of power or as co-founders. They have been trying to ramp-up their design credentials by putting together dedicated teams and giving designers a more prominent status in the business.[37]

Google has itself embarked on a project of infusing itself with design. Examples include the attempt to streamline and unify the interface across all its platforms; the work with physical objects such as phones and tablets (relatively successful via the expertise of LG), TV interfaces, media hubs Nexus Q and new formats (Google Glass) so far not so successful. Arguably, due to the multitude of activities Google has a bigger job on its hands when it comes to giving designers real power and a real say. If it wants to stay relevant it needs to find a way of systematically doing it, however.

There's no point in fudging it. In order for organisations to adopt design attitude and fully embrace the design culture, they must give designers more power internally. The ultimate company that does this is Apple. It not only transpired from my discussions with Jonathan Ive but also Job's biography that the influence of design and designers at Apple goes to the very top of the organisation. In Ive's biography Kahney says, 'Inside Apple, everybody defers to design studio.'[38] It is hard to imagine Apple without this high-level design input. It would simply not work. By not work I mean becoming the biggest company on the planet: collecting 70 per cent of profit on 9 per cent market share of mobile phones; turning industries upside down; making fans out of consumers; creating the most profitable physical retail environment; and enthusing people the world over to follow its brand.

'Steve Jobs was obviously a genius', says Kahney, 'But he couldn't code, wasn't an engineer, never designed anything. The reason Apple came up with as many breakthroughs under Jobs as they had is because he had a great system: he would set up small teams of people within the company and give them as much freedom as possible to get things done.'[38] No other department within Apple better exemplifies Jobs's system than the one headed by Ive. It is the central pillar of Apple and its beating heart. It is responsible for the iMac, the iPod, the iPhone, the iPad, and has helped make Apple the world's most valuable tech company, as well as revolutionise consumer design. If there's a lesson from Kahney's book, though, it's that more companies can achieve Apple's success, if only they recognised designers and gave them more power.

I believe that it is useful to look at how design and design attitude influence the world around us and, in particular, the inner workings of organisations. There are essentially three ways in which design impacts businesses: frameworks, outputs (products, services and environments) and designers themselves. Whenever we hear that design is used as a mediator or as an influencing force, we can understand how it is being applied.

If we do not allow designers access to the users in the development process, we are in danger of narrowing the bandwidth of empathy. As I explained in chapter on deep empathy (Chapter 5), designers have a particularly intimate access to popular culture that requires a direct, multi-sensory relationship with the user. If a business function or a unit, such as engineering or marketing, prevents the direct access to consumers, the ultimate products and services may not be as good as they could potentially be.

Designers impact organisations by spreading their values and ways of doing things. The connections between the closest professional group to designers, namely marketers, can potentially be detrimental to the way in which designers and design attitude are seen in organisations. The power balance is equalising, but it still is predominantly with marketers. Designers are the invaders of the corporate world, whilst marketers are the natives. This has consequences on the power balance, which usually is tipped towards marketers.

At the strategic level of integrating designers are as significant change agents who are transforming organisational cultures. By injecting their ways of doing things, their values and attitudes, they influence cultures and people in organisations directly. There has to be a sufficient number of them in sufficiently powerful positions to make a difference to organisational cultures.

References

Chapter 1: Design and the Design Profession

1. Kabani, S., Study Reveals Surprising Facts about Millennials in the Workplace. 2013, accessed: 10.05.2013; Available from: http://www.forbes.com/sites/shamakabani/2013/12/05/study-reveals-surprising-facts-about-millennials-in-the-workplace/

2. Garvin, D.A., *How Google sold its engineers on management*. 2013, *Harvard Business Review*, HBR Blog, accessed: 20.10.2013; Available from: http://hbr.org/2013/12/how-google-sold-its-engineers-on-management/ar/1

3. Olson, E.M., R. Cooper and S.F. Slater, Design Strategy and Competitive Advantage. *Business Horizons*, 1998, 41(2): pp. 55–61.

4. Simon, H.A., *The Sciences of the Artificial*. 3rd edn. 1996, Cambridge, MA: MIT Press.

5. Friedman, K., Theory construction in design research: Criteria, approaches, and methods. In 'Common Ground: Design Research Society International Conference 2002', London, September 2002 (pp. 388–414) Stoke-on-Trent, United Kingdom: Staffordshire University Press.

6. Friedman, K., Towards an Integrative Design Discipline, in *Creating Breakthrough Ideas: The Collaboration of Anthropologists and Designers in the Product Development Industry*, S. Squires and B. Byrne (eds). 2002, London: Bergin & Garvey, pp. 199–214.

7. Merriam-Webster, *Merriam-Webster's Collegiate Dictionary*. 10th edn. 1993, Springfield.

8. Cambridge University Press, *Cambridge Dictionaries Online*. 2003 [cited 20 March 2003]; Available from: http://www.cup.cam.ac.uk/elt/dictionary/.

9. Britannica-Webster's, *Encyclopedia Britannica Online*. 2003 [cited 12 April 2002]; Available from: http://www.britannica.com.

10. Borja de Mozota, B., *Design Management: Using Design to Build Brand Value and Corporate Innovation*. 2003, New York: Allworth Press.

11. Buchanan, R., Rhetoric, Humanism, and Design, in *Discovering Design: Explorations in Design Studies*, R. Buchanan and V. Margolin (eds). 1995, Chicago, IL: University of Chicago Press, pp. 23–66.

12. Schön, D., *The Reflective Practitioner: How Professionals Think in Action*. 1983, New York: Basic Books.

13. Schön, D., *Educating the Reflective Practitioner*. 1987, San Francisco, CA: Jossey-Bass.

14. Coyne, R. and A. Snodgrass, Is designing mysterious? Challenging the dual knowledge thesis. *Design Studies*, 1991, 12(3): pp. 124–131.

15. Cross, N., K. Dorst and N. Roozenburg (eds), *Research in Design Thinking*. 1992, Delft: Delft University Press.

16. Cross, N., H. Christiaans and K. Dorst (eds), *Analysing Design Activity*. 1996, Chichester: Wiley.

17. Akin, Ö. Editorial, Special Issue on descriptive models of design. *Design Studies*, 1997, 18(4): pp. 323–476.

18. Goldschmidt, G. and W. Porter (eds), *4th Design Thinking Research Symposium*. 1999, Cambridge, MA: MIT Press.

19. Cross, N., Designerly ways of knowing: design discipline versus design science, in S Pizzocaro, A Arruda & D De Moraes (eds.) *Design Plus Research*, Proceedings of Politecnico di Milano Conference, Politecnico di Milano, 2000, Milan, pp. 43–48.

20. Grant, D., Design methodology and design methods. *Design Methods and Theories*, 1979, 13(1): pp. 46–7.

21. Sargent, P. and C. Road, Design science or nonscience. *Design Studies*, 1994, 15(4): pp. 389–402.

22. Burrage, M. and R. Torstendahl (eds), *Professions in Theory and History*. 1990, London: Sage.

23. MacDonald, K.M., *The Sociology of the Professions*. 1995, London: Sage.

24. Leicht, K.T. and M.L. Fennell, *Professional Work: A Sociological Approach*. 2001, Oxford: Blackwell.

25. Walker, D., Managers and Designers: Two Tribes at War?, in *Design Management: A Handbook of Issues and Methods*, M. Oakley (ed.). 1990, Oxford: Blackwell, pp. 145–54.

26. Oakley, M., *Design Management: A Handbook of Issues and Methods*. 1990, Oxford: Blackwell.

27. Shaw, V. and C. Shaw, Conflict between engineers and marketers: The engineer's perspective. *Industrial Marketing Management*, 1998, 27: pp. 279–91.

28. Lester, R.K., M.J. Piore and K.M. Malek, Interpretive management: What general managers can learn from design. *Harvard Business Review*, 1998 Mar-Apr;76(2), pp. 86–96.

29. Shaw, V., C. Shaw and J. Tressider, Conflict between designers and marketers: A study of graphic designers in New Zealand. *Design Journal*, 2002, 5(3): pp. 10–22.

30. Cooper, R. and M. Press, *Design Agenda: A Guide to Successful Design Management*. 1995, Chichester: Wiley.

31. Bruce, M. and J. Bessant, *Design in Business: Strategic Innovation through Design*. 2002, Harlow: *Financial Times* / Prentice Hall.

32. Boland Jr., R.J. and F. Collopy (eds), *Managing as Designing*. 2004, Stanford, CA: Stanford University Press.

33. Ravasi, D. and G. Lojacono, Managing design and designers for strategic renewal. *Long Range Planning*, 2005, 38: pp. 51–77.

34. Banham, R., *Theory and Design in the First Machine Age*. 1960, London: Architectural Press.

35. Fuller, B., *World Design Science Decade 1965–75. Phase I (1064) Document 2: The Design Initiative*. 1964, Carbondale, IL: World Resource Inventory, Southern Illinois University.

36. Fuller, B., *World Design Science Decade 1965–75. Phase I (1065) Document 2: Comprehensive Thinking*. 1965, Carbondale, IL: World Resource Inventory, Southern Illinois University.

37. Fuller, B., *World Design Science Decade 1965–75. Phase I (1065) Document 5: Comprehensive Design Strategy*. 1967, Carbondale, IL: World Resource Inventory, Southern Illinois University.

38. Heskett, J., *Industrial Design*. 1980, London: Thames & Hudson.

39. Thackara, J., *Design after Modernism*. 1988, London: Themes & Hudson.

40. Walker, J., *A Design History and the History of Design*. 1989, London: Pluto Press.

41. Banham, R. and M. Pawley, *Theory and Design in the Second Machine Age*. 1990, Oxford: Blackwell.

42. Dormer, P., *The Meanings of Modern Design*. 1990, London: Thames & Hudson.

43. McDermott, C., *Essential Design*. 1992, London: Bloomsbury.

44. Dormer, P., *Design since 1945*. 1993, London: Thames & Hudson.

45. Dormer, P. (ed.), *The Culture of Craft: Status and Future*. 1997, Manchester: Manchester University Press.

46. Woodham, J., *Twentieth-Century Design*. 1997, Oxford: Oxford University Press.

47. McDermott, C., *The Product Book*. 1999, Hove: Rotavision.

48. Morgan, C., Lloyd, *Twentieth Century Design: A Readers' Guide*. 2000, Oxford: Architectural Press.

49. Woodham, J.M., A. Volker and K. Reyer (eds), *Icons of Design: The Twentieth Century*. 2000, London: Prestel.

50. McDermott, C., *Design Museum: Twentieth Century Design*. 2001, London: Carlton.

51. Heskett, J., *Toothpicks and Logos: Design in Everyday Life*. 2002, Oxford: Oxford University Press.

52. McDermott, C., *The Little Book of Design Classics*. 2002, London: Carlton.

53. Larson, M.S., *The Rise of Professionalism: A Sociological Analysis*. 1977, London: University of California Press.

54. Weber, M., *Economy and Society*. 1978, London: University of California Press.

55. Berger, P.L. and B. Berger, *Sociology: A Biological Approach*. 1976, London: Penguin.

56. Jenks, C., *Culture*. 1993, London: Routledge.

57. Weber, M., *The Methodology of the Social Sciences*. 1949, New York: Free Press.

58. Abbott, A., The order of professionalization: An empirical analysis. *Work and Occupations*, 1991, 18(4): pp. 355–84.

59. Bloor, G. and P. Dawson, Understanding professional culture in organizational context. *Organization Studies*, 1994, 15(2): pp. 275–95.

[60.] Wilensky, H.L., The professionalization of everyone? *American Journal of Sociology*, 1964, 70(2): pp. 137–58.

[61.] Wolek, F.W., The managerial principles behind craftsmanship. *Journal of Management History*, 1999, 5(7): pp. 401–13.

[62.] Forty, A., *Objects of Desire: Design and Society since 1750*. 1986, London: Thames & Hudson.

[63.] Press, M. and R. Cooper, *The Design Experience: The Role of Design and Designers in the Twenty-First Century*. 2003, Aldershot: Ashgate.

[64.] Flusser, V., *The Shape of Things: A Philosophy of Design*. 1999, London: Reaktion.

[65.] Broadbent, J. Generations in design methodology. In 'Common Ground: Design Research Society International Conference 2002, UK', 2002.

[66.] Cross, N. Design/Science/Research: Developing a discipline. In Keynote paper to the '5th Asian Design Conference', Seoul, South Korea, 2001 accessed: 10.11.05; Available from http://design.open.ac.uk/people/academics/cross/DesignScienceResearch.pdf.

[67.] Jones, J.C., A method of systematic design, in *Conference on Design Methods*, J.C. Jones and D.G. Thornley (eds). 1963, New York: Macmillan, pp. 53–74.

[68.] Cross, N., *Developments in Design Methodology*. 1984, Chichester: Wiley.

[69.] Simon, H.A., *The Sciences of the Artificial*. 1969, London: MIT Press.

[70.] Jimenez Narvaez, L.M., Design's own knowledge. *Design Issues*, 2000, 16(1): pp. 36–51.

[71.] Bucciarelli, L., *Designing Engineers*. 1994, Cambridge, MA: MIT Press.

[72.] Buchanan, R., Wicked problems in design thinking. *Design Issues*, 1992, 8(2): pp. 5–22.

[73.] Alexander, C., *Notes on the Synthesis of Form*. 1964, Cambridge, MA: Harvard University Press.

[74.] Alexander, C., S. Ishikawa and M. Silverstein, *A Pattern Language: Towns, Buildings, Construction*, Vol. 2. 1977, New York: Oxford University Press.

[75.] Friedman, K., Design Science and Design Education. In *The Challenge of Complexity*, P. McGrory (ed.). 1997, Helsinki: University of Art and Design, pp. 54–72.

[76.] Lockwood, T. (ed.), *Design Thinking: Integrating Innovation, Customer Experience, and Brand Value*. 2010, New York: Allworth Press.

[77.] Stickdorn, M. and J. Schneider (eds), *This is Service Design Thinking*. 2010, Amsterdam: BIS Publishers.

Chapter 2: A Few Words about Cultures

[1.] Williams, R., *Keywords: A Vocabulary of Culture and Society*. 1988, London: Fontana.

[2.] Clegg, S.R., W. Higgins, and T. Spybey, 'Post-Confucianism', Social Democracy and Economic Culture, in *Capitalism in Contrasting Cultures*, S.R. Clegg and S.G. Redding (eds). 1990, New York: Walter de Gruyter, pp. 31–78.

[3.] Ortner, S., Theory in anthropology since the sixties. *Comparative Studies in Society and History*, 1984, 26: pp. 126–66.

[4.] Borkowsky, R. (ed.), *Assessing Cultural Anthropology*. 1994, New York: McGraw-Hill.

[5.] Alvesson, M., *Understanding Organizational Culture*. 2002, London: Sage.

[6.] Ott, J.S., *The Organizational Culture Perspective*. 1989, Pacific Grove, CA: Brooks/Cole.

[7.] Martin, J., *Cultures in Organisations: Three Perspectives*. 1992, New York: Oxford University Press.

[8.] Martin, J., *Organizational Culture: Mapping the Terrain*. 2002, London: Sage.

[9.] Czarniawska-Joerges, B., Culture is the Medium of Life, in *Reframing Organizational Culture*, P. Frost, J. et al. (eds). 1991, London: Sage, pp. 285–97.

[10.] Peters, T. and R. Waterman, *In Search of Excellence: Lessons from America's Best Run Companies*. 1982, New York: Harper and Row.

[11.] Schein, E., *Organizational Culture and Leadership*. 2nd edn. 1992, San Francisco, CA: Jossey-Bass.

[12.] Gregory, K., Native-view paradigms: Multiple cultures and culture conflicts in organizations. *Administrative Science Quarterly*, 1983, 28: pp. 359–76.

13. Van Maanen, J. and S.R. Barley, Occupational Communities: Culture and Control in Organizations, in *Research in Organizational Behavior*, B.M. Staw and L.L. Cummings (eds). 1984, Greenwich: JAI Press, pp. 287–366.

14. Bloor, G. and P. Dawson, Understanding professional culture in organizational context. *Organization Studies*, 1994, 15(2): pp. 275–95.

15. Trice, H.M. and J.M. Beyer, *The Cultures of Work Organizations*. 1991, Englewood Cliffs, NJ: Prentice Hall.

16. Hofstede, G., *Culture's Consequences: International Differences in Work-Related Values*. 2nd edn. 2001, Thousand Oaks, CA: Sage.

17. Becher, T., Towards a definition of disciplinary cultures. *Studies in Higher Education*, 1981, 6(2): pp. 109–22.

18. Becher, T., The counter culture of specialisation. *European Journal of Education*, 1990, 25(3): pp. 333–47.

19. Hansen, C., Occupational cultures: Whose frame are we using? *Journal of Quality and Participation*, 1995, 18(3): pp. 60–65.

20. Deal, T. and A. Kennedy, *Corporate Cultures: The Rites and Rituals of Corporate Life*. 1982, Reading, MA: Addison-Wesley.

21. Barley, S.R., Semiotics and the study of occupational and organizational cultures. *Administrative Science Quarterly*, 1983, 28: pp. 393–414.

22. Denison, D., *Corporate Culture and Organizational Effectiveness*. 1990, New York: Wiley.

23. Kotter, J. and J. Haskett, *Corporate Culture and Performance*. 1992, New York: Free Press.

24. Meyer, A., Adapting to environmental jolts. *Administrative Science Quarterly*, 1982, 27: pp. 515–37.

25. Louis, M., An investigator's guide to workplace culture, in *Organizational Culture*, P. Frost et al. (eds). 1985, Beverly Hills, CA: Sage, pp. 73–94.

26. Barley, S.R., Technology as an occasion for structuring: Evidence from observations of CT scanners and the social order of radiology departments. *Administrative Science Quarterly*, 1986, 31: pp. 78–108.

27. Alvesson, M., *Cultural Perspectives on Organizations*. 1993, Cambridge: Cambridge University Press.

28. March, J. and J. Olsen, (eds), *Ambiguity and Choice in Organizations*. 1976, Bergen: Universitetsforlagert.

29. Weick, K., E., *The vulnerable system: An analysis of the Tenerife air disaster*, in *Reframing organizational culture*, P. Frost et al. (eds). 1991, Newbury Park, CA: Sage, pp. 117–30.

30. Meyerson, D., Uncovering socially undesirable emotions: Experiences of ambiguity in organizations. *American Behavioral Scientist*, 1990, 33(3): pp. 296–307.

31. Alvesson, M., Organization as rhetoric: Knowledge-intensive firms and the struggle with ambiguity. *Journal of Management Studies*, 1993, 30(6): pp. 997–1015.

32. Daft, R. and K.E. Weick, Toward a model of organizations as interpretation systems. *Academy of Management Review*, 1984, 9: pp. 284–95.

33. Bockus, S., Corporate values: A refutation of uniqueness theory. Unpublished manuscript, Stanford University, 1983.

34. Martin, J., C. Anterasian and C. Siehl, Externally espoused values and the legitimation of functional performance. Unpublished manuscript, Stanford University, 1983.

35. Schein, E., Three cultures of management: The key to organizational learning. *Sloan Management Review*, 1996, 38(1): pp. 9–20.

36. Mills, A., Organization, gender, and culture. *Organization Studies*, 1988, 9: pp. 351–70.

Chapter 3: The Making of a Designer

1. Schön, D., *The Reflective Practitioner: How Professionals Think in Action*. 1983, New York: Basic Books.

2. Lawson, B., Cognitive strategies in architectural design. *Ergonomics*, 1979, 22(1): pp. 59–68.

3. Lawson, B., *How Designers Think*. 1980, London: Architectural Press.

4. Lawson, B., *How Designers Think: The Design Process Demystified*. 3rd edn. 1997, Oxford: Architectural Press.

5. Cross, N., Discovering Design Ability, in *Discovering Design: Explorations in Design Studies*, R. Buchanan and V. Margolin (eds). 1995, Chicago, IL: University of Chicago Press, pp. 105–20.

6. Cross, N., Natural intelligence in design. *Design Studies*, 1999, 20(1): pp. 25–39.

7. Cross, N., Designerly ways of knowing: Design discipline versus design science, in S Pizzocaro, A Arruda & D De Moraes (eds.) *Design Plus Research*, Proceedings of Politecnico di Milano Conference, Politecnico di Milano, 2000, Milan, pp. 43–48.

8. Cross, N., H. Christiaans and K. Dorst, (eds), *Analysing Design Activity*. 1996, Chichester: Wiley.

9. Cross, N. and M. Nathenson, Design Methods and Learning Methods, in *Design: Science, Method*, J.A. Powell and R. Jacques (eds). 1981, Guildford: Westbury House, pp. 281–96.

10. Durling, D., N. Cross and J. Johnson. Personality and learning preferences of students in design and design related disciplines, in 'IDATER '96' (International Conference on Design and Technology Educational Research), Loughborough University of Technology, 1996.

11. Kirton, M.J., Adaptors and innovators: The way people approach problems. *Planned Innovation*, 1980, 33: pp. 51–4.

12. Kirton, M.J., Adaptors and innovators in organisations. *Human Relations*, 1980, 3: pp. 213–24.

13. Newland, P., J.A. Powell and C. Creed, Understanding architectural designers' selective information handling. *Design Studies*, 1987, 8(1): pp. 2–16.

14. Sacher, H., Semantics as Common Ground: Connecting the Cultures of Analysis and Creation, in *Creating Breakthrough Ideas: The Collaboration of Anthropologists and Designers in the Product Development Industry*, S. Squires and B. Byrne (eds). 2002, London: Bergin & Garvey, pp. 175–96.

15. Schön, D. and G. Wiggins, Kinds of seeing and their functions in designing. *Design Studies*, 1992, 13(2): pp. 135–56.

16. Lorenz, C., *The Design Dimension: Product Strategy and The Challenge of Global Marketing*. 1986, Oxford: Blackwell.

17. Margolin, V. and R. Buchanan (eds), *The Idea of Design*. 1995, Cambridge, MA: MIT Press.

18. Bruce, M. and J. Bessant, *Design in Business: Strategic Innovation through Design*. 2002, Harlow: *Financial Times* / Prentice Hall.

19. Bernstein, D., The design mind, in *Design talks!*, P. Gorb and E. Schneider (eds). 1988, London: London Business School, Design Management Seminars, The Design Council.

20. Polanyi, M., *The Tacit Dimension*. 1966, Garden City, NY: Doubleday.

21. Polanyi, M., *Personal knowledge*. 1973, London: Routledge and Kegan.

22. De Bono, E., *Lateral Thinking: A Textbook of Creativity*. 1970, London: Ward Lock Educational.

23. Goel, V. and P. Pirolli, The structure of design problem spaces. *Cognitive Science*, 1992, 16: pp. 395–429.

24. Lawson, B., *What Designers Know*. 2003, Oxford: Architectural Press.

25. Schön, D., *Educating the Reflective Practitioner*. 1987, San Francisco, CA: Jossey-Bass.

26. Schön, D., *The Reflective Turn: Case Studies in and on Educational Practice*. 1991, New York: Teachers College Press.

27. Chandran, K.K., *Modelling of the Curriculum within Engineering Design Education*. 1988, Surrey: University of Surrey.

28. Lewis, W.P. and E. Bonollo, An analysis of professional skills in design: Implications for education and research. *Design Studies*, 2002, 23: pp. 385–406.

29. Goel, V., *Sketches of Thought*. 1995, Cambridge, MA: MIT Press.

30. Lawson, B., *The Language of Space*. 2001, Oxford: Architectural Press.

31. Cross, N., *Developments in Design Methodology*. 1984, Chichester: Wiley.

32. Cross, N., K. Dorst, and N. Roozenburg, (eds), *Research in Design Thinking*. 1992, Delft: Delft University Press.

33. Durling, D., N. Cross and J. Johnson. CAI with style. In 'CEED '96' (Conference of Sharing Experience in Engineering Design), University of Bristol, 1996.

34. Feist, G., J., A meta-analysis of personality in scientific and artistic creativity. *Personality and Social Psychology Review*, 1998, 2(4): pp. 290–309.

35. Kirton, M.J., A. Bailey, and W. Glendinning, Adaptors and innovators: Preference for educational procedures. *The Journal of Psychology*, 1991, 125(4): pp. 445–55.

36. Lorenz, C., *The Design Dimension: The New Competitive Weapon for Product Strategy and Global Marketing*. 1990, Oxford: Blackwell.

37. Walker, D., Managers and Designers: Two Tribes at War?, in *Design Management: A Handbook of Issues and Methods*, M. Oakley (ed.). 1990, Oxford: Blackwell, pp. 145–54.

38. Gorb, P., The business of design management. *Design Studies*, 1986, 7(2): pp. 106–10.

39. Borja de Mozota, B., *Design Management: Using Design to Build Brand Value and Corporate Innovation*. 2003, New York: Allworth Press.

40. Bruce, M. and R. Harun. Exploring design capability for serial innovation in SMEs. In 'European Design Academy Conference', 2001. Portugal, April.

41. Shaw, V. and C. Shaw, T., Conflict between engineers and marketers: The engineer's perspective. *Industrial Marketing Management*, 1998, 27: pp. 279–91.

42. Shaw, V., C. Shaw, T. and J. Tressider, Conflict between designers and marketers: A study of graphic designers in New Zealand. *Design Journal*, 2002, 5(3): pp. 10–22.

43. Press, M. and R. Cooper, *The Design Experience: The Role of Design and Designers in the Twenty-First Century*. 2003, Aldershot: Ashgate.

44. Verganti, R., *Design-Driven Innovation: Changing the Rules of Competition by Radically Innovating What Things Mean*. 2009, Boston, MA: Harvard Business Press.

45. Martin, R., *The Design of Business: Why Design Thinking Is the Next Competitive Advantage*. 2009, Boston, MA: Harvard Business Press.

46. Alexander, C., S. Ishikawa and M. Silverstein, *A Pattern Language: Towns, Buildings, Construction*, Vol. 2. 1977, New York: Oxford University Press.

47. Alexander, C., *Notes on the Synthesis of Form*. 1964, Cambridge, MA: Harvard University Press.

48. Cross, N., *Engineering Design Methods: Strategies for Product Design*. 3rd edn. 2003, New York: Wiley.

49. Simon, H.A., *The Sciences of the Artificial*. 3rd edn. 1996, Cambridge, MA: MIT Press.

50. Buchanan, R., Wicked problems in design thinking. *Design Issues*, 1992, 8(2): pp. 5–22.

51. Smythe, M. Defining design thinking: The distinguishing factor in the design managers' approach to strategy. In proceedings of 'The Design Management Institute 11th International Forum on Design Management Research and Education', 2002, Boston, Massachusetts, accessed: 10.02.2005.

52. Alexander, C. and J.-P. Protzen, Value in design: A dialogue. *Design Studies*, 1980, 1(6): pp. 291–8.

53. Kolb, D.A., Toward a Theory of Experiential Learning, in *Theories of Group Process*, C. Cooper (ed.). 1975, London: Wiley, pp. 33–57.

54. Kolb, D.A., *Experiential Learning: Experience as the Source of Learning and Development*. 1985, Englewood Cliffs, NJ: Prentice Hall.

55. Carrol, J.B., *Human Cognitive Abilities: A Survey of Factor-Analytic Studies*. 1993, New York: Cambridge University Press.

56. Arvola, M. *Reflections on the concept of design ability: Telling apples from pears*. 2002 20 December 2005)]; Available from: http://homepage.mac.com/mattiasarvola/publications.html.

57. Cross, N. and M. Nathenson, Design Methods and Learning Methods, in *Design: Science, Method*, J.A. Powell and R. Jacques (eds). 1981, Guildford: Westbury House.

58. Kirton, M.J., Adaptors and innovators: The way people approach problems. *Planned Innovation*, 1980, 3: pp. 51–4.

59. Walker, D., Managers and Designers: Two Tribes at War?, in *Design Management: A Handbook of Issues and Methods*, M. Oakley (ed.). 1990, Oxford: Blackwell.

60. Kotler, P. and A.G. Rath, Design: A powerful but neglected strategic tool. *Journal of Business Strategy*, 1984, 5(2): pp. 16–21.

61. Cooper, R. and M. Press, *Design Agenda: A Guide to Successful Design Management*. 1995, Chichester: Wiley.

62. Thackara, J., *Winners! How Today's Successful Companies Innovate by Design*. 1997, Aldershot: Gower.

63. Lester, R.K., M.J. Piore and K.M. Malek, Interpretive management: What general managers can learn from design. *Harvard Business Review*, 1998, 76(2), pp. 86–96.

64. Lockwood, T. et al., Perspectives on communicating the value of design. *Design Management Journal*, 2001, 12(3): pp. 76–83.

65. Lockwood, T., Integrating design into organisational culture. *Design Management Review*, 2004, 15(2).

66. Lojacono, G. and G. Zaccai, The evolution of the design-inspired enterprise. *Sloan Management Review*, 2004, 45(3): pp. 75–9.

67. Ravasi, D. and G. Lojacono, managing design and designers for strategic renewal. *Long Range Planning*, 2005, 38: pp. 51–77.

Chapter 4: Embracing Uncertainty and Ambiguity

1. Martin, R. YouTube clip. 2010 [cited 2013 12 July]; Available from: http://www.youtube.com/watch?v=e-ySKaZJ_dU.

2. Ouden, H.E. den et al. (2013) Dissociable effects of dopamine and serotonin on reversal learning. *Neuron*, 80(4): pp. 1090–1100.

3. Weick, K., Rethinking Organizational Design, in *Managing as Designing*, R.J. Boland and Collopy, F. (eds). 2004, Stanford, CA: Stanford University Press, pp. 36–53

4. Lorenzoni, P., Where Lean Startups and Design Thinking Meet, in The Accelerators. 2004, *The Wall Street Journal*.

5. 2013 [cited 2013 July]; Available from: http://www.edibleapple.com/2010/04/29/why-the-newton-failed-and-the-ipad-is-poised-for-success/.

6. Stickdorn, M. and J. Schneider, (eds), *This is Service Design Thinking*. 2010, Amsterdam: BIS Publishers.

Chapter 5: Engaging Deep Empathy

1. Baron-Cohen, S., *Zero Degrees of Empathy*. 2011, London: Penguin.

2. New, S. and L. Kimbell, Chimps, designers, consultants and empathy: A 'Theory of mind' for service design. In '2nd Cambridge Academic Design Management Conference', Cambridge, 2013.

3. March, L., The Logic of Design, in *The Architecture of Form*, L. March (ed). 1976, Cambridge, MA: Cambridge University Press, pp. 1–40.

4. Rittel, H., On the planning crisis: Systems analysis of the first and second generations. *Bedrift Sokonomen*, 1972, 8: pp. 309–96.

5. Cross, N., Discovering Design Ability, in *Discovering Design: Explorations in Design Studies*, R. Buchanan and V. Margolin (eds). 1995, Chicago, IL: University of Chicago Press, pp. 105–20.

6. Buchanan, R., Wicked problems in design thinking. *Design Issues*, 1992, 8(2): pp. 5–22.

7. Kelley, T. and D. Kelley, *Creative Confidence: Unleashing the Creative Potential within Us All*. 2013, London: William Collins.

8. Kimbell, L., Before empathy. In '*Design Research Conference*', IIT Chicago, 2013.

9. Curedale, R.A., *Design Thinking Pocket Guide*. 2013, Design Community College Inc.

10. Stickdorn, M. and J. Schneider, (eds), *This is Service Design Thinking*. 2010, Amsterdam: BIS Publishers.

11. Hostyn, J., *Better Human Understanding, Not Big Data, Is the Future of Business*, 2010, accessed 17.11.2013, Available from: http://www.cmswire.com/cms/customer-experience/better-human-understanding-not-big-data-is-the-future-of-business-023088.php.

12. Boland, R.J. and F. Collopy (eds), *Managing as Designing*. 2004, Stanford, CA: Stanford University Press.

13. Senge, P., *The Fifth Discipline: The Art and Practice of the Learning Organisation*. 1990, New York: Doubleday.

14. Crabtree, J. *Agnes the Ageing Suit*. 2011, *Financial Times Magazine*, accessed: 15.11.2013, Available from: http://www.ft.com/cms/s/2/1fed1eee-b34b-11e0-9af2-00144feabdc0.html#axzz2d5f3kdG2

15. White, S., *Battery-powered fridge empowers Indian farmers*. 2013, YouTube, TEDx Talks Online.

16. Zobel, G., *Alfredo Moser: Bottle Light Inventor Proud to be Poor*. 2013, *BBC News Magazine*, accessed: 20.11.2013, Available from: http://www.bbc.co.uk/news/magazine-23536914.

17. Kelley, T., *The Art of Innovation: Lessons in Creativity from IDEO, America's Leading Design Firm*. 2001, New York: Random Books.

18. Squires, S. and B. Byrne (eds), *Creating Breakthrough Ideas: The Collaboration of Anthropologists and Designers in the Product Development Industry*. 2002, Westport, CT, and London: Bergin & Garvey, pp. 175–96.

19. Guillet de Monthoux, P., *The Art Firm: Aesthetic Management and Metaphysical Marketing*. 2004, Stanford, CA: Stanford University Press.

20. Goldschmidt, G., The Designer as a Team of One, in *Analysing Design Activity*, N. Cross, H. Christiaans and K. Dorst (eds). 1996, Chichester: Wiley, pp. 65–91.

21. Lawson, B., Cognitive strategies in architectural design. *Ergonomics*, 1979, 22(1): pp. 59–68.

22. Lawson, B., *How Designers Think: The Design Process Demystified*. 3rd edn. 1997, Oxford: Architectural Press.

23. Julier, G., *The Culture of Design*. 2000, London: Sage.

24. Friedman, K., Towards an Integrative Design Discipline, in *Creating Breakthrough Ideas: The Collaboration of Anthropologists and Designers in the Product Development Industry*, S. Squires and B. Byrne (eds). 2002, London: Bergin & Garvey, pp. 199–214.

25. Verganti, R., *Design-Driven Innovation: Changing the Rules of Competition by Radically Innovating What Things Mean*. 2009, Boston, MA: Harvard Business Press.

26. Margolin, V. and R. Buchanan (eds), *The Idea of Design*. 1995, Cambridge, MA: MIT Press.

27. Csikszentmihalyi, M., *The Meaning of Things: Domestic Symbols and the Self*. 1981, Cambridge: Cambridge University Press.

28. Kahney, L., *Jony Ive: The Genius behind Apple's Greatest Products*. 2013, London: Portfolio Penguin.

29. Simon, H.A., *The Sciences of the Artificial*. 1969, London: MIT Press.

Chapter 6: Embracing the Power of the Five Senses

1. Knutson, B. et al., Neural predictors of purchases. *Neuron*, 2007, 53(1): pp. 147–56.

2. Leone, C., *Come to Your Senses*. 2013, IIDA, accessed: 03.05.2013; Available from: http://www.iida.org/content.cfm/come-to-your-senses.

3. News, B., *Disney develops way to 'feel' touchscreen images*. November 2013; Available from: http://www.bbc.co.uk/news/technology-24443271.

4. Campbell-Dollaghan, K., *A cushy art exhibition that tickles all the senses*. 2012; Available from: fastcodesign.com.

5. Fulton Suri, J. and R.M. Hendrix, Developing Design Sensibilities. 2010, *Rotman Magazine*, pp. 58–63.

6. Kranowitz, C., Stock *The Out-of-Sync Child: Recognizing and Coping with Sensory Integration Dysfunction*. 1998, New York: Perigee.

7. Rivlin, R. and K. Gravelle, *Deciphering the Senses: The Expanding World of Human Perception*. 1984, New York: Simon & Schuster.

8. Williams, L. and J. Ackerman, *Please touch the merchandise*. 2011, *HBR*, HBR Blog.

9. *Information is Beautiful*. 2013; Available from: http://www.informationisbeautiful.net/.

10. Siegler, M., *Eric Schmidt: Every 2 days we create as much information as we did up to 2003*. 2010; Available from: techcrunch.com.

11. Lindstrom, M., *Brands Get Physical to Build Trust*. 2012, *Fastcompany*, accessed 10.11.13, Available from: http://www.fastcompany.com/1817965/brands-get-physical-build-trust.

12. Schifferstein, H.N.J. and P.M.A. Desmet, The effect of sensory impairments on product experience and personal well-being. *Ergonomics*, 2007, 50: pp. 2026–48.

13. Lindstrom, M., *Brand Sense*. 2010, New York: Free Press.

14. Ackerman, D., *A Natural History of the Senses*. 1992, New York: Random House.

15. Wikipedia. *Sematosensory*. 2013 [cited 2013 June]; Available from: http://en.wikipedia.org/wiki/Somatosensory.

16. McCabe, D.B. and S.M. Nowlis, The effect of examining actual products or product descriptions on consumer preference. *Journal of Consumer Psychology*, 2003, 13(4): pp. 431–9.

17. Spence, C. and A. Gallace, Multisensory design: Reaching out to touch the consumer. *Psychology & Marketing*, 2011, 28(3): pp. 267–308.

18. Zampini, M. and C. Spence, The role of auditory cues in modulating the perceived crispness and staleness of potato chips. *Journal of Sensory Science*, 2004, 19: pp. 347–63.

19. Sapherstein, M.B. *The trademark registrability of the Harley-Davidson roar: A Multimedia analysis.* 1998 [cited Jan 2014]; Available from: http://www.bc.edu/bc_org/avp/law/st_org/iptf/articles/content/1998101101.html.

20. Spence, C. and M. Zampini, Auditory contributions to multisensory product perception. *Acta Acustica*, 2006, 92: pp. 1009–25.

21. VW advert. 2013; Available from: http://www.tellyads.com/show_movie.php?filename=TA9403.

22. BMW. *The BMW sound designers. BMW quality.* 2013, accessed: 02.12.2013, Available from: https://www.youtube.com/watch?v=-PwRkh6vmwU.

23. Hui, A., The 5 Senses of Flavour: How Colour and Sound Can Make Your Dinner Taste Better. 2013, *The Globe and Mail*.

24. 27gen. *Engaging all 5 senses creates memory links.* 2013 [cited 2013 November]. Available from: http://27gen.com/2013/05/10/engaging-all-5-senses-creates-memory-links/.

25. Polanyi, M., *The Tacit Dimension.* 1966, Garden City, NY: Doubleday.

26. Vihma, S., Ways of Interpreting Design, in *No Guru, No Method? Discussion on Art and Design Research*, P. Strandman (ed.). 1998, Helsinki: Research Institute, University of Art and Design, pp. 7–13.

27. Julier, G., *The Culture of Design.* 2000, London: Sage.

28. Horizon, B. *Try the McGurk Effect! – Horizon: Is seeing believing?* 2010 [cited 20 October 2013]; Available from: https://www.youtube.com/watch?v=G-lN8vWm3m0.

29. Griffiths, S., *Taste without Smell.* 2008, *Guardian* Word of Mouth Blog, accessed: 20.11.2013, Available from: http://www.theguardian.com/lifeandstyle/wordofmouth/2008/jul/21/anosmiasensetaste.

30. Horizon, B., *The Rubber Hand Illusion – Horizon: Is Seeing Believing?* 2010; Available from: https://www.youtube.com/watch?v=sxwn1w7MJvk.

31. Coldewey, D., *IBM: 'Cognitive computers' to use all 5 senses.* 2012, NBC News Technology, accessed: 14.11.2013, Available from: http://www.nbcnews.com/technology/ibm-cognitive-computers-use-all-5-senses-1C7648130.

Chapter 7: Playfully Bringing Things to Life

1. Keil, S. *A manifesto for play, for Bulgaria and beyond*, accessed 01.05.14, Available from: http://www.ted.com/talks/steve_keil_a_manifesto_for_play_for_bulgaria_and_beyond?language=en

2. Joseph, R., Environmental influences on neural plasticity, the limbic system, emotional development and attachment: A review. *Child Psychiatry and Human Development*, 1999, 29(3): pp. 189–208.

3. Venema, V. *Odon childbirth device: Car mechanic uncorks a revolution*. 2013; Available from: http://www.bbc.co.uk/news/magazine-25137800.

4. New, S. and L. Kimbell, Chimps, designers, consultants and empathy: A 'Theory of Mind' for Service Design. In '2nd Cambridge Academic Design Management Conference', 2013, Cambridge.

5. Brown, T. *Tim Brown: Tales of creativity and play*. [Video] 2008 [cited 2013 December]; Available from: http://www.ted.com/talks/tim_brown_on_creativity_and_play.html.

6. Kelley, T. and D. Kelley, *Creative Confidence: Unleashing the Creative Potential within Us All*. 2013, London: William Collins.

7. *STEM to STEAM*. 2013 [cited November 2013]; Available from: http://stemtosteam.org/.

8. Verganti, R., *Design-Driven Innovation: Changing the Rules of Competition by Radically Innovating What Things Mean*. 2009, Boston, MA: Harvard Business Press.

9. *Third of adults 'still take teddy bear to bed'*. 2010; Available from: http://www.telegraph.co.uk/news/newstopics/howaboutthat/7947502/Third-of-adults-still-take-teddy-bear-to-bed.html.

10. Bason, C., *Design for Policy*. forthcoming. Ashgate, Gower.

11. Fulton Suri, J. and R.M. Hendrix, Developing Design Sensibilities. 2010, *Rotman Magazine*, pp. 58–63.

12. Williams, G. et al., The 2012 Wired 100. Jonathan Ive. 2012, *Wired*.

13. Rosling, H. *Hans Rosling: The best stats you've ever seen*. 2006 [cited June 2013]; Available from: http://www.ted.com/talks/hans_rosling_shows_the_best_stats_you_ve_ever_seen.html.

Chapter 8: Creating New Meaning from Complexity

1. Rittel, H., On the planning crisis: Systems analysis of the first and second generations. *Bedrift Sokonomen*, 1972, 8: pp. 309–96.

2. Conklin, J., *Dialogue Mapping: Building Shared Understanding of Wicked Problems*. 2006, Chichester: Wiley.

3. Boland, R.J. and F. Collopy, Design Matters for Management, in *Managing as Designing*, R.J. Boland and F. Collopy (eds). 2004, Stanford, CA: Stanford University Press, pp. 3–18.

4. Kelley, T. and D. Kelley, *Creative Confidence: Unleashing the Creative Potential within Us All*. 2013, London: William Collins.

5. Design Feast Series: Quotes 2013; Available from: http://www.designfeast.com/thoughts-on-design/.

6. Walker, D., Managers and Designers: Two Tribes at War?, in *Design Management: A Handbook of Issues and Methods*, M. Oakley (ed.). 1990, Oxford: Blackwell, pp. 145–54.

7. Bernstein, D., The Design Mind, in *Design talks!*, P. Gorb and E. Schneider (eds). 1988, London: London Business School, Design Management Seminars, The Design Council.

8. Sacher, H., Semantics as Common Ground: Connecting the Cultures of Analysis and Creation, in *Creating Breakthrough Ideas: The Collaboration of Anthropologists and Designers in the Product Development Industry*, S. Squires and B. Byrne (eds). 2002, London: Bergin & Garvey, pp. 175–96.

9. Guillet de Monthoux, P., *The Art Firm: Aesthetic Management and Metaphysical Marketing*. 2004, Stanford, CA: Stanford University Press.

10. Goldschmidt, G., *The Designer as a Team of One*, in *Analysing Design Activity*, N. Cross, H. Christiaans and K. Dorst (eds). 1996, Chichester: Wiley, pp. 65–91.

11. Lawson, B., Cognitive strategies in architectural design. *Ergonomics*, 1979, 22(1): pp. 59–68.

12. Lawson, B., *How Designers Think: The Design Process Demystified*. 3rd edn. 1997, Oxford: Architectural Press.

13. Julier, G., *The Culture of Design*. 2000, London: Sage.

14. Friedman, K., Towards an Integrative Design Discipline, in *Creating Breakthrough Ideas: The Collaboration of Anthropologists and Designers in the Product Development Industry*, S. Squires and B. Byrne (eds). 2002, London: Bergin & Garvey, pp. 199–214.

15. Verganti, R., *Design-Driven Innovation: Changing the Rules of Competition by Radically Innovating What Things Mean*. 2009, Boston, MA: Harvard Business Press.

16. Margolin, V. and R. Buchanan (eds), *The Idea of Design*. 1995, Cambridge, MA: MIT Press .

17. Csikszentmihalyi, M., *The Meaning of Things: Domestic Symbols and the Self*. 1981, Cambridge: Cambridge University Press.

18. Kahney, L., *Jony Ive: The Genius behind Apple's Greatest Products*. 2013, London: Portfolio Penguin.

19. Simon, H.A., *The Sciences of the Artificial*. 1969, London: MIT Press.

Chapter 9: How Design Attitude Influences Frameworks

1. Hertenstein, J.H., M.B. Platt and R.W. Veryzer, The impact of industrial design effectiveness on corporate financial performance. *Journal of Product Innovation and Management*, 2005, 22: pp. 3–21.

2. Rich, H., Proving the practical power of design. *Design Management Journal*, 2004, 15(4): pp. 28–34.

3. Roy, R. and S. Potter, The commercial aspects of investment in design. *Design Studies*, 1993. 14(2): pp. 171–93.

4. Ravasi, D. and G. Lojacono, Managing design and designers for strategic renewal. *Long Range Planning*, 2005, 38: pp. 51–77.

5. Borja de Mozota, B., *Design Management: Using Design to Build Brand Value and Corporate Innovation*. 2003, New York: Allworth Press.

6. Bruce, M. and J. Bessant, *Design in Business: Strategic Innovation through Design*. 2002, Harlow: *Financial Times* / Prentice Hall.

7. Kotler, P. and A.G. Rath, Design: A powerful but neglected strategic tool. *Journal of Business Strategy*, 1984, 5(2): pp. 16–21.

8. Lojacono, G. and G. Zaccai, The evolution of the design-inspired enterprise. *Sloan Management Review*, 2004, 45(3): pp. 75–9.

9. Cross, N. Designerly ways of knowing: Design discipline versus design science,. iIn S Pizzocaro, A Arruda & D De Moraes (eds.) Design Plus Research, Proceedings of Politecnico di Milano Conference, Politecnico di Milano, . 20002,. Milan , pp. 43–48.10.   Jimenez Narvaez, L.M., Design's own knowledge. *Design Issues*, 2000, 16(1): pp. 36–51.

11. Bertola, P. and J.C. Teixeira, Design as a knowledge agent. How design as a knowledge process is embedded into organizations to foster innovation. *Design Studies*, 2003, 24(2): pp. 181–94.

12. Buchanan, R., Wicked problems in design thinking. *Design Issues*, 1992, 8(2): pp. 5–22.

13. Thackara, J., *Winners! How Today's Successful Companies Innovate by Design.* 1997, Aldershot: Gower.

14. Bruce, M. and R. Harun. Exploring design capability for serial innovation in SMEs. In 'European Design Academy Conference', Portugal, 2001.

15. Squires, S. and B. Byrne (eds), *Creating Breakthrough Ideas: The Collaboration of Anthropologists and Designers in the Product Development Industry.* 2002, Westport, CT: Bergin & Garvey.

16. Papanek, V., *The Green Imperative: Natural Design for the Real World.* 1995, London: Thames & Hudson.

17. Margolin, V. and R. Buchanan (eds), *The Idea of Design.* 1995, Cambridge, MA: MIT Press.

18. Papanek, V., *Design for the Real World: Human Ecology and Social Change.* 1971, New York: Pantheon Books.

19. Stickdorn, M. and J. Schneider (eds), *This is Service Design Thinking.* 2010, Amsterdam: BIS Publishers.

20. Cross, N., Discovering Design Ability, in *Discovering Design: Explorations in Design Studies*, R. Buchanan and V. Margolin (eds). 1995, Chicago, IL: University of Chicago Press: pp. 105–20.

21. Simon, H.A., *The Sciences of the Artificial.* 3rd edn. 1996, Cambridge, MA: MIT Press.

22. Brown, T., *Change by Design: How Design Thinking Transforms Organizations and Inspires Innovation.* 2009, New York: HarperCollins.

23. Kelley, T. and D. Kelley, *Creative Confidence: Unleashing the Creative Potential within Us All*. 2013, London: William Collins.

24. Lockwood, T. (ed.), *Design Thinking: Integrating Innovation, Customer Experience, and Brand Value*. 2010, New York: Allworth Press.

25. Martin, R., *The Design of Business: Why Design Thinking Is the Next Competitive Advantage*. 2009, Boston, MA: Harvard Business Press.

26. Weick, K., Rethinking Organizational Design, in *Managing as Designing*, R.J. Boland and F. Collopy (eds). 2004, Stanford, CA: Stanford University Press, pp. 36–53.

27. Kelly, T., *The Art of Innovation*. 2001, New York: Random Books.

28. *Service Design Tools*. 2014; Available from: http://www.servicedesigntools.org/.

29. Kumar, V., *101 Design Methods: A Structured Approach for Driving Innovation in Your Organization*. 2012, Hoboken, NJ: Wiley.

30. Thinkers50. *Roger Martin biography*. 2013; Available from: http://www.thinkers50.com/biographies/roger-martin/.

31. Boland, R.J. and F. Collopy (eds), *Managing as Designing*. 2004, Stanford, CA: Stanford University Press.

32. Boland, R.J. and F. Collopy, Design Matters for Management, in *Managing as Designing*, R.J. Boland and F. Collopy (eds), 2004, Stanford, CA: Stanford University Press, pp. 3–18.

33. Cooper, R. and M. Press, *Design Agenda: A Guide to Successful Design Management*. 1995, Chichester: Wiley.

34. Press, M. and R. Cooper, *The Design Experience: The Role of Design and Designers in the Twenty-First Century*. 2003, Aldershot: Ashgate.

35. Design Council, *The Value of Design*. 2007, London: Design Council.

36. Westcott Michael et al., *The DMI design value scorecard*. DMI 2013. Winter 2013.

37. Mintzberg, H., *The Rise and Fall of Strategic Planning*. 1993, New York: Free Press.

38. Schön, D., *The Reflective Practitioner: How Professionals Think in Action*. 1983, New York: Basic Books.

39. Marzano, S., *Creating Value by Design: Thoughts and Facts*. 1999, Aldershot: Lund Humphries.

40. Manzini, E., Prometheus of the Everyday: The Ecology of the Artificial and the Designer's Responsibility, in *Discovering Design: Explorations in Design Studies*, R. Buchanan and V. Margolin (eds). 1995, Chicago, IL: University of Chicago Press, pp. 219–43.

41. Romme, A.G.L., Making a Difference: Organization as Design. *Organization Science*, 2003, 14(5): pp. 558–73.

42. Van Aken, J., E., Management research based on the paradigm of design science: The quest for field-tested and grounded technological rules. *Journal of Management Studies*, 2004, 41(2).

43. Van Aken, J., Management research as a design science: Articulating the research products of mode 2 knowledge production in management. *British Journal of Management*, 2005, 16(2): pp. 19–36.

44. Alexander, C., S. Ishikawa and M. Silverstein, *A Pattern Language: Towns, Buildings, Construction*, Vol. 2. 1977, New York: Oxford University Press.

45. Peto, J. (ed.), *Design, Process, Progress, Practice*. 1999, London: Design Museum.

46. Cross, N., H. Christiaans and K. Dorst (eds), *Analysing Design Activity*. 1996, Chichester: Wiley.

47. Cross, N., K. Dorst and N. Roozenburg (eds), *Research in Design Thinking*. 1992, Delft: Delft University Press.

48. Csikszentmihalyi, M., *The Meaning of Things: Domestic Symbols and the Self*. 1981, Cambridge: Cambridge University Press.

49. Csikszentmihalyi, M., *The Idea of Design*. 1996, Cambridge, MA: MIT Press.

50. Dewey, J., *Art as Experience*. 1934, New York: Perigee.

51. Dewey, J., *How we Think*. 1991, Amherst, NY: Prometheus.

52. Verganti, R., *Design-Driven Innovation: Changing the Rules of Competition by Radically Innovating What Things Mean*. 2009, Boston, MA: Harvard Business Press.

[53.] Byrne, B. and E. Sands, Creating Collaborative Corporate Cultures, in *Creating Breakthrough Ideas: The Collaboration of Anthropologists and Designers in the Product Development Industry*, S. Squires and B. Byrne (eds). 2002, Westport, CT: Bergin & Garvey, pp. 45–70.

[54.] Myerson, J., *IDEO: Masters of Innovation*. 2001, London: Laurence King.

[55.] Nussbaum, B., The Power of Design. *Business Week*, 2004, pp. 86–94.

[56.] Pine, J., II and J. Gilmore, H, Welcome to the experience economy. *Harvard Business Review*, 1998.

[57.] Pine, J., II and J. Gilmore, H, *The Experience Economy*. 1999, Cambridge, MA: Harvard Business School Press.

[58.] Sherry, J.F., Foreword: Ethnography, Design, and Customer Experience: An Anthropologist's Sense of It All, in *Creating Breakthrough Ideas: The Collaboration of Anthropologists and Designers in the Product Development Industry*, S. Squires and B. Byrne, (eds). 2002, London: Bergin & Garvey.

[59.] Dawson, M., Anthropology and Industrial Design: A voice from the Front Lines, in *Creating Breakthrough Ideas: The Collaboration of Anthropologists and Designers in the Product Development Industry*, S. Squires and B. Byrne, (eds). 2002, Westport, CT: Bergin & Garvey.

[60.] Sutton, R.I. and A. Hargadon, Brainstorming groups in context: effectiveness in a product design firm. *Administrative Science Quarterly*, 1996, 41: pp. 685–718.

[61.] Bason, C. *MindLab*. 2013; Available from: http://www.mind-lab.dk/en.

Chapter 10: How Design Attitude Influences Outputs

[1.] Olins, W., *International Corporate Identity 1*. 1995, London: Laurence King Publishing.

[2.] Gobé, M., *Emotional Branding: The New Paradigm for Connecting Brands to People*. 2001, Oxford: Windsor Books.

[3.] Strati, A., *Organization and Aesthetics*. 1999, London: SAGE.

[4.] Strati, A., The Aesthetic Approach in Organization Studies, in *The Aesthetics of Organization*, S. Linstead and H. Höpfl (eds). 2000, London: Sage, pp. 13–34.

[5.] Gagliardi, P. (ed.), *Symbols and Artifacts: Views of the Corporate Landscape*. 1990, New York: Aldine de Gruyter.

6. Schein, E., *Organizational Culture and Leadership*. 2nd edn. 1992, San Francisco, CA: Jossey-Bass.

7. Kelly, T., *The Art of Innovation*. 2001, New York: Random Books.

8. Anderson, C., *The shared genius of Elon Musk and Steve Jobs*. 2013, *CNN Money*.

9. Cooper, R. and M. Press, *Design Agenda: A Guide to Successful Design Management*. 1995, Chichester: Wiley.

10. Myerson, J., *New Workspace, New Culture: Office Design as a Catalyst for Change*. 1998: Aldershot: Ashgate.

11. Heskett, J., *Toothpicks and Logos: Design in Everyday Life*. 2002, Oxford: Oxford University Press.

12. Heskett, J., *Industrial Design*. 1980, London: Thames & Hudson.

13. Csikszentmihalyi, M., *The Meaning of Things: Domestic Symbols and the Self*. 1981, Cambridge: Cambridge University Press.

14. Norman, D., A., *The Psychology of Everyday Things*. 1988, New York: Basic Books.

15. Sudjic, D., *Cult Objects: The Complete Guide to Having It All*. 1985, London: Paladin.

16. Forty, A., *Objects of Desire: Design and Society since 1750*. 1986, London: Thames & Hudson.

17. Julier, G., *Encyclopaedia of Twentieth Century Design*. 1993, London: Thames & Hudson.

18. Woodham, J., *Twentieth-Century Design*. 1997, Oxford: Oxford University Press.

19. Eric, J. *Using good design to eliminate medical errors*. 2013; Available from: http://www.fastcodesign.com/3021303/evidence/using-good-design-to-eliminate-medical-errors?partner=rss.

20. Meetod. *270 Design principles*. 2013; Available from: http://designprinciplesftw.com/?page=1.

21. Hovding. *Invisible helmet*. 2014; Available from: http://www.hovding.com.

22. ODE. *The world's first fragrance device that uses smell to help people recover their appetite and remember to eat*. 2013; Available from: http://www.myode.org/.

23. Fred, V., *And Then Steve Said, 'Let There Be an iPhone'*. 2013, *New York Times* online.

24. Kahney, L., *Jony Ive: The Genius behind Apple's Greatest Products*. 2013, London: Portfolio Penguin.

25. Tom, S., Nest's Smarter Home. 2013, *Technology Review*.

26. Participle. *The Circle Movement*. 2013 [cited 2013 November]; Available from: http://www.participle.net/projects/view/5/101/.

27. Gov.uk, *GOV.UK wins design of the year 2013*. 2013, gov.uk, accessed 12.12.13, Available from: https://www.gov.uk/government/news/govuk-wins-design-of-the-year-2013.

28. Digital, F. *Giffgaff*. 2013, accessed 10.10.13, Available from: http://www.figarodigital.co.uk/case-study/giffgaff.aspx .

29. Austin, C., Most innovative companies 2012, Airbnb. 2012, *Fastcompany*.

30. Driscoll Tony and LaRosa Craig, 'Live Labs': Prototyping Environments to Measure Customer Experience, in *Consumer Understanding, Service Design*. 2013, Continuum Innovation website: Continuum Innovation website.

31. Kelley, T. and D. Kelley, *Creative Confidence: Unleashing the Creative Potential within Us All*. 2013, London: William Collins.

32. Hunter, T.C. *Offices*. 2014 [cited 2014 January]; Available from: http://www.thecoolhunter.co.uk/offices.

33. Oliver, B., Open-Plan Offices were Devised by Satan in the Deepest Caverns of Hell, in *Oliver Burkeman's blog*. 2013, *The Guardian* online.

Chapter 11: How Designers Directly Impact Organisations

1. Martin, R. *Rotman Dean Roger Martin on Design Thinking*. 2010; Available from: http://www.youtube.com/watch?v=e-ySKaZJ_dU.

2. Buchanan, R., *Management and Design*, in *Managing as Designing*, R.J. Boland Jr. and F. Collopy (eds). 2004, Stanford, CA: Stanford University Press, pp. 54–63.

3. Bruce, M. and J. Bessant, *Design in Business: Strategic Innovation through Design*. 2002, Harlow: *Financial Times* / Prentice Hall.

4. Peto, J. (ed.), *Design, Process, Progress, Practice*. 1999, London: Design Museum.

5. Sherry, J.F., Foreword: Ethnography, Design, and Customer Experience: An Anthropologist's Sense of It All, in *Creating Breakthrough Ideas: The Collaboration of Anthropologists and Designers in the Product Development Industry*, S. Squires and B. Byrne, (eds). 2002, London: Bergin & Garvey.

6. Morello, A., 'Discovering Design' means [re-] discovering users and projects, in *Discovering Design: Explorations in Design Studies*, R. Buchanan and V. Margolin (eds). 1995, Chicago, IL: University of Chicago Press, pp. 69–76.

7. Woodhusyen, J., The relevance of design futures, in *Design Management: A Handbook of Issues and Methods*, M. Oakley (ed.). 1990, Oxford: Blackwell, pp. 265–73.

8. Sacher, H., Semantics as Common Ground: Connecting the Cultures of Analysis and Creation, in *Creating Breakthrough Ideas: The Collaboration of Anthropologists and Designers in the Product Development Industry*, S. Squires and B. Byrne, (eds). 2002, London: Bergin & Garvey, pp. 175–96.

9. Verganti, R., *Design-Driven Innovation: Changing the Rules of Competition by Radically Innovating What Things Mean*. 2009, Boston, MA: Harvard Business Press.

10. Ramirez, R. and N. Arvidsson, The Aesthetics of Business Innovation: An Exploratory Distinction of Two Archetypes. 2005, *Innovation: Management Policy and Practice*, 7(4): pp. 373–388.

11. Stickdorn, M. and J. Schneider (eds), *This is Service Design Thinking*. 2010, Amsterdam: BIS Publishers.

12. Walter, I., *Steve Jobs by Walter Isaacson*. 2011, London: Little, Brown.

13. Cooper, R. and M. Press, *The Design Experience: The Role of Design and Designers in the Twenty-First Century*. 2003: Ashgate.

14. Lorenz, C., *The Design Dimension: The New Competitive Weapon for Product Strategy and Global Marketing*. 1990, Oxford: Blackwell.

15. Ravasi, D. and G. Lojacono, Managing Design and Designers for Strategic Renewal. *Long Range Planning*, 2005, 38: pp. 51–77.

16. Borja De Mozota, B., *Design Management: Using Design to Build Brand Value and Corporate Innovation*. 2003, New York: Allworth Press.

17. Lockwood, T. (ed), *Design Thinking: Integrating Innovation, Customer Experience, and Brand Value*. 2010, Allworth Press: New York.

18. Kotler, P. and A.G. Rath, Design: A powerful but neglected strategic tool. *Journal of Business Strategy*, 1984, 5(2): pp. 16–21.

19. Thinkers50. *Roger Martin Biography*. 2013; Available from: http://www.thinkers50.com/biographies/roger-martin/.

20. Europe, S.E. *The Design Ladder*. 2013 [cited 2013 December].

21. Brown, S., Art or science?: Fifty years of marketing debate. *Journal of Marketing Management*, 1996, 12(4): pp. 243–67.

22. Thomas, H., Designers don't want to agree. *Marketing*, 1993, p. 26.

23. Bruce, M. and R. Cooper, *Marketing and Design Management*. 1997, London: Thompson Business Press.

24. Roy, R. and S. Potter, The commercial aspects of investment in design. *Design Studies*, 1993, 14(2): pp. 171–93.

25. Bruce, M. and G. Docherty, It's all in a relationship: A comparative study of client-design consultant relationships. *Design Studies*, 1993, 14(4): pp. 402–22.

26. Shaw, V., C. Shaw and J. Tressider, Conflict between Designers and Marketers: A Study of Graphic Designers in New Zealand. *Design Journal*, 2002, 5(3): pp. 10–22.

27. Lorenz, C., *The Design Dimension: Product Strategy and The Challenge of Global Marketing*. 1986, Oxford: Blackwell.

28. Squires, G., Management as a professional discipline. *Journal of Management Studies*, 2001, 38(4): pp. 474–87.

29. Johansson, U. and L. Svengren. One swallow doesn't make a summer: About the need for critical mass of designers to make a design strategy. In 'The 11th International Forum on Design Management Research and Education', Boston, Massachusetts, 2002.

30. Nussbaum, B., The Power of Design. 2004, *Business Week*, pp. 86–94.

31. Sutton, R.I. and A. Hargadon, Brainstorming groups in context: effectiveness in a product design firm. *Administrative Science Quarterly*, 1996, 41: pp. 685–718.

32. Kelley, T. and D. Kelley, *Creative Confidence: Unleashing the Creative Potential within Us All*. 2013, London: William Collins.

33. De Geus, A., *The Living Company*. 1997, Boston, MA: Harvard Business School Press.

34. Reingold, J., The Interpreter. 2005, *Fastcompany*, p. 95.

35. Reingold, J., Creating a Design-Centric Culture. 2005, *Fastcompany*, p. 95.

36. [cited 11 November 2013]; Available from: http://www.theguardian.com/fashion/shortcuts/2013/apr/03/hagfish-slime-new-lycra.

37. Aronowitz, K., *Facebook's Design Director, On Crafting A Design-Led Organization*. 2012, accessed 11.10.13, Available from: http://www.fastcodesign.com/welcome.html?destination=http://www.fastcodesign.com/1669610/kate-aronowitz-facebooks-design-director-on-crafting-a-design-led-organization.

38. Kahney, L., *Jony Ive: The Genius behind Apple's Greatest Products*. 2013, London: Portfolio Penguin.

Index

Bold page numbers indicate figures, *italic* numbers indicate tables.

If you have found this book useful you may be interested in other titles from Gower

**Design Leadership:
Securing the Strategic Value of Design**
Raymond Turner
Hardback: 978-1-4094-6323-8
e-book: 978-1-4094-6324-5 (PDF)
e-book: 9978-1-4094-6325-2 (ePUB)

**Open Design and Innovation:
Facilitating Creativity in Everyone**
Leon Cruickshank
Hardback: 978-1-4094-4854-9
e-book: 978-1-4094-4855-6 (PDF)
e-book: 978-1-4094-7475-3 (ePUB)

**Creating Innovative Products and Services:
The FORTH Innovation Method**
Gijs van Wulfen
Hardback: 978-1-4094-1754-5
e-book: 978-1-4094-1755-2 (PDF)
e-book: 978-1-4094-5905-7 (ePUB)

Visit **www.gowerpublishing.com** and

- search the entire catalogue of Gower books in print
- order titles online at 10% discount
- take advantage of special offers
- sign up for our monthly e-mail update service
- download free sample chapters from all recent titles
- download or order our catalogue